# Al-Inṣāf fī Bayān Sabab al-Ikhtilāf
and
# ʻIqd al-Jīd fī Aḥkām al-Ijtihād wa-l-Taqlīd

# Shāh Walī Allāh's Treatises on Juristic Disagreement and Taqlīd

## Al-Inṣāf fī Bayān Sabab al-Ikhtilāf

and

## 'Iqd al-Jīd fī Aḥkām al-Ijtihād wa-l-Taqlīd

Translated by
Marcia Hermansen

FONS VITAE

First published in 2010 by
Fons Vitae
49 Mockingbird Valley Drive
Louisville, KY 40207
http://www.fonsvitae.com
Email: fonsvitaeky@aol.com


Library of Congress Control Number: 2010936399
ISBN 9781891785467



Printed in Canada

# Table of Contents

# Foreword

Translation deepens our appreciation of the "source culture," the language from where the text originates, as well as the "target culture," the vernacular into which it is translated.[1] Yet there is more to translation than merely making a work accessible from a foreign tongue into a familiar language. Apart from sharing with us the horizons, the anxieties and the insights of an author, familiar or unfamiliar, close or distant, translation also enriches our own universe of meaning. As the German-Jewish writer, Walter Benjamin, so aptly pointed out, translation also deepens the recipient language, compelling the 'target' language to expand its own semantic possibilities in order to receive and make sense of the new text. The renowned literary critic, George Steiner, has reminded us that each language--irrespective of its spread, significance or insignificance--projects a set of possible worlds, what he described as "geographies of remembrance."[2] It is the accumulation of these pasts, in their infinite diversity, that constitute what we call history.

In the pages that follow this preface, Professor Marcia Hermansen has provided for us one instance of a "geography of remembrance." She unfolds a distinct moment of human history through her excellent translations of the writings of Shāh Walī Allāh of Delhi (d. 1762), arguably one of the most influential thinkers and scholars of eighteenth century India. Hermansen's impeccable linguistic skills have furnished scholars, students and general readers, with a nuanced understanding of various aspects of Islamicate civilization. English-speaking readers are already in her debt for translating a good part of Walī Allāh's veritable classic in Muslim religious literature, *Ḥujjat Allāh al-Bāligha, The Conclusive Argument of God*.[3] Now, she has provided in English two critical essays on the much vaunted themes of *ijtihād* and *taqlid* by the same author. Both concepts are as explosive as they are opaque. They can only be rendered into English as "independent derivation of juridical opinions" (*ijtihād*), and "intellectual effort and its impulse to comply with juro-moral authority" (*taqlīd*). Students of Islamic law and Muslim culture will no doubt profit immensely from Professor Hermansen's labor to provide us translations of *'Iqd al-jīd fī aḥkām al-ijtihād wa al-taqlīd-The Chaplet Concerning the Rules of Independent Authority and Binding Authority and al-Inṣāf fī bayān sabab al-ikhtilāf—Doing Justice in Explaining the Cause of Juristic Disagreement.*

1. Roger Allen, "Translation and Culture: Theory and Practice," *Journal of Social Affairs* 21, no. 83 (2004).

2. George Steiner, *After Babel: Aspects of Language and Translation* (Oxford: Oxford University Press, 1998).

3. Shāh Walī Allāh ad-Dihlāwī and Marcia K. Hermansen (trans), *The Conclusive Argument of God: Shāh Walī Allāh of Delhi's Ḥujjat Allāh Al-Bāligha* (Leiden: Brill, 1996), 1:34.

In penning this foreword, I follow the advice of Shaykh Abū'l Ḥasan ʻAlī al-Nadwī (d. 1999), one of the foremost Indian traditional scholars and thinkers of recent times, who counseled writers of prefaces to ensure that their reflections on introducing a book "stem from an exuberance, harmony and the fulfillment of a desire in their soul" about the subject to be discussed.[4] I am grateful to Professor Hermansen for giving me an opportunity to comment on a subject of great importance to me and I trust that both the translator and the readers of what follows will pardon my exuberance.

Translation is often a thankless job and translators suffer an uneasy afterlife having to brave the endless nitpicking of critics like dreaded ministrations. Despite the challenges, translation is not only necessary, but also imperative, since translation also involves interpretation. The Andalusian mystic and polymath, Muḥyī al-Dīn Ibn ʻArabī (d. 1240) wrote that translation was to grasp the meaning of the signifier or word used by the speaker or author.[5] In other words, translation is nothing but an intense and more demanding form of what we do whenever we are engaged in reading.[6] Why then should we read/translate Walī Allāh? I would argue that reading this pivotal thinker gives us an opportunity to explore the historical understanding of the past and its resonance in the present.

Walī Allāh's footprints mark contemporary Muslim perceptions of religion and its practices, not only in South Asia, but also beyond. He is a giant who has elicited different receptions. While he was widely regarded as a reformer and scholar par excellence, different Muslim audiences put him to use for various ideological and political projects at times, aiming to satisfy radically different ends. Since translations are also acts of reading, we glean diverse portraits of Walī Allāh, proving yet again that translation as an act of reading is not merely a mechanical rendering of antique facts.[7] Translations of classics not only advance our knowledge of the past but also force us to refine our historical understanding. Sometimes one wishes that scholars of Islam in traditional institutions of learning in Muslim majority contexts, as also scholars of Islam in the Western academy, would heed this point and rethink their own preconceptions of the past.

The South African-born novelist, John Coetzee, astutely observed:

---

4. Abū'l-Ḥasan ʻAlī al-Ḥasanī al-Nadwī and compiled by Muḥammad Muntaẓar ʻAbd al-Ḥafīz, *Muqaddimāt Al-Imām Al-ʻAllāma Al-Dāʻiya Al-Mufakkir Al-Islāmī Al-Shaykh Abī 'l-Ḥasan ʻAlī Al-Ḥasanī Al-Nadwī* (Beirut: Mu'assasa al-Risāla, 1425/2004), 10.

5. Abū Bakr Muḥyī al-Dīn ibn ʻArabī and Aḥmad Shams al-Dīn (ed), *Al-Futūḥāt Al-Makkīya*, 1st ed., 9 vols., vol. 1 (Beirut: Dār al-Kutub al-ʻIlmīya, 1420/1999), 1:220-21.

6. J.M. Coetzee, *Stranger Shores: Literary Essays* (New York: Penguin Books, 2001), 70.

7. Steiner, *After Babel: Aspects of Language and Translation.*

> Historical understanding is understanding of the past as a shaping force upon the present. Insofar as the shaping force is tangibly felt upon our lives, historical understanding is part of the present. Our historical being is part of our present. It is that part of our present—namely, the part that belongs to history—that we cannot fully understand, since it requires us to understand ourselves not only as objects of historical forces but as subjects of our own historical self-understanding.[8]

How can we be "subjects of our own historical self-understanding"? Especially, since Marx once quipped that "Men make history but they do not know the history they make"? At a time of deep cultural and political disruption on a global scale, I believe that translations can offer a unique, and uniquely valuable, window to intercultural self-understanding, just as the absence of translation renders certain communities and cultures invisible within human history. The task of the translator is to etch the past in order to embolden the present and make possible what seems only opaque in the future.

To study great writers and thinkers of the past, like Walī Allāh (1703-1762) requires historical imagination. Cross-cultural comparison is also of value. The French scholar, Jacques Berque, imagined Walī Allāh to be the Indian equivalent of Jean-Jacques Rousseau (1712-1778), who was a contemporary of the Delhi-based scholar.[9] Walī Allāh was troubled by the machinations and instability of the monarchy and the turpitude of the institutions of state under India's Moghul rulers, just as Rousseau was disturbed by the doings of the French monarchy and Genovese aristocracy. While these realities formed the larger background to each thinker's context, they still pursued different paths to address the challenges of their societies. However, we can learn a great deal about ideas, politics, and the impact of thinkers in the eighteenth century by following events as they occurred in both south Asia and Europe concurrently, especially on the eve of British colonization of the subcontinent.

There is also great benefit to scholarship if a figure like 'Abd al-Raḥmān ibn Khaldūn (1332-1406), author of the highly noted *Prolegomena* (*Muqaddima*) to history were to be examined in cross-cultural and comparative perspective with Michel de Montaigne (1533-1592), author of *The Complete Essays*. Each of their major works is a veritable encyclopedia brimful with wisdom of every kind.

Walī Allāh, like Ibn Khaldūn, de Montaigne, Rousseau, and others, was troubled by the follies of his contemporary fellow Muslims, yet he also found his intellectual and spiritual calling within that social and cultural maelstrom. He was convinced of the necessity to improve the human condi-

8. Coetzee, *Stranger Shores*, 13.

9. Jacques Berque, "*Un Contemporain Islamo-Indien De Jean-Jacques Rousseau*," in *L'islam Au Temps Du Monde* (Paris: Sindbad, 1984).

tion guided by the hand of Providence. Walī Allāh's advocacy took the form of writing, with an almost dizzying rate of productivity. In the *Conclusive Argument* he re-situated the metaphysical architecture that underscored the proposed political and ethical paths he advocated. In nuanced and subtle meditations he imagined a new moral and political order in advancing a re-furnished vocabulary for Islamic thought in his time, a theme that Professor Hermansen had fruitfully elaborated in her introduction to that book.

But the proverbial elephant in the room ignored by most historians of Muslim South Asia is this: was Walī Allāh's inquiry into the technical details of the different kinds of independent thinking (*ijtihād*), and discussions about authority (*taqlīd*) merely a question of doctrinal integrity or did he envisage to address broader social and political issues with these concepts? We know that in sparking this debate, he vexed a good number of jurists in his time. We also know that he vacillated between opposing positions. At first, he opposed established juro-moral authority (*taqlīd*) and advocated the necessity of independent reasoning (*ijtihād*), a form of intellectual autonomy permitted for scholars, albeit in limited forms. After extended reflection on this matter, he endorsed a version of informed *taqlīd* as an acceptable practice for scholars. But this explanation remains, for this writer at least, unsatisfactory since it does not explain why Walī Allāh returned to endorsing a version of *taqlīd*. Was he apprehensive that in advocating *ijtihād* against the communal consensus of the scholars he could be marginalized or stigmatised for abandoning an established juro-moral discursive school (*madhhab*)? In the absence of a convincing explanation one might be encouraged to seek other explanations in pursuit of which I offer some threads for further inquiry.

Much has been made of Walī Allāh's tolerant attitude towards other law schools, his eclectic bent and openness to new ideas, in particular a commitment to the authority and meaning of prophetic reports (*ḥadīth*). Professor Hermansen and others have argued that his two-year sojourn to Arabia between 1731-1733 where he immersed himself in the study of the different juro-moral traditions of Islam with several distinguished teachers shaped this attitude.

Before putting too much weight on Arabian influences on his disposition, it would be worth exploring what factors in India, prior to his travels abroad, could have shaped Walī Allāh's tolerant disposition to different facets of Sunnī teachings. Recall that his father, Shāh 'Abd al-Raḥīm (1644-1718), was himself a scholar, steeped in mysticism, and adopted a less rigid approach to Ḥanafī law compared to his contemporaries. And, since traditional Muslim scholars placed a great deal of emphasis on the psychological factors that shaped and formed students and disciples, it might well be that Walī Allāh's resistance to doctrinaire Indian Ḥanafism was a predisposition passed on from father to son.[10]

Ḥanafī scholarship and hegemony on the Indian subcontinent in the latter half of the seventeenth century, in the words of one writer, was a "general milieu of stagnant and inflexible jurists (*fuqahā'*)."[11] Concerns about Ḥanafī intolerance dated back to earlier times. For centuries Ḥanafīs had to countenance charges that they zealously defended their viewpoints in the face of countervailing evidence derived from hadith reports. Some conscientious Ḥanafīs, like the Egyptian scholar Abū Ja'far al-Ṭaḥāwī (d. 933), moderated the school's attitude and practices towards prophetic reports. In his prolific writings Ṭaḥāwī tried to realign the mandates and directives in Ḥanafī juro-moral teachings with the teachings found in the corpus of prophetic reports.[12] However, Ḥanafīs on the Indian subcontinent and Central Asia, had perhaps not fully internalized this hadith-friendly Ḥanafī genealogy prior to the eighteenth century much to the chagrin of their detractors.

Legend has it that Indian Ḥanafīs often preferred to cling to the opinions generated by their juro-moral school (*madhhab fī al-fiqh)* instead of following the warrant of the prophetic report (*ḥadīth*). The Delhi-based mystic, Nizām al-Dīn Awliyā' (d. 1325), recounted an incident when he was rebuffed by the city's Ḥanafī jurists while debating the status of listening to spiritual music (*samā'*) for esoteric purposes. Rejecting his view on the permissibility of spiritual music, the Ḥanafī jurists left the mystic in no doubt what they recognized as authority, when they said, "In this city we prefer the juristic tradition over the reported tradition (*ḥadīth*)."[13] This same group of Ḥanafī jurists then allegedly claimed that embracing the teachings of *hadith en passant* was to capitulate to the method of their rivals, the Shāfi'ī school.[14] Another account claims that during the reign of 'Alā' al-Dīn Khiljī (d. 1316), a visiting Egyptian hadith scholar in a letter to the ruler of the day complained bitterly about the Indian Ḥanafī *'ulamā*'s utter disregard for hadith. The missive never reached the ruler, some historians report, by a conspiracy of fate and cunning on the part of the Ḥanafī

10. Nadvi explicitly recommends that biographers take into account psychological factors in shaping the predispositions of a subject. See Sayyid Abū'l Ḥasan 'Alī Ḥasanī Nadvī, *Ḥayāt-e 'Abd Al-Ḥayy* (Lucknow: Majlis-i Taḥqiqāt va Nashariyāt-i Islam, 1425/2004), 20.

11. Mujībullāh Nadvī, *Fatāwā 'Ālamgīrī Aur Us Ke Mu'allifīn* (Delhi: Taj Company, 1422/2001), 85.

12. I am grateful to my friend Dr Muneer Fareed for reminding me of Ṭaḥāwī's role in the Ḥanafī school and the predisposition of Sūfīs to favor hadith much more readily than the fuqahā'.

13. Ḥakīm Sayyid 'Abd al-Ḥayy, "Hindūstān kā Niṣāb-i Dars aur us ke Tahayyurāt (Part 1)," *Tarjumān Dārul 'Ulūm* (2000): 61.

14. Ibid.

*'ulamā'*![15] Of course, these sensational nuggets cannot be taken at face value; they need to be located in a larger context and require further vetting in order to give us a full sense of the situation. We do not only learn that Indian Ḥanafīs prior to the eighteenth century were being painted in unflattering colors by their rivals from these snippets but they paradoxically also whet our appetite to unravel the deeper social and political cleavages which our historiography of the period had shrouded.

Complicating the somewhat exaggerated indictment of the pre-eighteenth century Indian Ḥanafīs for their allergy toward hadith was the element of pietism displayed in the attitudes of many influential scholars. In the historiography of hadith studies Muslim pietists and mystics were generally charged for circulating weak, unsubstantiated, and sometimes even forged prophetic reports (*ḥadīth*).[16] Passionate in their love for the Prophet Muḥammad, it is alleged that pietists often uncritically attributed teachings to him that were never sanctioned by specialists in hadith studies. By the methodology of the jurists, on the other hand, individual prophetic reports (*aḥādīth*) do not automatically amount to knowledge as to what was a normative prophetic practice (*sunna*). Jurists employed a forensic and hermeneutical approach to the content of the prophetic reports. By contrast, hadith specialists (*muḥaddithūn*), many of whom were moved by pious impulses, used different criteria for vetting a report. They primarily vetted a report on the credibility and integrity of a reporter of hadith and verified the existence of actors identified in a chain of transmission linked to the report. And often, hadith specialists implied that a verified report was tantamount to the prophetic norm, *sunna.* Jurists (*fuqahā'*) disagreed with such an approach and adopted a more dispassionate approach to hadith materials by also verifying the content of prophetic reports. Aḥmad ibn Ḥanbal's legendary statement that he would readily act on the mandate of a weak prophetic report instead of relying on a teaching indirectly derived by jurists from solid reports by way of analogy typified the attitude of the hadith scholars debate from a very early period onwards.[17] One might, therefore, have to be more circumspect in uncritically accepting the charge that Indian Ḥanafīs were cavalier in their approach to hadith until careful studies had shed more light on the verity of such claims. For indeed, hadīth scholarship

---

15. Ibid. This view is reinforced by 'Abd al-Ḥayy's son, Abu'l Hasan Ali Nadwi in his preface to Muḥammad Zakariyya al-Kandhlawi's book, "Awjaz al-masālik ila Muwaṭṭa' Mālik" see al-Nadwī and 'Abd al-Ḥafīz, *Muqaddimāt*, 30.

16. See Yūsuf al-Qarḍāwī, *Kayfa Nata'āmal Ma'a al-Sunna al-Nabawiyya* (Herndon, Va: The International Institute of Islamic Thought, 1411/1990), Muḥammad Ghazālī, *al-Sunna al-Nabawiyya bayna Ahl Al-Fiqh wa Ahl Al-Ḥadīth* (Beirut: Dār al-Shurūq, 1409/1989).

17. Later Ḥanbalīs believe their founder meant hadith in the 'hasan' category not forged or weak. al-Qarḍāwī, *Kayfa Nata'āmal*, 75.

in India before Walī Allāh reached the stage, had an impressive history. Figures such as Ḥusām al-Dīn 'Alī al-Muttaqī al-Hindī (d. 1567), his student, Muḥammad Ṭāhir bin 'Alī al-Fatanī (Patani) (d. 1578), followed by 'Abd al-Ḥaqq al-Dihlawī (d.1642) among others, were renowned for their diligent scholarship in the discipline of hadith studies. More importantly, the noted early twentieth century scholar Muḥammad Zāhid al-Kawtharī levelled a barrage of bruising critique at Walī Allāh's intellectual project.[18] Walī Allāh's intellectual promiscuity, al-Kawtharī believed, led him into serious confusion resulting in his embrace of cosmologies and viewpoints that were unsustainable by the standards of traditional Sunnī dogmatics. Moreover, Walī Allāh's lack of skill to distinguish flawed reports from authentic ones resulted in several questionable conclusions he reached, al-Kawtharī pointed out. Among those were Walī Allāh's uneven and skewed views on the topic of *ijtihād*.

There might be more than meets the eye in terms of factors that shaped Walī Allāh's preference for hadith above the claims of Ḥanafī law in certain issues, notably the approach of his father. A conscientious scholar like Shāh 'Abd al-Raḥīm dissented from Ḥanafī doctrine on a number of issues related to ritual practice, as his son later confirmed.[19] More interesting is the fact of his gradual disenchantment from the Moghul court and its project to promote the Ḥanafī school. At first Shāh 'Abd al-Raḥīm was part of the panel of scholars employed to prepare the prestigious *Fatāwā 'Ālamgīrī* also known as the *Fatāwā Hindiyya*, under the royal patronage of Emperor 'Ālamgīr Awrangzeb. The latter is reported to have spent the princely sum of a million rupees (10 lakhs) on the compilation of the prestigious fatwā project.[20] As an assistant to a former classmate, Mullah Ḥāmid Jawnpūrī, a senior member of the editorial board of the fatwā manual under preparation, Shāh 'Abd al-Raḥīm had a ring-side seat to observe the workings of the Moghul court and the predilections of the Ḥanafī *'ulamā'* who worked closely with it.[21]

For reasons of piety he apparently preferred to keep arm's length from the ruling establishment but pecuniary forced him to seek employment at the royal court. One incident gave him the perfect opportunity to exit his detested job. Emperor Awrangzeb and his close confident, Mulla Niẓām Burhānpūrī, who was assigned to direct the fatwā compilation project, held weekly review sessions to discuss progress. On one such occasion Burhānpūrī had reason to reproach Jawnpūrī for lapses in rigor in the writ-

18. Muḥammad Zāhid al-Kawtharī, *Ḥusn Al-Taqāḍī Fī Sīra al-Īmām Abī Yūsuf al-Qāḍī* (Homs: Maṭba'a al-Andalūs, 1388/1968), 116-21.

19. Nadvī, *Fatāwā 'Ālamgīrī*, 85.

20. Ibid., 22.

21. Abd al-Ḥayy bin Fakhr al-Dīn al-Ḥasanī, *Nuzhat al-Khawāṭir wa Bahjat al-Masāmi' wa Al-Nawāẓir* (Multan & Rae Bareli: Tayyab Academy/ Dār 'Arafāt, 1413/1992), 6:65.

ing of the chapters assigned to him.[22] It turned out that the errors stemmed from the work of Jawnpūrī's assistant, Shāh 'Abd al-Raḥīm. An embarrassed Jawnpūrī, it turned out, was an unforgiving mentor and the incident soured his relationship with his assistant. Chastened by the petty scholarly rivalries and driven by his pious impulses, Shāh 'Abd al-Raḥīm was either forced to resign or his services were terminated.[23] Whatever the impact of the bruising professional relations with his fellow Ḥanafī *'ulamā'*, we know for certain that when it came to ritual observances Shāh 'Abd al-Raḥīm recited the *sūra Fātiḥa* as part of his liturgy while praying in congregation. In doing so, he followed the Shāfi'ī practice and abandoned the Ḥanafī requirement of absolute silence. The Ḥanafī school deemed even the silent recitation of a congregant's liturgical formula, while following a prayer-leader in a communal prayer, to be an act that was strictly proscribed.

So did Walī Allāh inherit some paternal traits with respect to observing school doctrine? Were his theological sensibilities disturbed by the Ḥanafī zealotry? Did he think such zealousness skirted dangerously close to deifying the discursive opinions of mortals while ignoring the teachings of the Messenger as expressed in the hadith? What are the layers of subtext for Walī Allāh's reflections on *ijtihād* and *taqlīd*? There are no easy answers to these speculative questions. The two essays translated here, however, do provide some glimpses as to what Walī Allāh's goals might have been. One got the sense that he was trying to say that differences in juro-moral traditions, in other words, normativity, were the product of sociological, anthropological, historical and cognitive factors coalescing unpredictably at different junctures in history. Modern readers of Walī Allāh could well conclude that he tried to show the constructed nature of juridical rulings and gently attempted to move away from the perception that the juro-moral schools of Islam were part of some sacred dogmatic order.

In these essays Walī Allāh signals his displeasure at the predilection of some Ḥanafīs for abstract rationality, while ignoring the direct, concrete, and compelling mandate of the prophetic practices documented in the hadith literature. The rhetorical strategy by which he attempted to dissuade the Ḥanafīs of their wayward methodology was interesting. He reminded his readers that abstract thinking and polemical reasoning were elements first introduced to Islamdom by the Mu'tazilites. Without using vituperative language, Walī Allāh impishly linked rational modes of thinking to the Mu'tazilite sect within Islamdom hoping the associated would repel his readers. One can palpably observe Walī Allāh's attempt to shame-face a Pharisee-like approach to the law. His glowing references to Muḥammad bin Idris al-Shāfi'ī, one of the four founders of the Sunnī law schools, must surely have galled many a doctrinaire Ḥanafī scholar. For the latter, al-

22. Ibid, Nadvī, *Fatāwā 'Ālamgīrī*, 79. al-Ḥasanī, *Nuzhat Al-Khawāṭir* 5:404.
23. Nadvī, *Fatāwā 'Ālamgīrī*, 77-79.

Shāfi'ī was undoubtedly the foremost intellectual rival. Perhaps in highlighting the merits of al-Shāfi'ī, Walī Allāh was also trying to signal to the Ḥanafīs to end their futile polemics against the Shāfi'ī school. Anti-Shāfi'ī polemics were a favorite past time in the seminaries (*madrasas*) of South Asia and a feature of the Ḥanafī pedagogical law (*fiqh*) manuals used to this very day in the curricula there.

A generous reading of Walī Allāh's essays might lead one to conclude that he was merely attempting to rattle the cage of doctrinaire Ḥanafīsm, but he never intended to undermine the discursive juridical tradition of this school or any of the other schools (*madhāhib*) per se. His contribution was that of a corrective, to return the law schools to equilibrium and inject in them a modicum of dynamism. Those Islamic trends in south Asia who viewed themselves as Walī Allāh's heirs, like the Deoband school, certainly do not view his project as inaugurating a radical questioning of the intellectual tradition. Similarly, adherents of the Barelwi school also deemed him an intellectual icon, but perhaps more for Walī Allāh's heady mystical thought and for confessing to ultimately remaining a follower of the Ḥanafī school.[24]

Admirers of Walī Allāh included a spectrum of trends in traditional and modern interpretations of Islam. Conventional wisdom has it that Walī Allāh's project inspired the revival of the study of hadith and by implication, the prophetic *sunna*. In so doing, it laid the groundwork to combat unsanctioned religious practices (*bid'a*) and the revitalization of the idea of an Islamic polity in the form of an emirate governed by Sharī'a law. This view has gained widespread currency in the wake of the social activism and *jihād* activities of Sayyid Aḥmad Rai Barelī (d.1831) and Walī Allāh's grandson, Shāh Ismā'īl Shahīd (d.1831), following their unsuccessful bid to establish an Islamic emirate in parts of northwestern India during the colonial period.

Those committed to a version of scriptural traditionalism, known as the Ahl-i Ḥadīth school of pre-partition India, doctrinal rivals to both the Deoband and Barelwi schools, took great inspiration from Sayyid Aḥmad and Ismā'īl Shahīd. Members of the Ahl-i Ḥadīth fraternity viewed Walī Allāh's critique of the juro-moral schools as a vindication of their renunciation of all forms of juro-moral authority (*taqlīd*). None other than the premier advocate of the Ahl-i Ḥadīth, Nawwāb Sayyid Ṣiddīq Ḥasan Khān al-Qannaujī (d.1890) offered a shimmering *ex post facto* endorsement of Walī Allāh.[25] Walī Allāh, al-Qannaujī wrote, was "the spokesman for his epoch and its sage" because of his outstanding intellectual labor (*ijtihād*) in studying hadith. Turning the eighteenth century scholar into ally of the

24. For more on the Barelwi school see Usha Sanyal, *Devotional Islam & Politics in British India* (Delhi: Oxford University Press, 1999).
25. al-Ḥasanī, *Nuzhat al-Khawāṭir* 6:418.

cause of the Ahl-i Ḥadīth movement, al-Qannaujī stated that reason why he thought so. Walī Allāh, he said, "gave preference to the science of prophetic traditions (*'ilm al-sunna*) above all other disciplines or modes of learning (*'ulūm*) and made the science of jurisprudence (*fiqh*) subservient to the science of *sunna*."[26] Al-Qannaujī's statement brilliantly distilled the fundamental difference between the Ḥanafīs and their Ahl-i Ḥadīth rivals on the Indian subcontinent.

Walī Allāh's preference to ground Islamic law in the authority of hadith materials whose authenticity could be regularly reviewed and updated, rather than adhere to the transmitted view of the Ḥanafī juro-moral discursive tradition and its sometimes arcane logic, placed him close to the orbit of the Ahl-i Ḥadīth. Only Walī Allāh's testimony as a Ḥanafī redeemed him from being totally identified with the hadith movement. But his arguments in support of the 'other side,' so to speak, riled many Ḥanafīs resulting in some chafing and carping till very recently. A contemporary admirer like Salmān al-Ḥusaynī al-Nadwī, a professor at Nadwatul 'Ulamā' seminary in Lucknow, among others, gingerly disagreed with some of Walī Allāh's critiques of the Ḥanafī school.[27]

The founders of the Deoband seminary glowingly endorsed Walī Allāh's legacy with pronouncements of loyalty to his philosophical and spiritual outlook. Therefore Walī Allāh's view on the centrality of hadith in Muslim juro-moral discourse has been fervently promoted by a large segment of the Deoband school and their allies while simultaneously remaining loyal to the Ḥanafī tradition. The inclusion of the six canonical Sunnī books on hadith in the revamped Nizāmī *madrasa* (seminary) curriculum was a direct outcome of the campaigns mounted by Walī Allāh and his disciples to alter the curriculum of the *madrasas*. Abū'l-Ḥasan 'Alī Nadwī triumphantly proclaimed that thanks to Walī Allāh's labors "the study of hadith became a precondition for intellectual excellence (*kamāl*), a symbol for the pious and the votaries of sound dogma, to the extent that a scholar of religion was not deemed 'learned' unless he demonstrated excellence in hadith studies."[28]

And some Deobandī scholars went so far as to admit that in the end, Walī Allāh forced Indian Ḥanafī thought to come to terms with hadith scholarship in an unprecedented way. Whether the Deoband school conceded to the mandate of the hadith and amended the traditional Ḥanafī *fiqh* doctrines, or whether they merely used the discourse of hadith to affirm and legitimate pre-existing Ḥanafī doctrines through elaborate and tortured

26. Ibid., 6:419.

27. Salmān al-Ḥusaynī al-Nadwī, *Ārā' Al-Īmām Walī Allāh Al-Dihlawī Fī Ta'rīkh Al-Tashrī' Al-Islāmī Wa Asbāb Al-Ikhtilāf Fī'l Madhāhib Al-Fiqhīya Wa Bayna Ahl Al-Ra'y Wa Ahl Al-Ḥadīth* (Lucknow: Dār al-Sunna li al-Nashr wa al-Tawzī', 1407/1986).

28. al-Nadwī and 'Abd al-Ḥafīz, *Muqaddimāt*, 31.

hermeneutical forays, was a topic that needed to be treated elsewhere. However, it is worth noting the nuanced tones among the Deobandī scholars when it came to their support for Ḥanafī doctrines. Sa'īd Aḥmad Pālanpūrī, currently a professor at the Deoband seminary, is the editor of a new Arabic edition of Walī Allāh's *magnum opus*, *Ḥujjat Allāh al-Bāligha-The Conclusive Argument of God,* as well as the author of a sprawling translation cum-commentary in Urdu of the same work. In the last mentioned work Pālanpūrī noted Kawtharī's critique of Walī Allāh and conceded that the latter occasionally relied on dubious reports.[29] A stellar figure in the Deobandī pantheon and a renowned hadith scholar, Anwār Shāh Kashmīrī (d. 1933) also maintained a critical admiration for Walī Allāh. While he shared some of Kawtharī's misgivings regarding some of the eighteenth century scholars' views, Kashmirī remained unfazed by Walī Allāh's periodic skepticism about adherence to the juro-moral schools and remained a staunch Ḥanafī. Ẓafar Aḥmad 'Uthmānī, a Pakistan-based Deoband scholar, often vigorously defended the Ḥanafī doctrine in his extensive writings on hadith. Clearly the historiography of hadith studies in India requires careful scrutiny and deepening. Such studies will surely have one benefit; scholars will hopefully not dim Indian achievements in hadith studies prior to Walī Allāh in order to shine all the light on his accomplishments.

Different from Walī Allāh's admirers among the *'ulamā'* were foremost thinkers in pre-partition India like the poet-philosopher Muḥammad Iqbāl, the religious scholar Shiblī Nu'mānī, other intellectuals, and leaders of revivalist movements, all of whom viewed Walī Allāh as advocating a more thoroughgoing reform of Islam. Iqbal went as far as crediting Walī Allāh to be qualified to "rethink the whole system of Islam without completely breaking with the past."[30] "Perhaps the first Muslim who felt the urge of a new spirit in him was Shāh Walī Allāh of Delhi," Iqbal said confidently, adding that "the only course open to us is to approach modern knowledge with a respectful but independent attitude and to appreciate the teachings of Islam in the light of that knowledge, even though we may be led to differ from those who have gone before us."[31] But the social, political, and intellectual projects advanced by figures like Sir Sayyid Aḥmad Khān (d. 1898), Shiblī Nu'māni (d. 1914), Muḥammad Iqbāl (d. 1938), and Abū'l A'lā Mawdūdī (d. 1979), among others, viewed Walī Allāh's project to be more ambitious.

29. Shāh Walī Allāh Dihlawī and ed. Pālanpūrī, Sa'īd Aḥmad, *Raḥmatullāh Al-Wāsi'a Sharḥ Ḥujjatullāh Al-Bāligha*, 5 vols. (Deoband: Makataba Ḥijāz, 1422/2001), 1:34. Also see his Aḥmad bin 'Abd al-Raḥīm Shāh Walī Allāh al-Dihlawī and ed. al-Bālanbūrī (Pālanpūrī), Sa'īd Aḥmad bin Yūsuf, *Ḥujjat Allāh Al-Bāligha*, 2 vols. (Deoband: Maktaba Ḥijāz, 1426AH/2005).
30. Sir Muhammad Iqbal, *The Reconstruction of Religious Thought in Islam* (Lahore: Javid Iqbal/Shaikh Muhammad Ashraf, 1960), 97.
31. Ibid.

And each also viewed himself as either following him or supplementing his vision through their distinct contributions to Islamic thought.

'Ubaydullāh Sindhī (d. 1944), a convert from Sikhism and a graduate of the Deoband seminary, must certainly count as the foremost scholar-activist on the sub-continent who most strongly appreciated the revolutionary appeal of Walī Allāh's thought and grasped the salience of his pan-Islamic ambitions. Charismatic, brilliant, and itinerant, he was somewhat of a non-conformist in certain issues, which set him apart from the rest of the Deoband scholars and marginalized him. He nevertheless remained a close companion and comrade of the anti-colonial Deoband scholar and activist Maḥmūd al-Ḥasan (d. 1920). In all his ventures scholarly and political, Sindhī fearlessly elaborated and applied Walī Allāh's ideas to the human condition of twentieth century India. A realist and rationalist par excellence, hindsight proved that he struck the proper balance between adhering to tradition while critically updating tradition in its encounter with modernity, especially the use of science and technology.[32] Some sceptics might cry that some of the most grandiose interpretations of Walī Allāh's project were either still-born or at best, resulted in mixed fortunes. Whatever the polemic on that score, what was undeniable is that these perspectives had accumulated many adherents over the decades.

Apart from the multiple traces Walī Allāh left behind, more interesting questions lurk behind his stoking the debate on *ijtihād*. It would be fair to say that in light of some of the activities undertaken in his name, that Walī Allāh envisaged a mode of religiosity that not only favored moderation and tolerance, but more importantly he envisaged an understanding of tradition that was dynamic and not static. Like his intellectual predecessors, Ibn Taymiyya and Ibn Qayim al-Jawziyya, among others, he relied on fresh readings of hadith literature in order to create social dynamism and ethical re-visioning. For many reformers the appeal to hadith in the manner that al-Shāfi'ī did centuries earlier, and, whom Walī Allāh held up as an icon, was the safest and most acceptable way of breaking the monopoly of *madhhab*-based juro-moral thinking that was often wedded to the establishment of political and economic agendas. Richard Bulliet's study of eleventh century Iraq has shown how Shāfi'ism allied to Islamic mysticism broke the aristocratic base of the Ḥanafīs in Iraq and ushered in new and dynamic modes of thinking.[33] While India in the eighteenth century was very different to Iraq eight centuries earlier, there was a sense that a hadith-friendly Islamic ideology was "progressive" not in the modern sense of the word, but in "...

32. See Sayyid Muḥammad Aḥmad, *Islām Aur Aṣr-e Jadīd: Mawlānā 'Ubaydullāh Sindhī Special Issue*, vol. xxxvii (New Delhi: Zakir Husain Insitute of Islamic Studies, 2005).

33. Richard W. Bulliet, *The Patricians of Nishapur: A Study in Medieval Islamic Social History* (Cambridge, Massachusetts: Harvard University Press, 1972), 39.

supporting those trends which were comparatively new in society...."[34]

Somehow one gets the sense that Walī Allāh and other anti-establishment figures like him configured that expunging philosophical rationality from religious discourse had its benefits. In his case it might well be that he attempted to unsettle not so much the Ḥanafī law but the complacent guardians of the law, the court-friendly *'ulamā'* who were coveted by the political establishment. Scripturalism was a necessary step to enliven projects for social reform like the one pursued by Walī Allāh. Needless to say, this hypothesis still has to be proven. Yet, in times of crisis, Walī Allāh, like Muslim thinkers prior to him, promoted mysticism, emphasized fraternal solidarity and made faith the basis of religion. Reason, in turn, was tethered to the dictates of faith and mediated by the prophetic wisdom contained in the hadith while abjuring abstract rationality.[35] Walī Allāh tried to do all this by avoiding a self-defeating collision-course with the Ḥanafīs. And, while earlier followers of primitive scriptural traditionalism (*salafīs*) did favor piety and devotion, Walī Allāh personally flaunted such extravagant cosmologies of Islamic mysticism (*taṣawwuf*) that would scandalize the puritan temperaments of the likes of Ibn Ṣalāḥ and Ibn Taymiyya.

Despite the moderate growth in Walī Allāh studies over the years, much remains to be done. Our understanding and impressions of the multiple dimensions of this extraordinary figure and his times will continue to be refined by fresh readings of his work. To do so requires a better grasp of his society and a critical examination of his views. In order to reach such ends postures of faux piety and misplaced reverence for the subject of inquiry would of necessity have to be foresworn, a trait that saddles many studies, with some exceptions, of course.

As to the question of why we read Walī Allāh or any major thinker or text of the past, the answer is in part that such acts of reading provide us with an historical understanding. Add to that the observation of Michel de Certeau "that any reading of the past--however much it is controlled by the analysis of documents--is driven by a reading of current events. Readings of both past and present are effectively organized in relation to problematic issues which a historical situation is imposing."[36] Much to the chagrin of pretentious objectivists and dyed-in-the-wool empiricists, human subjectivity is part of the knowledge process and cannot be disentangled from it. If we acknowledge its place, we could also curb its excesses.

Ebrahim Moosa
Associate Professor of Islamic Studies
Duke University, Durham, North Carolina

34. Ibid.
35. Ibid., 46.
36. Michel de Certeau, *The Writing of History*, trans. Tom Conley (New York: Columbia University Press, 1988), 23.

## Bibliography


'Abd al-Ḥayy, Ḥakīm Sayyid. "Hindūstān Kā Niṣāb-e Dars Aur Us Ke Taghayyurāt (Part 1)." *Tarjumān Dārul 'Ulūm* (2000).

Aḥmad, Sayyid Muḥammad. *Islām Aur Aṣr-e Jadīd: Mawlānā 'ubaydullāh Sindhī Special Issue*. Vol. xxxvii. New Delhi: Zakir Husain Insitute of Islamic Studies, 2005. Allen, Roger. "Translation and Culture:Theory and Practice." *Journal of Social Affairs* 21, no. 83 (2004): 13-23.

Berque, Jacques. "Un Contemporain Islamo-Indien De Jean-Jacques Rousseau." In *L'islam Au Temps Du Monde*, 113-46. Paris: Sindbad, 1984.

Bulliet, Richard W. *The Patricians of Nishapur: A Study in Medieval Islamic Social History*. Cambridge, Massachusetts: Harvard University Press, 1972.

Coetzee, J.M. *Stranger Shores: Literary Essays*. New York: Penguin Books, 2001.

de Certeau, Michel. *The Writing of History*. Translated by Tom Conley. New York: Columbia University Press, 1988.

al-Dihlawī, Aḥmad bin 'Abd al-Raḥīm Shāh Walī Allāh, and ed. al-Bālanbūrī (Pālanpūrī), Sa'īd Aḥmad bin Yūsuf. *Ḥujjat Allāh Al-Bāligha*. 5 vols. Deoband: Maktaba Ḥijāz, 1426AH/2005.

al-Dihlāwī, Shāh Walī Allāh, and Marcia K. Hermansen (trans). *The Conclusive Argument of God: Shāh Walī Allāh of Delhi's Ḥujjat Allāh Al-Bāligha*. Leiden: Brill, 1996.

al-Dihlawī, Shāh Walī Allāh, and ed. Pālanpūrī, Sa'īd Aḥmad. *Raḥmatullāh Al-Wāsi'a Sharḥ Ḥujjatullāh Al-Bāligha*. 5 vols. Deoband: Makataba Ḥijāz, 1422/2001.

Ghazālī, Muḥammad. *Al-Sunna Al-Nabawiyya Bayna Ahl Al-Fiqh Wa Ahl Al-Ḥadīth*. Beirut: Dār al-Shurūq, 1409/1989.

al-Ḥasanī, 'Abd al-Ḥayy bin Fakhr al-Dīn. *Nuzhat Al-Khawāṭir Wa Bahjat Al-Masāmi' Wa Al-Nawāẓir*. Multan & Rae Bareli: Tayyab Academy/ Dār 'Arafāt, 1413/1992.

Ibn 'Arabī, Abū Bakr Muḥī al-Dīn, and Aḥmad Shams al-Dīn (ed). *Al-Futūḥāt Al-Makkīya*. 1st ed. 9 vols. Vol. 1. Beirut: Dār al-Kutub al-'Ilmīya, 1420/1999.

Iqbal, Sir Muhammad. *The Reconstruction of Religious Thought in Islam*. Lahore: Javid Iqbal/Shaikh Muhammad Ashraf, 1960.

al-Kawtharī, Muḥammad Zāhid. *Ḥusn Al-Taqāḍī Fī Sīra Al-Īmām Abī Yūsuf Al-Qāḍī*. Homs: Maṭba'a al-Andalus, 1388/1968.

Nadvī, Mujībullāh. *Fatāwā 'Ālamgīrī aur us ke Mu'allifīn*. Delhi: Taj Company, 1422/2001.

al-Nadwī, Abū'l-Ḥasan 'Alī al-Ḥasanī, and compiled by Muḥammad

Muntaẓar ʻAbd al-Ḥafīz. *Muqaddimāt Al-Īmām Al-ʻAllāma Al-Dāʻiya Al-Mufakkir Al-Islāmī Al-Shaykh Abī'l-Ḥasan ʻAlī Al-Ḥasanī Al-Nadwī.* Beirut: Mu'assasa al-Risāla, 1425/2004.

al-Nadwī, Salmān al-Ḥusaynī. *Ārā' Al-Īmām Walī Allāh Al-Dihlawī Fī Ta'rīkh Al-Tashrīʻ Al-Islāmī Wa Asbāb Al-Ikhtilāf Fī'l Madhāhib Al-Fiqhīya Wa Bayna Ahl Al-Ra'y Wa Ahl Al-Ḥadīth.* Lucknow: Dār al-Sunna li al-Nashr wa al-Tawzīʻ, 1407/1986.

Nadvī, Sayyid Abū'l Ḥasan ʻAlī Ḥasanī. *Ḥayāt-e ʻAbd Al-Ḥayy.* Lucknow: Majlis-i Taḥqiqāt va Nashariyāt-i Islām, 1425/2004.

al-Qarḍāwī, Yūsuf. *Kayfa Nataʻāmal Maʻa al-Sunna al-Nabawiyya.* Herndon, Va: The International Institute of Islamic Thought, 1411/1990.

Sanyal, Usha. *Devotional Islam and Politics in British India.* Delhi: Oxford University Press, 1999.

Steiner, George. *After Babel: Aspects of Language and Translation.* Oxford: Oxford University Press, 1998.

# Translator's Introduction[1]

Shāh Walī Allāh's (1703-1762) two treatises on *fiqh*, *al-Inṣāf fī Bayān Sabab al-Ikhtilāf* and *'Iqd al-Jīd fī Aḥkām al-Ijtihād wa-l-Taqlīd*, deal with several technical aspects of juristic theory, in particular, *ikhtilāf* (disagreement among the jurists), *ijtihād* (independent reasoning in deriving legal opinions), and *taqlīd* (complying only with the rulings of one school of law or a single jurist within a school). Concern about these subjects, in particlar, *ijthād* and *taqlīd*, came into increasing prominence among Muslim scholars struggling with changing circumstances in the eighteenth and nineteenth centuries. They are not, however, new within Islamic legal approaches to the interpretation of jurisprudential method.

The first treatise translated here, *al-Inṣāf* of Shāh Walī Allāh deals with the issue of juristic disagreement (*ikhtilāf*) among Muslim jurists and the types and scope of individual reasoning (*ijtihād*) within the Islamic legal system. There are pressing questions about the composition and even the authorship of al-*Inṣāf.* A considerable portion of its text is duplicated in four chapters that appear to have been appended to the first volume of the author's major work, *Ḥujjat Allāh al-Bāligha.*[2] The original Indian editors of the Arabic text note that this additional section was found in only one of the manuscript copies available to them[3] although its inclusion became standard in the subsequent printed versions. At the conclusion of these chapters appended to the *Ḥujjat Allāh al-Bāligha*, Shāh Walī Allāh indicates his desire to compose a further text on the subject of juristic disagreement.[4] Normally it has been concluded that ultimately he had to content himself with amending the material in these chapters by the addition of some new elements. This text was thus prepared with some additions and modifications as a separate treatise under the title *al-Inṣāf fī-Bayān Sabab al-Ikhtilāf.* The changes in the separate treatise *al-Inṣāf* consist primarily of a long quote

1. In the English translation I have numbered certain paragraphs in order to set off and clarify the argument in some areas, following the practice of many modern Arabic editors. I have also added certain sub-headings in brackets. This, of course, was not the convention in the time of the author.

2. *Ḥujjat Allāh al-Bāligha I* ed. al-Sayyid Ṣābiq (Cairo: Dar al-Ṭab' wa-l-Nashr, 1952), 296-340. The references to volume two in this translation are cited by the chapter headings in order to facilitate references to other editions.

3. *Ḥujjat Allāh al-Bāligha I*, 296.

4. At the conclusion of the final one of these chapters included as part of the *Ḥujjat Allāh* Shāh Walī Allāh writes, "I have had the intention of composing a treatise entitled, 'The Summit of Justice in Explaining the Cause for Disagreement'... but I have not been free to do this until this time, so that when the argument drew near the origin of (juristic) disagreement I was led by my inner motivation to explain whatever I easily could with regard to this subject." *Ḥujjat Allāh* I, 340.

from al-Khaṭṭābī added at the end of Chapter Three, an extended discussion of the topics of *ijtihād* and the Shāfi'ī school in Chapter Four, and a reorganization of the original text to constitute an additional fifth chapter.[5]

Some doubt is cast on this interpretation of its composition by the fact that certain material in this work is identical to text found in a treatise, *al-Iqāf 'alā Sabab al-Ikhtilāf*[6] by Muḥammad Ḥayāt al-Sindī (1750),[7] a slightly older contemporary of Shāh Walī Allāh who lived in Arabia and was part of the same circle of hadith scholars who studied with al-Kurdī (d. 1733). The fact that Shāh Walī Allāh must have encountered al-Sindī during his stay in Mecca and Madina and yet never mentions him in his works, although Shāh Walī Allāh scrupulously documents his *ijāzas* in other fields in numerous locations, suggests the hypothesis that these chapters were in fact added by another hand without the sanction of Shāh Walī Allāh. The contravening evidence is a purported *ijāza* that has Shāh Walī Allāh giving permission to transmit these works to a student. This is said to date to the year 1759.[8] What is not verifiable at present is whether the work for which the *ijāza* was given is identical to the text currently in circulation. In addition, the fact that the title of Shāh Walī Allāh's work rhymes with that of al-Sindī could suggest a direct emulation or at least response. My conclusion is that the treatise *al-Inṣāf* was composed soon after the *Ḥujjat Allāh al-Baligha* and that four chapters based on *al-Inṣāf* were probably added to the first volume of the larger work after its initial composition. It is also possible to conclude that the chapters were originally conceived and written as part of the larger work and later issued separately with the previously mentioned modifications. Most scholars believe that *Ḥujjat Allāh al-Bāligha* was composed during the decade after the author's return from the pilgrimage in 1732.[9] A certificate (*ijāza*) given in 1759 mentions the author's permission to teach the *Inṣāf*, so

5. 'Abd al-Faṭṭāh Abū Ghuddah rearranges the text of the final chapter of the *Inṣāf* in his edition (Beirut: Dār al-Nafā'is, 1978). There do seem to be some problems with the consistency of structure and expression of chapter five, possibly due to its having been reworked later based on material composed as part of the *Ḥujjat Allāh al-Bāligha.*

6. Muḥammad Ḥayāt al-Sindhī, "*al-Iqāf 'alā Sabab al-Ikhtilāf,*" published with others treatises under the title *al-Ittibā* (Lahore: Maktaba al-Salafiyya, 1981), 107-115.

7. On Muḥammad Ḥayāt al-Sindī see Basheer M. Nafi, "A Teacher of Ibn 'Abd al-Wahhāb: Muḥammad Ḥayāt al-Sindī and the Revival of Aṣḥāb al-Ḥadīth's Methodology," *Islamic Law and Society13* (2, 2006): 208-241.

8. *al-Muṣawwā* (Mecca: Maṭba'a al-Salafiyya, 1932), 43.

9. I have been unable to verify a note in Maẓhar Baqā', *Uṣūl-e-Fiqh aur Shāh Walī Allāh*, (Islamabad: Idāra Taḥqīqāt Islāmī, 1979), 81 note #2 in which he mentions an observation by Muḥammad Ikrām, *Thaqāfat* (Lahore: Jan. 1967), 71 that a manuscript of *al-Inṣāf* in the India Office, London was written in 1153/1741.

that the work can definitely be said to predate this year.[10]

The second treatise translated here entitled *ʻIqd al-Jīd fī Aḥkām al-Ijtihād wa-l-Taqlīd* (The Chaplet for the Neck concerning the Rules of Ijtihād and Taqlīd) is mentioned in the same *ijāza*.[11] Some pages from this second treatise are found duplicated both in the treatise *al-Inṣāf* and in the material appended to the *Ḥujjat Allāh al-Bāligha*. Some further material in this treatise has been located in the work *Tuḥfa al-Anām fī-l ʻAmal bi-Ḥadīth al-Nabī* of the same Muḥammad Ḥayāt al-Sindī,[12] again raising questions of the authorship of these portions of the works.[13]

These issues of authorship are important and controversial because the opinions of Shāh Walī Allāh on matters of *fiqh* and *ijtihād* have been claimed as normative by succeeding generations of South Asian scholars—scholars whose opinions have often diverged on these very issues. It is quite possible that parties inclined to the more literalist *Ahl-i ḥadīth* perspective of interpretation that would have been closer to al-Sindī's view, were able at an early period to have these insertions assumed into Shāh Walī Allāh's corpus. This has in fact happened with other works of Shāh Walī Allāh that would style him as a reformer who opposed practices of popular Sufism. An example of such a work is the treatise *al-Balāgh al-Mubīn* studied and deemed spurious by the French scholar, Marc Garborieau.[14] The other possibility is that both authors may have had access to a common text that has not yet been identitfied.

In preparing these translations I need to acknowledge the important contributions of earlier scholars from India and Pakistan who edited the Arabic versions of the texts and who also prepared pioneering Urdu translations, in many cases supplying valuable notes and clarifying ambiguous references and allusions in the original Arabic text. These Urdu translations

---

10. Baqā', 40.

11. *ʻIqd al-Jīd fī-Aḥkām al-Ijtihād wa-l-Taqlīd*, (Cairo: Maktaba al-Salafiyya, 1965). Partially translated by Da'ud Rahbar. "Shah Waliullah and Ijtihād." *The Muslim World* 45 (December 1955), 346-358.

12. Muḥammad Ḥayāt al-Sindī, *Tuḥfa al-Anām fī-l ʻAmal bi-Ḥadīth al-Nabī* (ed. Abū Bakr Ṭā Ḥā Bū Sarīḥ) (Beirut: Dār Ibn Ḥazm, 1993). Some scholars have claimed that Muḥammad Ḥayāt al-Sindī was a direct pupil of Shaykh Muḥammad Muʻīn al-Sindī, a student of Shāh Walī Allāh *al-Muṣawwā* (Mecca edition), preface, p. 6. This claim has been refuted by Basheer M. Nafi in his article "A Teacher of Ibn ʻAbd al-Wahhāb: Muḥammad Ḥayāt al-Sindī."

13. Martin Riexinger, *Sanaullah Amritsari (1868-1948) und die Ahl-i Hadis im Punjab unter britischer Herrschaft, Mitteilunungen zur Sozial und Kulturgeschichte der Islamischen Welt* (Würzburg, Germany: Ergon, 2004), 74.

14. Gaborieau, Marc, "A XIXth Century Indian Wahhabi Tract against the Cult of Muslim Saints: al-Balāgh al-Mubīn," in Christian W. Troll (ed.), *Muslim Shrines in India* (Delhi: Oxford University Press, 1989), 198-239.

and editions are mentioned in the bibliography and cited in various places among the footnotes to this edition.[15]

Trying to formulate a chronology of Shāh Walī Allāh's works is a lengthy and complex process. The most recent annotated list appears in J. M. S. Baljon, *Religion and Thought of Shāh Walī Allāh Dihlawī*.[16] Including the author's brief treatises, the list is composed of some forty works.

## Biography

Shāh Walī Allāh was a great intellectual figure of eighteenth-century Islam in India and a prolific writer in Arabic and Persian. He was born on the 4th of Shawwāl, 1214 A.H. or February 21, 1703. Biographical material and anecdotes concerning his life and family may be found in his brief autobiography *Al-Juz' al-Laṭīf fi Tarjama al-'Abd al- Ḍa'īf*[17] and in his work *Anfas al-'Ārifīn*[18] (Souls of the Gnostics) which features accounts of his father, his uncle, and his spiritual teachers in India and the Hijaz.

His father, Shāh 'Abd al-Raḥīm, was a noted scholar and mystic. He had been engaged for a time to work on the compilation of Ḥanafī legal rulings known as the *Fatāwā 'Ālamgīrī* commissioned by the Mughal ruler Aurangzeb (d. 1707). Shāh 'Abd al-Raḥīm devoted considerable attention to the education of his precocious son. With his father, young Walī Allāh studied hadith works such as *Mishkāt al-Maṣābiḥ*[19] and *Ṣaḥīḥ al-Bukhārī*, works on Qur'ān interpretation, Islamic jurisprudence, and theology. In addition, he was exposed to works of Sufism by such masters as Ibn 'Arabī and 'Abd al-Raḥmān Jāmi. He took over his father's position as head of the Raḥīmiyya madrasa on his death in 1719.

In about April 1731, Walī Allāh departed India to perform the pilgrimage to Mecca and Medina where he stayed for some fourteen months, returning to India in December 1732. This stay in the Hijaz was an important formative influence on his thought and subsequent life. While in the Hijaz he studied hadith, *fiqh*, and Sufism with various eminent teachers whom he mentions in the *Anfas al-'Ārifīn*, the most important influences being Shaykh Abū Ṭāhir al-Kurdī al-Madanī (al-Shāfi'ī) (d. 1733),[20] Shaykh

15. An Urdu translation *Silk al-Mawārīd* (*Stringing the Unbored Pearl*) of this text was made in 1309 by Maulānā Muḥammad Aḥsan Ṣiddiqī Nānautvī and published by Maṭba'a Mujtabā'ī, Delhi, 1344 (1925/6).

16. Leiden: E. J. Brill, 1986, 9-14.

17. *Al-Juz' al-Laṭīf fi-Tarjamat al-'Abd al-Ḍa'īf* in *Journal of the Asiatic Society of Bengal* 14 (1912), 161-175 with English translation by M. Hidayat Husain.

18. *Anfas al-'Ārifīn.* (Urdu translation of the Persian original). Sayyid Muḥammad Farūqī al-Qādirī. (Lahore: Al-Ma'ārif, 1974).

19. *Mishkāt al-Maṣābīḥ* compiled by al-Tabrīzī, trans. James Robson (Lahore: Ashraf, 1963).

20. Son of the famous hadith scholar and Sufi of the Hijāz, Shaykh Ibrāhīm al-Kurānī (d. 1690). See A. H. Johns, "al-Kurānī, Ibrāhīm" in *Encyclopeadia of Islam*

Wafd Allāh al-Makkī (al-Mālikī), and Shaykh Tāj al-Dīn al-Qala'ī (al-Ḥanafī) (d. 1734). These teachers in Mecca exposed Shāh Walī Allāh to the trend of increased cosmopolitanism in hadith scholarship which began to emerge there in the eighteenth century due to a blending of the North African, Hijazi, and Indian traditions of study and evaluation.[21] While in the Holy Cities, Shāh Walī Allāh developed a particular respect for Mālik's work, the *Muwaṭṭā'*, on which he later was to write two commentaries, *Musawwā* (The Rectified) and *Muṣaffā* (The Purified). During his stay in the Holy Cities, Shāh Walī Allāh had many mystical experiences, dreams, and visions of Prophet Muhammad in which his questions were answered and he was instructed to carry out a mission of teaching. He felt that these visions confirmed his religious purpose and his exalted state, and later included them in a work entitled *The Emanations of the Two Holy Cities*.[22] At times these same spiritual experiences influenced his attitude to legal issues such as the need to follow one particular legal school (*taqlīd*) and the primacy of one legal school over another.[23]

Shāh Walī Allāh's writing career began in earnest on his return from pilgrimage. While the *Ḥujjat Allāh al-Bāligha* was composed sometime during the decade after his return, it seems that the inspiration to compose the work came to him while on the pilgrimage. At that time, he saw a vision of the grandsons of the Prophet Muḥammad, Ḥasan and Ḥusayn, holding a broken pen out to him, then repairing it, and later bestowing upon him a robe of the Prophet. From this he understood that he had a mission to restore the Islamic sciences through the study of the reports of the Prophet.[24] This revitalization of hadith studies as a discipline has been associated by some scholars with the rise of 18$^{th}$ century Islamic reform movements ad-

---

2nd edition. V. (Leiden: E. J. Brill, 19), 242-243. Shāh Walī Allāh has composed his biographical notice in *Anfās al-'Ārifīn*, 386-389. Alexander Knysh, "Ibrāhīm al-Kūrānī (d. 1101/1690), an Apologist for *waḥdat al-wujūd*" in *Journal of the Royal Asiatic Society* Series 3, 5, 1 (1995): 39-47.

21. John O. Voll, "Hadith Scholars and Tarīqahs: An 'Ulema' Group." J*ournal of Asian and African Studies* 15 (July-October 1980), 264-273.

22. *Fuyūḍ al-Ḥaramayn.* Arabic with Urdu translation. (Karachi: Muḥammad Sa'īd, n.d). The practice of writing accounts of both inner and outer event of the pilgrimage seems to have been a tradition of Indian Naqshbandīs of the Mujaddidī line, see for example, *Ḥasanāt al-Ḥaramayn* which features the visions of Khwāja Muḥammad Ma'ṣūm (1662) and was compiled by his son Muḥammad 'Ubayd Allāh. Persian version edited and annotated by Muḥammad Iqbāl Mujaddidī (Dera Ismail Khan, Pakistan: Maktaba Sirājiyya, 1981).

23. *Fuyūḍ al-Ḥaramayn.* Vision # 10, 89-90; Vision # 33, 187-8.

24. *Ḥujjat Allāh* I, 12. This vision is recounted in the author's book, *Fuyūḍ al-Ḥaramayn*, "The Emanations of the Two Sacred Mosques," 65-66 and *al-Tafhīmāt al-Ilāhiyya II*, 300. See also Baqā', 39, *Fuyūḍ,* 180-181.

vocating social and moral reconstruction.[25] The connection of this renewal of hadith studies with reformist tendencies in Sufism during this period was first noted by Fazlur Rahman who coined the term Neo-Sufism for such developments.[26] Some aspects of this "new" expression of Sufism included a revival of hadith studies and increased devotion centered on the figure of the Prophet Muhammad. Subsequently a scholarly debate continued for some time as to the nature and novelty of "Neo-Sufism."[27] In a later article, for example, O'Fahey criticized the concept of neo-Sufism based on developments in African Sufi traditions. It does, however, seem to the present author that South Asian Sufi thought exhibits some of the tendencies described by Voll and Rahman.

More recently with the publication of more treatises and more detailed academic work on the scholars of the Ḥaramayn during that period such as al-Kurānī and Muḥammad Ḥayāt al-Sindī, it becomes possible to trace further intellectual connections and gain understanding of how they incorporated the approaches of literalist and brilliant figures such as Ibn Ḥazm (d. 456/1064) and Ibn Taymiyya (d. 728/1328). The fact that their ideas were being appropriated by eighteenth century Sufi oriented *'ulamā'* formed within *madhhab* traditions of *taqlīd* and acceptance of the authority of past methodologies and opinions within legal schools discloses that some sort of synthesis among competing methodological currents was being attempted by scholars at this time.

It is interesting that today the most important Islamic religious movements in South Asia construe Shāh Walī Allāh as an intellectual progenitor. In the Indian subcontinent the scholars of Deoband have perhaps the most direct link to his heritage in combining the Sufi tradition of spiritual lineage with intellectual learning in hadith and legal studies.[28]

Those who have a more reformist and puritanical outlook such as the Ahl al-Ḥadīth movement and even the followers of Maulānā Maudūdī (d. 1978) find in Shah Walī Allāh's elucidation of the *sharī'a* and call for reform a precursor to their own beliefs. From Shāh Walī Allāh's legal works such as *al-Inṣāf* it is clear that he did not go so far as some of these reformers who were prepared to completely reject following the four legal schools.[29]

The third major inclination in contemporary South Asia is that of the

25. On neo-Sufism see the new preface by John O. Voll to Trimingham's, *The Sufi Orders in Islam* (New York: Oxford University Press, 1998).
26. F. Rahman, *Islam* (Chicago: University of Chicago, 1979), 206.
27. R. S. O'Fahey. *Enigmatic Saint.* (Evanston: Northwestern U. P., 1990), 1-9.
28. On the Deoband Madrasa see Barbara Daly Metcalf, *Islamic Revival in British India: Deoband, 1860-1900* (Princeton: Princeton University Press, 1982).
29. Maẓhar Baqā', *Uṣūl-e-Fiqh aur Shāh Walī Allāh* (Islamabad: Idāra Taḥqīqāt Islāmī, 1979), 35-6.

Bareilvis or the *Ahl-e Sunna wa-l Jamā'a*,[30] who are more oriented to popular religious practices within Sufism. They support the Ḥanafī *madhhab* and have a particular reverence for Abū Ḥanīfa, its founder. The Bareilvis would therefore find some of the author's statements in support of maintaining Ḥanafī practice among the Muslims of the sub-continent to be in agreement with their position. This aspect of Shāh Walī Allāh's teaching is best exemplified in his son-in-law and disciple, Muḥammad 'Āshiq, whose memorial work on his teacher known as *al-Qaul al-Jalī fī Akhbār al-Walī* merits further study.[31]

*Al-Inṣāf* was composed in Arabic, not only because this was the preferred language for scholarly religious literature, but also because this allowed the work to appeal to a wider reading public of which the author was in contact as part of a cosmopolitan network of learned scholars concerned with the revival of hadith scholarship among Muslims in the eighteenth century.[32]

Outside of the Indian sub-continent, *Ḥujjat Allāh al-Bāligha*, *al-Inṣāf fī Bayān Sabab al-Ikhtilāf*, and *'Iqd al-Jīd* are the most readily available of Shāh Walī Allāh's works. The former remains popular among the present generation of reformers in the Arab Middle East, as well as in South and South East Asia. At the same time, twentieth century Islamic liberals such as Muhammad Iqbal (d. 1938) and Fazlur Rahman (d. 1988) have seen in Shāh Walī Allāh a thinker who responded to the crisis of his time with moderation and a search for the spirit behind the *sharī'a* injunctions.[33]

## Juristic Disagreement

The subject of juristic disagreement, or *ikhtilāf*, among scholars was often treated by Muslim jurists once legal schools began to form.[34] Among

30. On this school of thought and the life of its founder, Reza Khān Bareilvī, see Usha Sanyal, *Devotional Islam and Politics in British India: Ahmad Reza Khan Barelwi and his Movement* (Oxford: Delhi, 1996).

31. al-Qaul al-Jalī

32. John O. Voll, "Hadith Scholars and Tarīqahs: An 'Ulema' Group." *Journal of Asian and African Studies* 15 (July-October 1980), 265.

33. Fazlur Rahman, "The Thinker of Crisis—Shāh Waliy-Ullah." *The Pakistan Quarterly* (Summer 1956), 44-48. A. Halepota, "Affinity of Iqbāl with Shāh Walī Allāh." *Iqbal Review* XV (1,1974), 65-72, and Halepota, "Shāh Waliyullah and Iqbal. The Philosophers of the Modern Age." *Islamic Studies* 13 (December 1974), 225-234.

34. For a list of some early *ikhtilāf* works see, al-Ṭaḥawī, *Ikhtilāf al-Fuqahā'* ed. M. Ḥasan Ma'ṣūmī (Islamabad: Islamic Research Institute, 1971), 24-30. A French translation of another early *ikhtilāf* work is Gérard Lecomte, *Le traité des Divergences du Ḥadīt d'Ibn Qutayba d. 889*, (Institut Français de Damàs, 1962). A very useful work is Ibn Rushd's *Bidāyat al-mujtahid fī nihāyat al-muqtaṣid ll* (Cairo: Maktaba al-Azhariyya, 1970). An excellent English translation has been prepared

the most influential of these works on Shāh Walī Allāh's formulations are al-Shāfi'ī's *Risāla*, al-Sha'rānī's *Mīzān,* and al-Suyūṭī's (1505) works on *ijtihād.*

Shāh Walī Allāh felt that one of his contributions to understanding the topic of jusristic disagreement was his being able to discern that there are actually various types of these disagreements. He lists these as falling into four categories: "refuted" disagreements which are not admissible; disagreements which may be permitted as long as no hadith definitely rules on the issue; admissible disagreements in which the revealed sources have allowed clear and absolute choice regarding the case; and disagreements wherein two admissible alternatives have been ascertained on the basis of *ijtihād* and deduction from the Prophet's pronouncements. The final type can only become religiously obligating (*mukallif*) subsequent to the process of *ijtihād* and the confirmation of jurists' opinions about the case.[35]

Shāh Walī Allāh's position concerning complying with the rulings of a particular legal school (*taqlīd*) seems to have modified over the course of his lifetime. The Pakistani scholar, Maẓhar Baqā', categorizes these developmental stages chronologically as: (1) inherited tendencies; (2) the youthful outcome of his own reflections; (3) influences acquired during his stay in the Hijāz; and (4) the effects of the practical environment in which he later taught in India.[36]

As previously indicated, his family background would have stressed the Ḥanafī school, which was by far the dominant legal school in Central Asia and India. While his father was a prominent Ḥanafī jurist, he was known to have disagreed with the school on a number of issues.[37] Before performing the pilgrimage in 1731, Shāh Walī Allāh seems to have independently arrived at a rejection of *taqlīd*, the need for an individual to accept the rulings of only one among the four main legal schools.[38] He writes in *Fuyūḍ al-Ḥaramayn* that personally he had been inclined to reject *taqlīd* but that he was commanded to support it in a vision of the Prophet that he had during his pilgrimage.[39]

This vision may also have reflected the influence of his experiences with his various teachers in the Ḥaramayn who belonged to the other legal schools. His own research into the early works of Islamic law, specifically

---

by Imran Ahsan Nyazee, *The Distinguished Jurist's Primer* 1 & 11 (London: Garnet Press, 1994-6).

35. *al-Tafhīmāt al-Ilāhiyya* (Hyderabad, Sindh: Shāh Walī Allāh Academy, 1970)1:208.

36. Baqā', *Uṣūl-i-Fiqh aur Shāh Walī Allāh*, 24-31.

37. Baqā', 24-25. See also Ebrahim Moosa's preface to the present work, xiv.

38. J. M. S. Baljon, *Religion and Thought of Shāh Walī Allāh*, (Leiden: E. J. Brill, 1986), 165 quotes *al-Juz' al-Laṭīf* regarding his position at this time.

39. *Fuyūḍ al-Ḥaramayn*, Vision #33, 187-8. Discussed in Baqā', 24-25.

the *Muwaṭṭā* of Mālik, led him to examine the earliest sources and original texts in search of a solution to this dilemma. In other words, he undertook his own process of *ijtihād*, or independent investigation, rather than following any one of the schools absolutely. These factors led him to modify his anti-*taqlīd* position so as to allow following one particular legal school in the case of the general public.[40] At the same time, he tried to mitigate antagonism and controversy among followers of various schools by tracing the original rationales for the rulings and historical circumstances underlying any apparent disagreements.[41]

In Walī Allāh's time the Hanbalī school was of limited scope. He was acquainted with the literalist trend of Ibn Ḥazm and some works of Ibn Taymiyya.[42] His most influential teacher, al-Kurdī, followed the Shāfi'ī school and this seems to have been the dominant influence on Walī Allāh's theoretical jurisprudence. The present treatise *al-Inṣāf* reflects this influence of Shafi'īsm.

Later in his life Shāh Walī Allāh came to see his mission in the Indian context as one of performing *taṭbīq* or the accommodation of the Ḥanafī and Shāfi'ī schools, as well as other divergent approaches and methodologies.[43] It is reported that in a personal note in his own writing dated 1159 A.H./ 1746 found on a manuscript of al-Bukhārī that he used in teaching hadith that Shāh Walī Allāh stated that he followed the Ḥanafī school in his own practice while teaching both Ḥanafī and Shāfi'ī *fiqh*.[44]

In *Fuyūḍ al-Ḥaramayn*, a work that was composed soon after his return from the pilgrimage, several notes extol the virtues of Ḥanafīsm,[45] although elsewhere Shāh Walī Allāh stated that the Shāfi'ī school was most in con-

40. In the treatise *'Iqd al-Jīd* Shāh Walī Allāh includes a chapter on why most people should remain within the four legal schools, pp. 96-101. One reason is that these schools have preserved the historical continuity of the tradition going back to the Prophet. The second is that they represent the accurate consensus of the community. Thirdly, it is more reliable to follow the sayings of these schools than to follow a scholar of one's own age who may have been co-opted or corrupted.

41. In *Fuyūḍ* Vision # 10, 89-91 he is informed that the Prophet dislikes conflict among the schools and considers them to be equal.

42. In fact, one of his letters defends the orthodoxy of Ibn Taymiyya against his critics. "Maktūb dar manāqib va difā' az Taqī al-Dīn ibn-e-Taymiyya" in *Maktūbāt-e-Shāh Valī Allāh Dihlavī* ed. by Muḥammad 'Aṭā' Allāh Ḥanīf (Lahore: Maktaba al-Salafiyya, 1983).

43. *Musawwā* 1, 12-13. *al-Tafhīmāt* 1, 212.

44. Baqā', 40.

45. *Fuyūḍ* Vision # 19, 136-137. Here he is informed of the greatness of the Ḥanafī school. Vision # 31, 179-183. This vision concerns the necessity of following the Ḥanafī madhhab for Muslims in India. On pages 311-320 he recounts being inspired regarding the superiority of the Ḥanafī school.

formity with the Prophet's Sunna.[46] He seems to have envisioned that some sort of accommodated version of both schools was the most suitable form of jurisprudence, although in theory all four legal schools were deemed acceptable by him.[47]

Views on *Ijtihād* and *Taqlīd*

Historically certain Muslim scholars have disallowed the following of legal schools, for example, Ibn Ḥazm. By Shāh Walī Allāh's time the commonly held position was that the "gate of *ijtihād*" was closed, so that, in fact, only *taqlīd* was possible for Muslims including those with scholarly acomplishments, had been advanced and accepted by many jurists. This discussion became increasingly important for Muslims during the 18th century, with an increasing numbers of reformist scholars advocating scholarly recourse to *ijtihād*. It should also be pointed out that *ijtihād*, or making one's utmost effort to derive the correct ruling on an issue, has two major forms. In one case the scholar goes directly to the texts of the Qur'ān and the Sunna, especially to seek rulings in cases which have not previously arisen. In the second, more limited, type of *ijtihād*, the scholar decides upon the most correct ruling among scholarly opinions that already exist.

Shāh Walī Allāh's position resembles that of the Shāfi'ī school in that he concludes that all but the most radical forms of *ijtihād* remain possible, while rejecting blind or absolute imitation of any scholar or school (*taqlīd*).[48] He follows the theory worked out by Shāfi'ī masters such as al-Nawawī (1277) that absolute *ijtihād* remains possible as the level of the "affiliated absolute *mujtahid*" while the higher degree of absolute *ijtihād* of the original founders of the legal schools is no longer in existence. Rudolph Peters notes that, "This theory recognizes the possibility that there were still absolute mujtahids without, however, compromising the superiority of the founders of the madhhabs."[49]

In terms of his own affiliation to a legal school, Shāh Walī Allāh was a Ḥanafī in practice, but intellectually and preponderantly in his analysis of cases he often gave preference to the Shāfi'ī school.[50] In the treatise *al-Inṣāf* he speaks highly of this school, for example:

As for the *madhhab* of al-Shāfi'ī, it is the legal school having the most

46. *al-Khayr al-Kathīr* Khizāna # 10, cited in Baljon, 166. "The madhhab of al-Shāfi'ī, which gets to the root of things, is among the four the most in agreement with the Sunna."

47. *Fuyūḍ*, Vision # 10, 89-91.

48. *Inṣāf,* present translation, Chapter Four, 88-9.

49. Rudolph Peters, "Idjtihād and Taqlīd in 18th and 19th Century Islam," *Die Welt des Islams*, XX (3-4, 1980 ), 137.

50. Baqā', 27 and also 502 where he show that Shāh Walī Allāh prefers Shāfi'ī rulings in 70% of cases.

> absolute *mujtahids* and *mujtahids* within the school. It is also the legal school with the most developed legal theory and theology and the one that has provided the most Qur'ān interpretation and commentary on the hadith. It is the strongest in (establishing) chains of hadith reporters and transmission, the most accomplished in verifying the statements of the founder, the strongest in distinguishing between the opinions of the founder and the points of view of his associates, and the most scrupulous when giving certain opinions and points of view of prominent scholars preference over others.[51]

In terms of his own categories Shāh Walī Allāh could be considered a *mujtahid* affiliated (*mujtahid muntasib*) to this legal school[52] based on his criterion of preferring the analytical principles of Imam Shāfi'ī. According to his own statements as well as the prevailing legal theory, this level of affiliated *ijtihād* had died out in the Ḥanafī school after the third century due to the fact that hadith analysis was not a primary activity of this school. Meanwhile Hanbalīs and some Shāfi'īs had permitted the higher level of *ijtihād* to continue.[53] *al-Inṣāf* reflects the author's recognition of limited degrees of *ijtihād* for qualified persons while accepting *taqlīd* as normative among the general public.

The context of this treatise along with later nineteenth century works arguing for *ijtihād* has been clarified in an article by Rudolph Peters, who finds *al-Inṣāf* to be more conservative than the comparable but later works of al-Shawkānī (1760-1832) and al-Sanūsī (1787-1859).[54] Shāh Walī Allāh's views on *ijtihād* also participate in a tradition that both Voll and Peters suggest as having pan-Islamic roots going back to a circle of pious and learned scholars in the Hijaz, in particular to Ibrahīm al-Kūrānī (1690).[55] This is, in fact, the circle frequented by Shāh Walī Allāh during his two year stay in the Holy Cities.[56]

---

51. Present translation, Chapter Four, p. 58.

52. Baqā', 48. "This, however, cannot be regarded as *taqlīd* since the affiliated mujtahid accepts his Imam's ruling with complete understanding of its bases and arguments." Peters, 137.

53. Wael B. Hallaq, "Was the Gate of Ijtihād Closed?" *International Journal of Middle East Studies* 16 (1984), 30.

54. Peters studied Muḥammad ibn 'Alī al-Shawkānī's (1760-1832), *al-Qaul al-Mufīd fī adillat al-ijtihād wa-l-taqlīd* and *Irshād al-Fuḥūl* and Muḥammad ibn 'Alī al-Sanūsī's (1787-1859) *Īqāẓ al-asnān fī-l-'amal bi-l-ff wa-l-Qur'ān* and *Kitāb al-Masā'il al-'Ashar al-Musammā Bughyat al-Maqāṣid fī Khulāṣat al-Marāṣid*, 142-144.

55. Peters, 144-145.

56. Basheer M. Nafi, "Taṣawwuf and Reform in Pre-Modern Islamic Culture: In Search of Ibrāhīm al-Kūrānī," *Die Welt des Islams* 42 (3, 2002): 264-273 is recommended for a deeper understanding of the roles of al-Kūrānī and his article "A

It can therefore be shown that over his lifetime Shāh Walī Allāh went from a position of rejecting *taqlīd*[57] to an acceptance of following the four madhhabs in general, although he acknowledged the possibility of being able to go outside of them in specific cases. The following two treatises reflect this attitude. They demonstrate the author's mastery of both theoretical and practical jurisprudence, his position within a long tradition of debate over juristic disagreement, and his attitude to issues of *ijtihād* and *taqlīd*.

Teacher of Ibn 'Abd al-Wahhāb: Muḥammad Ḥayāt al-Sindī and the Revival of Aṣḥāb al-Ḥadīth's Methodology,"*Islamic Law and Society 13* (2, 2006): 208-241 for the role of al-Sindī.

57. *Fuyūḍ,* "Although it went against my temperament the Prophet ordered me to follow in practice one of the four legal schools, and not to go beyond them, although by nature I disliked and rejected *taqlīd.*,"187-8.

# Shāh Walī Allāh's
# al-Inṣāf fī Bayān Sabab al-Ikhtilāf
# (Doing Justice in Explaining the Cause of Juristic Disagreement)

# Shāh Walī Allāh's Preface

In the name of Allah, the Merciful, the Compassionate. Praise be to Allah who sent our master Muḥammad, may God's blessings be upon him, to be humanity's guide to Allah through His permission and to be an illuminating light. Then He inspired the Companions of the Prophet and the following generation and the jurists who carry out *ijtihād* to keep to the course[1] of their Prophet, generation after generation, until the world will be apprised of its end, so that His blessing may be fulfilled, and He is able to do whatsoever He wills.

I testify that there is no God but Allah, who is One, and has no partner, and I testify that our master Muḥammad is His servant and messenger after whom there will be no other Prophet. May God send blessings on him, his family, and his Companions, one and all.

To proceed, I who am in need of the mercy of Allah, the Bountiful One; Walī Allāh, son of 'Abd al-Raḥīm, may God (ﷻ) fulfill His blessing upon us both, in this life and the hereafter, say that:

God (ﷻ) placed in my heart on one occasion a measure through which I might recognize[2] every disagreement occurring in the community of Muḥammad, may blessings and peace be upon its leader, and through which I could recognize what is the truth according to Allah and His messenger. This standard also enabled me to explain the causes of juristic disagreement in such a way that there would remain neither doubt nor ambiguity.

Then I was asked about the reason for the disagreement among the Companions and among those who came after them, in particular with respect to positive legal rulings (*furū'*). I therefore undertook at that moment

---

1. Following the Cairo edition "*sair*" (course of their Prophet), rather than the Lahore edition's "*sirr*" (secret of their Prophet).

2. This refers to a vision that Shāh Walī Allāh recounts in a number of his works, "While I was sitting one day after the afternoon prayer with my concentration turned to God, suddenly there appeared the spirit of the Prophet, may the peace and blessings of God be upon him. It covered me from above with something that appeared to me to be a robe cast upon me. It was inspired in my heart in that situation that this was an indication of the manner of expounding the religion. At this I found in my breast a light that does not cease to expand every minute. Then my Lord inspired me, after a time, of what He had written for me with the exalted Pen, that some day I would undertake this important work, and that 'the earth would be illuminated with the light of its Lord' and that the rays of light would be reflected at the time of sunset, and that the divine law of Muḥammad would shine forth in this age by being presented in long and loose-fitting robes of demonstrative proof." *Hujjat Allāh al-Bāligha* I, 12. English translation p. 7.

to explain some of what God had disclosed to me, to the extent that time permitted me and at a level which the questioner could comprehend. What has emerged is a useful treatise on this topic that I have entitled, *Doing Justice to Explaining the Cause for Juristic Disagreement*.

Allah is sufficient for me and the best of guardians, and there is no refuge and no strength except in Allah the Exalted, the Magnificent.

# Chapter 1
# The Causes for the Disagreement of the Companions and the Followers Concerning Positive Law (*al-Furū'*)

You should know that in the noble time of the Messenger of God (ﷺ) law had not yet been put into writing. The mode of investigating legal rulings at that time was not like the investigative method of today's jurists who make great efforts in expounding the pillars, conditions, and principles governing[1] each matter as distinguished from other matters on the basis of its indicant (*dalīl*).[2] They posit hypothetical cases that they discuss and they formulate definitions for whatever may be defined, and stipulate limits for whatever may be limited, and so on with the rest of their accomplishments.

As for the Messenger of God (ﷺ), he used to perform ablution and the Companions would see his manner of ablution and imitate it without him explaining what was a [necessary] pillar (*rukn*) and what was his preferred mode of behavior (*adab*).[3] He used to pray, and they observed his prayers so they prayed just as they had seen him praying. He performed the pilgrimage and the people noted the way he performed the pilgrimage and followed what he had done. This was his (ﷺ) customary way. He did not explain whether there were six or four obligatory aspects to the ablution,[4] nor did he hypothesize that it would be possible that a person should do the ablution in any way other than in an uninterrupted sequence, so that he should rule on the soundness or invalidity of this, except on rare occasions. The Companions only rarely asked him about these things.

It is reported from Ibn 'Abbās (ﷺ) that he said, "I never saw any group better than the Companions of the Messenger of God (ﷺ). Up to the time of his death they had only asked him about thirteen issues, all of which were found in the Qur'ān. Among those issues were 'They will ask you about fighting in the sacred month. Say, fighting in it is a great sin,'[5] and 'They

1. The pillars are the necessary elements of a ruling. The conditions are attributes or elements which bring a ruling into force, for example, purity is a prerequisite of prayer; and the time for a certain prayer having arrived is a necessary condition for the valid performance of that prayer.
2. "Indicants" are features of the textual statement that can signify the reason for or force of an Islamic legal injunction.
3. The Prophet did not usually specify which elements of his actions were obligatory (*farḍ*) or which were his usual his practice and therefore fall under the *sharī'a* category of being recommended (*mustaḥabb*).
4. Ḥanafites hold that the obligatory elements are four, Shāfi'ites, six.
5. Qur'ān 2:217.

will ask you about menstruation.'" [6] He (Ibn 'Abbās])said, "They only used to ask about what would be beneficial for them." [7] Ibn 'Umar said, "Don't ask about things which haven't yet arisen, for I heard 'Umar ibn al-Khaṭṭāb curse someone who asked about something hypothetical." [8] Al-Qāsim said, "You are asking about things that we didn't use to ask about and you are probing into things into which we didn't use to probe. You are asking about things that we didn't know about and if we had known them we would not have been permitted to keep them hidden." It is reported that 'Umar ibn Isḥāq said, "Those of the Companions of the Prophet (ﷺ) whom I have met outnumber those who had passed away before me and I never saw any group more easygoing in behavior and more lacking in severity than them." It is reported about 'Ubāda ibn Bisr al-Kindī that he was asked about a woman who died while among a group of people where she had no guardian.[9] In response he said, "I have met many groups of people who weren't as severe as you and who didn't ask about [these] issues the way that you do." Al-Dārimī reported these accounts.[10]

The Prophet (ﷺ) was asked by people to give legal opinions about things as they came up, so he gave opinions concerning them, and cases were brought before him to adjudicate, so he judged them. He saw people doing something good, so he praised it; or a bad thing, so he forbade it. Whenever he issued a legal opinion on something, passed a judgement, or forbade an action, this occurred in public situations. Similar (was the procedure of) the two Shaykhs (Abū Bakr and 'Umar), who when they didn't have any authoritative knowledge (*'ilm*) about an issue would ask the people for a hadith of the Messenger (ﷺ).

Abū Bakr (رضي الله عنه) said, "I didn't hear the Messenger (ﷺ) say anything about her," i.e., the grandmother, and therefore he asked the people. After he led the noon prayer he asked, "Did any of you ever hear the Prophet of God (ﷺ) say anything about the grandmother?" Al-Mughīra ibn Shu'ba (669/70) said, "I have." Abū Bakr said, "What did he say?" He replied, "The Prophet of God (ﷺ) accorded her one-sixth [as a share of the inheritance]. Abū Bakr then asked, "Does any one else besides you know of

6. Qur'ān 2:222.

7. Al-Dārimī I, 51.

8. Al-Dārimī I, 50.

9. Therefore there was no representative (*walī*) available to arrange washing her corpse for burial.

10. 'Abd al-Raḥmān al-Dārimī, 797-869, from whose hadith collection *Sunan* (Beirut: Dār Iḥyā' al-Sunan al-Nabawiyya, 197-) Shāh Walī Allāh draws a number of examples in these pages. The ones cited above are drawn from hadiths in the chapter, "The Repugnancy of Asking for Legal Opinions," 50-51 Pālanpūrī emends "Ubāda ibn Bisr" to "Ubāda ibn Nusayy" II:607

this?" Then Muḥammad ibn Salama said, "He has spoken truly." So Abū Bakr accorded the grandmother one-sixth as a share.[11]

[An example of the same type is] the story of 'Umar asking the people about the case of the compensation for causing the death of the fetus, then his having recourse to the report of Mughīra;[12] and his asking them about the plague, then his accepting the report of 'Abd Al-Raḥmān ibn 'Awf.[13] A similar example is his having recourse to 'Abd al-Rahmān ibn 'Awf's report in the story of the Magians,[14] and the joy of 'Abd Allāh ibn Mas'ūd at the report of Ma'qil ibn Yasār when it agreed with his opinion,[15] and the story of Abū Mūsā turning back from the door of 'Umar who asked him about the hadith and Abū Sa'īd (al-Khudrī's) bearing witness in his favor.[16] Examples of this are well-known and abundantly reported in the two *Ṣaḥīḥ*s and the *Sunan*.[17]

In general, this was the Prophet's noble habit, may the peace and blessings of God be upon him. Thus each Companion saw whatever God enabled

11. This hadith is reported in al-Dārimī II, 359, Tirmidhī, Muwaṭṭa, and other collections.

12. This was the compensation which Mughīra reported that the Prophet had established: "I heard him judging that a male or female slave should be given as compensation (*diya*)." Al-Bukhārī IX , trans. M. M. Khan (Lahore: Kazi, 1979), 32-33. See al-Shāfi'ī, *al-Risāla*, trans. Majid Khadduri (Baltimore: Johns Hopkins, 1962), 263-264, for a discussion of this issue.

13. On an expedition to Syria in 639, 'Umar was informed that the country had been struck by a plague, and during consultation with other Companions he did not obtain a definite answer concerning a precedent of whether he and his men should continue into the afflicted territory. Then 'Abd al-Raḥmān ibn 'Awf informed him that the Prophet had said, "If you hear that a territory is afflicted by plague, don't enter it, and if you are in a place where plague strikes, don't flee from it." Shāh Walī Allāh, *Muṣaffā* 2 (Karachī: Muḥammad 'Alī Karkhāna, 1980), 206-207. Bukhārī Ṭibb 30, Muslim, *Muwaṭṭa* trans. Muhammad Rahimuddin (Lahore: Ashraf, 1980), 372-373. al-Shāfi'ī, *al-Risāla*, 264.

14. 'Abd al-Raḥmān reported that the Prophet had treated the Magians of Hajar according to the same rules as the People of the Book. Therefore the *jizya* tax was levied on them. *Muṣaffā* 2, 167. al-Shāfi'ī, *al-Risāla*, 265-6.

15. Recounted in detail on the next page.

16. According to a hadith, Abū Mūsā al-Ash'arī came to 'Umar's door and knocked three times, then went away when it was not opened. 'Umar sent after him and asked, "Why did you not come in?" Abū Musā replied that he had heard the Prophet say, "Ask permission to enter three times and if you are given it, enter, and if not, then leave." 'Umar said, "Who can confirm this?" Abū Mūsā went to the mosque and found that Abū Sa'īd al-Khudrī had heard the same statement. 'Umar assured Abū Mūsā that he had not doubted his veracity but rather he had done this as a deterrent to the circulation of false, unconfirmed hadiths. al-Shāfi'ī, *al-Risāla*, 267.

17. The three most authoritative hadith collections of al-Bukhārī, Muslim, and Abū Dāwūd.

him to see of his acts of worship, legal opinions, and judgements, then he committed them to memory, reflected upon them and recognized the reason for each thing due to the convergence of contextual evidence.[18] Thus the Companions interpreted some things as being permitted (*ibāḥa*), some as being recommended (*istiḥbāb*), and some as being abrogated due to textual signs (*amārāt*) and contextual evidence that satisfied them. What was most salient for them was the sense of confidence and assurance and they scarcely ever resorted to methods of legal reasoning, just as you observe that Arabic speakers understand the meaning of a conversation among themselves as they become assured through declarations, signals and allusions, without doing this consciously. The noble era of the Prophet came to a conclusion while the Companions were still proceeding in this manner.

Once the Companions had dispersed among different regions and each one had become the exemplar for some region, new legal problems proliferated and questions began to arise so that they were asked to give legal opinions about these. Each one answered on the basis of his recollection of the texts or resorted to legal inference. If he didn't find in what he knew about or had been about to deduce something that could serve to respond then he would perform *ijtihād* based on his own opinion and he would ascertain the rationale for legislation on which the Messenger of God (ﷺ) had based the ruling in his pronouncements. Thus he would search for the rationale underlying a ruling wherever he could find this rationale and he would spare no effort in order to remain consistent with the Prophet's (ﷺ) intent.

At this point disagreement of various types arose among them.

> [Type 1] One Companion heard a ruling about a judgement or legal opinion while some other one did not, and then the latter one used his own opinion to perform *ijtihād* in the case.

This *ijtihād* could also turn out in various ways.

A) One of them is that the second Companion's *ijtihād* might turn out to concur with the hadith. An example of this is what Al-Nasā'ī[19] and others recounted about Ibn Mas'ūd (ؓ). He was asked about a woman whose husband had passed away without settling her dowry portion (*mahr*).[20] Then he

18. *Qarā'in*. For the nuances of this term see, Wael Hallaq, "Notes on the Term *Qarīna* in Islamic Legal Discourse," in *Journal of the American Oriental Society* #109 (1989), 475-480.

19. Ahmad ibn Shu'ayb al-Nasā'ī, 830/31-915. He compiled of one of the six standard hadith collections.

20. That is, they had not yet had conjugal relations. Abū Dāwūd Nikāḥ 31, II p. 237 #2114. Tirmidhī, Nasā'ī, Ibn Māja, Ibn Ḥanbal. This tradition and Schacht's analysis of its ramifications concerning the retroactive attribution of hadith reports to the Prophet are discussed in Schacht, *The Origins of Muhammadan Jurisprudence*, (Oxford: Oxford University Press, 1975), 29, 226-227.

replied, "I did not see the Prophet of God (☙) making a judgement in such a case." However, people kept on coming one after the other and asking him for a month, and remained insistent. Finally he performed *ijtihād* based on his own opinion, and ruled that she should receive the dowry of his other wives, neither less nor more, and that she should observe the waiting period, and that she was entitled to inherit. Then Ma'qil ibn Yasār[21] stood up and testified that the Prophet, may the peace and blessings of God be upon him, had ruled similarly in the case of another woman. At this Ibn Mas'ūd was overjoyed to a greater extent than he had been at anything else since accepting Islam.[22]

B) Otherwise a debate might have arisen between two Companions. Then a hadith could become known in such a way that it would get accorded the rank of being the most probable opinion (*ghālib al-zann*) so that one Companion would retract his *ijtihād* in favor of the narrated hadith. An example of this is what the Imams report about Abū Hurayra (☙) who held that whoever got up in the morning in a state of ritual impurity could not keep the fast, until some of the wives of the Messenger of God (☙) informed him of a hadith which was contrary to his opinion, so he withdrew it.[23]

C) A further case is that a Companion would come to know of a hadith but not at that level which brings with it the rank of being highly probable (*ghālib al-zann*), so that he would not abandon his *ijtihād*, but rather would impugn the authenticity of the hadith. An example is what the masters of theoretical jurisprudence relate about Fāṭima bint Qays who testified before 'Umar ibn al-Khaṭṭāb that she had been divorced by the triple formula, and that the Prophet of God (☙) had neither granted her maintenance nor residence. He rejected her testimony saying, "I will not abandon the Book of God[24] on the basis of the statement of a woman when I don't know if she is telling the truth or lying. A divorced woman should receive maintenance and residence." 'Ā'isha (☙) said to Fāṭima, "Don't you fear God!" i.e., because of her statement (that a divorced woman should receive) "neither residence nor maintenance."[25]

---

21. In al-Nasā'ī's version the Companion is Ma'qil ibn Sinān al-Ashjā'ī.
22. Nasā'ī, *Sunan* VI, 164. This hadith concerns the case of Birwa' bint Wāshiq. See also *'Iqd al-Jīd*, p. 128.
23. al-Bukhārī, Fasting, Vol. III, 81. When asked about Abū Hurayra's ruling 'Ā'isha and Umm Salama reported. "At times Allāh's Apostle used to get up in the morning in a state of *janāba* (ritual impurity after having had sexual relations). He would then take a bath and keep the fast." *Muṣaffā* 1, 239.
24. For example, Qur'ān 65:6, "Lodge them where you are lodging" and 60:11, "Give to those wives who have gone away the like of what they have expended."
25. *Ṣaḥīḥ Muslim*, Hadith #3524, 772. The wording is slightly different from this version in the main hadith collections. 'Abd al-Fattāḥ Abū Ghuddah discusses this hadith in detail in his notes on *al-Inṣāf*, 24-25. The issue is whether an irrevocable

Another example of this type is that the two shaykhs (al-Bukhārī and Muslim) reported that 'Umar ibn al-Khaṭṭāb held that the ablution with sand was not sufficient for someone in a state of major ritual impurity who did not find water. Then 'Āmmār reported to 'Umar that he had been with the Messenger of God (ﷺ) on a journey and had become ritually impure and did not find any water so that he rolled himself in the dirt. Then he mentioned this to the Prophet of God (ﷺ). The Prophet of God (ﷺ) said, "It would have been sufficient for you to have done thus," and he lightly struck his hands against the earth and rubbed both of them across his face and arms.[26] However, 'Umar did not accept this and the proof of it according to him was not established due to a concealed defect that he saw in it.

Later that hadith became abundantly transmitted by many chains in the next generation, and the suspicion that it was defective faded into obscurity so that they implemented it.

D) The fourth case occurs when the hadith doesn't reach the Companion at all. For example, what Muslim related about Ibn 'Umar who ordered women to unbind their hair when they were taking the ritual bath. 'Ā'isha heard this and said, "I'm amazed at Ibn 'Umar—He commands women to unbind their hair, why didn't he order them to shave their heads too! I used to take a bath together with the Prophet of God (ﷺ) using the same vessel, and I did no more than pour water over my head three times."[27] Another example is what al-Zuhrī mentioned about Hind, i.e., that she had not heard about the Prophet allowing women to pray in the case of slight bleeding after the regular menstrual period,[28] so she used to cry because she could not pray.

### [Type 2] Differences in Evaluating Actions of the Prophet

Among [causes for disagreement among the Companions] are that they saw the Prophet carrying out an action, and some interpreted it as a means of drawing nearer to God (*qurba*) and others as being (merely) a permitted action.[29] An example of this is what the experts in legal theory relate about the ruling on *taḥṣīb*, (stopping to relax at a place called al-Abṭaḥ between Mina and Mecca when returning from Mina during the pilgrimage)—i.e., that the

divorce still entitles the woman to both maintenance and residence, as would be the case with revocable divorce. Ibn Rushd, *Distinguished Jurist's Primer* II, trans. Imran Ahsan Nyazee (London: Garnet Publishing, 1994-6), 204-5.

26. Bukhārī Tayammum 8. Nasā'ī Ṭahāra 195, 199-201.

27. Muslim Ḥaiḍ 29, Ibn Māja Ṭahāra 108, Ibn Ḥanbal. 'Abd Allāh ibn 'Amr, not Ibn 'Umar in Muslim's version.

28. For example, the hadith about the case of Fāṭima bint Abū Ḥubaysh is found in most collections in the chapter on "*Mustaḥāda.*" If the regular menstrual period is over but some bleeding occurs, the woman can perform the full ablution once and then the lesser ablution before each prayer.

29. In other words, should the action be legally recommended or neutral.

Prophet (ﷺ) had stopped there to rest. Abū Hurayra and Ibn ʻUmar held that this was done by way of performing an act of "drawing near to God" and thus they took it to be one of the normative Hajj practices (*sunan*). On the other hand, ʻĀ'isha and Ibn ʻAbbās held that it was coincidental and not one of the normative practices of the pilgrimage.[30]

Another example is that the majority held that walking with a fast gait *(ramal)* during the circumambulations of the Kaʻba was a normative practice of the Prophet. Ibn ʻAbbās held that the Prophet (ﷺ) had only done this as a response to an incidental situation which was the polytheists' saying that the fever of Yathrib had overcome the Muslims. Therefore this ramal was not a normative practice (*sunna*) of the Prophet.[31]

[Type 3] Disagreements based on misconstruing (*wahm*).

An example is that when the Messenger of God (ﷺ) performed the pilgrimage people saw him, so that some of them held that he entered the state of consecration (*iḥrām*) for ʻUmra and then later performed the Hajj (*tamattuʻ*), while others said that he had entered *iḥrām* for ʻUmra and Hajj together (*qirān*). Some said that he had entered the state of *iḥrām* for performing the Hajj only (*ifrād*).[32]

Another example that Abū Dāwūd reported from Saʻīd ibn Jubayr is that he said,

> "I said to ʻAbd Allāh ibn ʻAbbās, ʻO Ibn ʻAbbās, I am surprised at the disagreement of the Companions of the Messenger of God (ﷺ) about when the Prophet began to observe the *Iḥrām*.' He replied, 'In fact I am the most knowledgeable person about this. It occurred due to the fact that the Prophet only performed the Hajj once and their disagreement occurred for this reason. The Prophet (ﷺ) set out (from Medina) on the pilgrimage and when he had prayed one *rakʻa* in the mosque of Dhū Ḥulayfa he entered the state of *Iḥrām* while he was sitting and made the exclamation "Labbaika" when he had finished his two *rakʻas*, so that

---

30. *Saḥīḥ Muslim*. Arabic II, #337-345, pp. 951-952, Siddiqi trans. Hadiths #3005-3015, pp. 659-660. Ibn Māja, Ibn Ḥanbal. Shāh Walī Allāh prefers the latter in *Ḥujjat Allāh al-Bāligha* II (Cairo: Dār al-ṭabʻ wa-l-nashr, 1952-3), 548 ff. "Account of the Farewell Hajj."

31. Bukhārī Hajj 55, Muslim Hajj 247, Abū Dāwūd, Ibn Māja.

32. *Iḥrām* is the state of consecration maintained by the pilgrims during the pilgrimage to Mecca. There are three types of *iḥrām*. A pilgrim may declare at the outset the intention of either remaining in the state of *iḥrām* throughout the period of performing *ʻumra* and *ḥajj* without any break of the sanctified state (*qirān*); the pilgrim may break the *iḥrām* state after the *ʻumra* and then resume it for the *ḥajj* (*tamattuʻ*); or the pilgrim may perform only a *ḥajj* without undertaking any *ʻumra* (*ifrād*). This is discussed in *Ḥujjat Allāh al-Bāligha* II, Chapter "Account of the Farewell Hajj," 548 ff.

some groups of people heard him do this. I have preserved the recollection of his doing this. Then he mounted, and when his camel stood up bearing him he cried out "I am at your service O Lord" and (other) people saw that he did this. This is due to the fact that people were coming to him group by group so that some heard him say "Labbaika" only when his camel stood up bearing him, so that they said, "The Messenger of God (ﷺ) began saying 'Labbaika' when his camel rose up bearing him." Then the Prophet (ﷺ) set out on the journey, and when he had climbed the heights of Baida', he called out "I am at your service, O Lord" and some of the people saw this so that they said, 'He began saying "Labbaika" when he had climbed the heights of al-Bayda'.' By God's oath he entered the state of Iḥrām at his place of prayer and said 'Labbaika' both when his camel rose up with him, and also when he reached the heights of al-Bayda'."[33]

[Type 4] Disagreement due to lack of attention and forgetting.

An example is that it is reported that Ibn 'Umar used to say that the Prophet (ﷺ) had made 'Umra during the month of Rajab, then 'Ā'isha heard this and judged that Ibn 'Umar had been inattentive.[34]

[Type 5] Disagreements on how to construe a situation.

An example is what either Ibn 'Umar or 'Umar related from the Prophet, may the peace and blessings of God be upon him, about the dead person being tormented by the weeping of his family over him. Then 'Ā'isha adjudged that he had not construed the hadith properly. The Messenger of God (ﷺ) was passing by the funeral of a Jewish woman whose family was weeping over her so that he said, "They are weeping over her while she is being tormented in her grave."[35] He (Ibn 'Umar) had supposed that the torment was causally related to the weeping, so that the ruling was generally applicable to the case of every dead person.

[Type 6] Disagreement over the rationale for the legislation (*'illa*) behind the ruling.

One example concerns (the reason for) standing up as a funeral procession passes. One opinion is that it is out of respect to the angels so it should be generalized to funerals of both Believers and Unbelievers. Another says that it is due to the awe of death, so it should be done for either a Believer or a Unbeliever. Al-Ḥasan ibn 'Alī (may God be pleased with him and his father) said, "The funeral bier of a Jew was passing by the Messenger of God (ﷺ) and he stood up because he disliked that it should be raised above

33. Abū Dāwūd Manāsik 21. Vol II, p. 150 #1770.
34. Ibn Māja Manāsik 47, Bukhārī 'Umra 3, Tirmidhī, Ibn Ḥanbal.
35. Bukhārī Janā'iz 12, 36; Muslim, Tirmidhī, Nasā'ī.

his head,"[36] so that he considered that this practice applied only in the case of Unbelievers.

[Type 7] Disagreement over how to reconcile two conflicting rulings.

For example, the Prophet (ﷺ) gave permission for temporary marriage during the year of Khaybar and the year of Awṭās, then he forbade it. Then Ibn 'Abbās said, "The dispensation was based on an extenuating circumstance and the prohibition came due to the cessation of that circumstance, thus the prohibition remains in force."[37] The majority of the scholars held that the dispensation (*rukhṣa*) had made it allowable (for a time) and that the prohibition had abrogated this. Another example is the Prophet's (ﷺ) forbidding facing the direction of prayer (*qibla*) while performing *istinjā'*,[38] so one group held this ruling to be generally applicable and not abrogated. Jābar saw him urinating while facing the *qibla* a year before his death, so he held that this abrogated the previous prohibition. Ibn 'Umar saw him relieving himself with his back to the *qibla* and his face toward Syria,[39] so he used this to refute their opinions. Another group reconciled the two reports: al-Sha'bī and others held that the prohibition applied in the particular circumstance of being outside in the desert, but that if the person were in an enclosed toilet, then there would be no importance given to either facing towards or to having one's back turned to the *qibla*. One group held that the Prophet's statement of prohibition was definitive and universally in force (*'āmm muḥkam*), and that what he himself had done might possibly apply to his case only, so that it could neither abrogate nor restrict the practice to specific circumstances.[40]

In summary, the opinions of the Companions of the Prophet (ﷺ) varied and each one of the Followers learned whatever he was able from them, in like manner. Thus the Follower memorized whichever hadiths of the

---

36. This story is found in Bukhārī, Muslim, Nasā'ī, and Ibn Ḥanbal, but none mention the phrase about his disliking the bier being raised above his head. al-Nadvī, Salmān al-Husaynī, *Ārā' al-imām Walī Allāh al-Dihlavī fī ta'rīkh al-tashrī' al-islāmī* (A study of *al-Inṣāf fī Bayān Sabab al-Ikhtilāf*) (Lukhnow: *Dār al-sunna l-il-nashr*, 1986), 14-5.

37. That is, Ibn 'Abbās had, according to some reports, considered temporary marriage permissible in times of need, but then changed his opinion. Tirmidhī, chapter forbidding temporary marriage. Bukhārī Khan trans. VII, 36-37,

38. *Istinjā'*—cleaning with water after urination.

39. Bukhārī Khan trans. I, 108. By facing Syria is meant facing Jerusalem, which some also considered to be forbidden.

40. In *Muṣaffā* 1 (Karachi: Muḥammad 'Alī Karkhāna-e-Islāmī Kutub, 1980), 40-41, Walī Allāh notes that al-Shāfi'ī forbade both facing towards Mecca or Jerusalem while outside, not while indoors, while Abū Ḥanīfa considered both reprehensible in all circumstances. al-Shāfi'ī, *al-Risāla*, 217-218.

Prophet (ﷺ) and opinions of the Companions that he heard and reflected on them. Then he reconciled the disagreements in so far as he was able and preferred some opinions over others. Some of the sayings vanished from their consideration even though they had been reported from some of the most important Companions. For example, the opinion reported from 'Umar and Ibn Mas'ūd concerning [the invalidity of] performing the ablution with sand on the part of a person who was in a state of major ritual impurity (*junūb*), faded away once the hadith reports from 'Ammār and 'Umrān ibn al-Ḥaṣīn and others became abundantly transmitted.[41] At this point each learned scholar among the Followers came to have his very own school, so that within every city there stood out a leading scholar like Sa'īd ibn al-Musayyab (713) and Sālim ibn 'Abd Allāh ibn 'Umar (725) in Medina, and after them al-Zuhrī (742) and al-Qāḍī Yaḥyā ibn Sa'īd (761) and Rabī'a ibn 'Abd al-Raḥmān (753), and 'Aṭā' ibn Abī Rabāḥ (732) in Mecca, and Ibrāhīm al-Nakha'ī (715) and al-Sha'bī (c. 728) in Kufa, and Al-Ḥasan al-Baṣrī (728) in Basra, and Ṭāwūs ibn Kaysān (c. 720) in Yemen, and Makḥūl (736) in Syria. Thus God made people avid and desirous for their knowledge so that they learned hadiths of the Prophet and the legal opinions and sayings of the Companions from these scholars, while they also learned their own legal opinions and verifications from them. Those who needed legal opinions would consult them, legal issues were discussed among them, and cases were put before them to judge. Sa'īd ibn al-Musayyab and Ibrāhīm (al-Nakha'ī) and their peers compiled together all of the categories of jurisprudence, and for each topic of jurisprudence they had principles which they had learned from the pious ancestors.

Sa'īd and his associates believed that the people of the two Holy Cities were the most reliable in jurisprudence. Therefore they based their school on the legal opinions and judgments of 'Umar and 'Uthmān, and the fatwas of 'Abd Allāh ibn 'Umar, 'Ā'isha, and Ibn 'Abbās, and on the verdicts of the judges of Medina. They compiled whatever they were able of these, then they examined them with respect to reliability and thorough research. They firmly upheld whatever they found to be agreed upon by the learned scholars of Medina. Whenever they found them to be in disagreement, they adopted the strongest and the prevaling opinion, either due to it being held by the majority, or due to its agreeing with a strong analogy or a clear inference from the Qur'ān and Sunna, or due to other similar reasons. When they didn't find any response on the issue among what they had learned from those scholars (of Medina) then they derived a response on the basis of their sayings, or they traced allusions or logical entailments (within the

41. Bukhārī I, 208-209. Tayammum 8, has both versions. Also Muslim, Nasā'ī Ṭahāra 195, 199-201.

revealed sources).[42] Thus they came up with many cases (in jurisprudence) in which each topic has various sub-divisions.

Ibrāhīm and his associates thought that 'Abd Allāh ibn Mas'ūd and his circle were the most reliable persons in jurisprudence. This is shown by what 'Alqama (680/81) said to Masrūq (682/83), "Is anyone of them more reliable than 'Abd Allāh (Ibn Mas'ūd)?"[43] and by the saying of Abū Ḥanīfa (ﷺ) to Al-Awzā'ī, "Ibrāhīm is more adept at jurisprudence than Sālim, and if not for the virtue of ('Abd Allāh Ibn 'Umar's) having been a Companion, I would have said that 'Alqama had more legal acumen than 'Abd Allāh ibn 'Umar; and 'Abd Allāh (ibn Mas'ūd) is in a class by himself."[44]

The basis of his (al-Nakha'ī's) school consists of the fatwas of 'Abd Allāh ibn Mas'ūd, the judgements and fatwas of 'Alī (ﷺ) along with the judgments of Shurayḥ and other Kufan judges, so that he combined whatever he was able of this. Then he did for their reports what the Medinan scholars had done for the reports of the Medinans. He derived as they had derived, and then outlined the issues of jurisprudence according to sub-divisions under each topic.

Sa'īd ibn al-Musayyab was the spokesman for the jurists of Medina and had memorized more judgments of 'Umar and hadith narrated by Abū Hurayra than any of them, while Ibrāhīm (al-Nakha'ī) was the spokesman for the Kufan jurists. Thus, when they spoke about a matter without attributing it to someone else, this usually became attributed to one of the Companions or Followers either explicitly, by allusion, or in some other way. The jurists of their two respective cities concurred on the accuracy of these two figures, learned from them, reflected on what they had learned, and then drew further inferences on the basis of this, and God knows best.

---

42. The allusions (*īmā'āt*) are meanings implied by a text while the logical entailments (*iqtidā'āt*) are meanings which are necessarily understood from a text although they are not explicitly stated. Both are forms of textual indication (*dalālat al-naṣṣ*).

43. The occasion is explained in more detail in the following chapter on p. 16.

44. The occasion of this remark was that al-Awzā'ī had asked Abū Ḥanīfa why he did not lift his hands at various points during the ritual prayer, while he knew of a hadith transmitted by Zuhrī from Sālim from Ibn 'Umar that the Prophet used to raise his arms at the times of the *takbīr* of respect, bowing, and returning to the upright position. Abū Ḥanifa said that he had heard a hadith from Ḥammād from Ibrāhīm from 'Alqama from Asad from 'Abd Allāh ibn Mas'ūd that the Prophet raised his hands only at the beginning of the prayer. *Kashshāf fī Tarjuma al-Inṣāf*, Urdu trans. by Muḥammad 'Abd Allāh Balyavī (Lucknow: 1886), 18.

# Chapter 2
# The Causes for Disagreement Among the Legal Schools of the Jurists

You should know that God (ﷻ) brought into being a generation of scholars after the era of the Followers who conveyed religious knowledge. This fulfilled the promise of the Prophet (ﷺ) when he said, "A just person from every succeeding generation will convey this knowledge."[1] Thus these later persons learned the manner of performing the lesser and greater ablutions, prayer, pilgrimage, marriage, business transactions, and all other commonly occurring things from those who had been with the Prophet. They transmitted the hadith reports of the Prophet (ﷺ), heard the judgments of the judges (*qāḍīs*) of the various cities and the fatwas of their muftīs and they inquired about legal issues, and performed *ijtihād* concerning all of these things. Then when they became leaders of the community and were consulted about all religious matters, they followed in the footsteps of their teachers and did not fail to study the allusions (*īmā'āt*) and logical implications (*iqtiḍā'āt*) (of revealed texts). Thus they judged, gave legal opinions, transmitted, and taught. The procedure of (all of the) scholars (*'ulamā'*) of this generation was similar.

The essence of the procedure of these scholars was:

1) To uphold both those hadiths that were transmitted in uninterrupted chains reaching back to the Prophet (*musnad*) and those reports related about him that were transmitted directly on a Companion's authority.[2] They deduced knowledge using the sayings of the Companions and Followers which might have been hadiths transmitted from the Messenger of God (ﷺ) but were considered to be less authoritative, so they termed them (these hadith) as being interrupted (*mawqūf*) before reaching the Prophet. An example is what Ibrāhīm (al-Nakha'ī) said while he was narrating a hadith about the Prophet (ﷺ) forbidding crop futures contracts and the sale of fresh dates still on the tree for dried dates.[3] It was asked of him, "Have you learned from the Prophet of God any other hadith than this (that could shed light on the issue)?" He answered, "Yes, but I prefer to say (in such a case), 'Abd Allāh

1. *Mishkāt*. Hadith cited in the chapter on knowledge. p. 57. Related in al-Bayhaqī's *Madkhal*.

2. Such hadith are termed "*mursal*."

3. *Muzābana* (exchanging dry harvested dates for fresh dates in equal quantities) and *Muhāqala* (renting land in return for part of the wheat harvest) was forbidden in the Shāfi'i school due to its being interest and according to Mālik due to its being gambling. *Muṣaffa* I, 352. al-Shāfi'ī, *al-Risāla*, 235-6, 325-6.

said,' or 'Alqama[4] said.'" Likewise al-Sha'bī[5] said, when he was asked about a hadith which was said to go back to the Prophet (ﷺ), "I prefer to say that it goes back to a great person at a lesser rank than the Prophet(s) so that if there should be any addition to or deletion from it, it would come from someone lesser than the Prophet."[6] In other cases they deduced conclusions from sayings of the Companions using inferences (*istinbāṭ*) that they based on revealed sources or they employed a process of independent reasoning (*ijtihād*) based on their own opinions. In all of these matters the procedure of the Followers and Successors was better (than those who came later). This is because they were more accurate, closer in time, and knew more religious sources by heart, than those who came after them. For this reason implementing their rulings was prescribed unless they disagreed among themselves or a hadith of the Prophet of God (ﷺ) overtly conflicted with their opinion.

2) It was also the procedure of the early scholars to refer to the opinions of the Companions in cases when the hadith reports of the Prophet of God(s) were at variance with one another about some issue. If the Companions held that some hadiths were abrogated or that their literal meaning should be disregarded; or if they did not pronounce them abrogated, but concurred on leaving them aside and not holding them obligatory—this would be tantamount to rejecting any legalistic rationale (*'illa*) in them, or to ruling that they were abrogated or required interpretation. The jurists used to follow the Companions in all of these matters. An example is the doctrine of Mālik concerning the hadith about a dog's saliva,[7] when he said, "This hadith has been reported but I don't understand what it really means." Ibn Ḥājib[8] related this in his *Mukhtaṣar al-Uṣūl*, but I do not see the jurists implementing it.

3) When the opinions of the Companions and the Followers differed about an issue, then the preference of every scholar was for the school of

4. 'Alqama ibn Qays, a Successor and Kufan legal expert, d. 721-83.
5. 'Amīr ibn Sharāḥīl al-Sha'bi, a Successor who compiled hadith and was a legal expert.
6. al-Dārimī I, 84.
7. This refers to the hadith, "If a dog drinks from one of your utensils it must be washed seven times to be pure." Mālik held the view that the water should be disposed of and the utensil washed but not for any special number of times since prey caught by a dog is considered ritually clean (Qur'ān 5:4). Malikites therefore hold that this ruling could be implemented as an act of piety but was not obligatory which seems to be at variance with the explicit meaning of the hadith. Bukhārī Wuḍū' 33, Muslim, Abū Dāwūd, Tirmidhī, Nasā'ī, Ibn Māja, al-Dārimī, Ibn Ḥanbal. Ibn Rushd, *Bidāyat al-Mujtahid wa-nihāyat al-muqtaṣid* 1, trans. *The Distinguished Jurist's Primer* 1, trans. Imran Ahsan Nyazee (London: Garnet Publishing, 1994), 27.
8. 'Uthmān ibn 'Umar Ibn Ḥājib, 1175-1249 who wrote *Mukhtaṣar al-Muntahā al-Uṣūlī,* a manual of Shāfi'ī *fiqh.* (Beirut: Dār al-Kutub al-'Ilmiyya,1983).

the people of his city and his teachers. This is because he was more able to distinguish their sound opinions from their faulty ones, and was more cognizant of the principles underlying their opinions, and therefore would be predisposed toward their superiority and erudition.

The way of 'Umar, 'Uthmān, Ibn 'Umar, 'A'isha, Ibn 'Abbās, Zayd ibn Thābit, and their associates such as Sa'īd ibn al- Musayyab, who best knew 'Umar's judgments and the hadith narrated by Abū Hurayra; and those such as 'Urwa, Sālim, 'Ikrama,[9] 'Aṭā' ibn Yasār, Qāsim, 'Ubayd Allāh ibn 'Abd Allāh, al-Zuhrī, Yaḥyā ibn Sa'īd, Zayd ibn Aslam, and Rabī'a were more worthy of being followed than others since they were people of Medina. This is due to what the Prophet (ﷺ) had explained about the virtues of Medina, and due to its being the abode of the jurists and the gathering place of the scholars in every age. Therefore, you find Mālik following their methods of reasoning and it is well-known that Mālik upheld the consensus of the Medinan scholars and that al-Bukhārī consecrated a chapter to "Adhering to What is Agreed Upon by the People of the Two Holy Cities."

According to the Kufan scholars, the school of 'Abd Allāh ibn Ma'sūd and his associates, and the judgments of 'Alī, Shurayḥ, and al-Sha'bī, and the fatwas of Ibrāhīm, were more worthy of being followed than others. This is represented by 'Alqama's saying when Masrūq[10] inclined to the opinion of Zayd ibn Thābit concerning giving equal shares of inheritance. 'Alqama said, "Is anyone of you more reliable than 'Abd Allāh (ibn Mas'ūd)?" Then Masrūq replied, "No, but I saw Zayd ibn Thābit and the people of Medina practicing *tashrīk*.[11] If the people of a region concur about something they firmly adhere to it."[12] Mālik said about this same type of issue, "The established practice (sunna) about which there is no disagreement in our view is such and such." If people differed, then they accepted the stronger and preferable opinion—either due to the majority upholding it, or due to its agreeing with a strong analogy, or due to it being derived from the Qur'ān and the practice of the Prophet. This is the type of instance in which Mālik said, "This is the most correct (opinion) among those that I have heard."

If the scholars did not find a response to an issue among the sources that they had preserved, they derived it on the basis of their (the Compa-

9. 'Ikrama's name does not appear in the same list when it is found in the *Ḥujjat Allāh*. 'Abd al-Faṭṭāh Abū Ghuddah, 36, notes that the omission is more accurate since 'Ikrama was from Mecca, not Madīna.

10. Masrūq ibn al-Ajda' (d. 682), a Kufan Successor in the tradition of 'Abd Allāh ibn Mas'ūd.

11. *Tashrīk* is that a woman's husband, mother, mother's brothers, and parent's brothers will inherit from her and that the parent's brothers will share in a third. 'Umar had said that they should not inherit.

12. al-Dārimī *Sunan* II, Farā'iḍ, 349-350. 'Alī didn't give these shares and Zayd did.

nions') sayings and sought out allusions and logical implications (within these revealed texts).

In this generation scholars were inspired to record hadiths so that Mālik and Muḥammad ibn 'Abd al-Raḥmān ibn Abī Dhi'b (775) recorded them in Medina, and Ibn Jurayj (767) and Ibn 'Uyayna (814) in Mecca, and al-Thaurī (778) in Kufā, and Rabī' ibn al-Ṣabīḥ (777) in Baṣra. All of them followed the procedure that we mentioned.

When (the Caliph) Manṣūr performed the pilgrimage he said to Mālik, "I have decided to order that the books that you have compiled (*The Muwaṭṭa'*) should be copied and then I will send copies to every garrison town of the Muslims and command them to follow what is in them, and not to go beyond them to any other source." Mālik replied, "O Commander of the Faithful, don't do this, for sayings (of the Companions and Followers) are already known to people, and they have heard hadith and have transmitted the reports. Each group follows what they already know and differences have (already) arisen, so leave people with what each locality has chosen for itself."

A similar story has also been told about (the Caliph) Harūn al-Rashīd, that he consulted Mālik if he could have the *Muwaṭṭa'* hung up in the Ka'ba, and urge the people to act according to it. Mālik replied, "Don't do that, for the Companions of the Messenger of God (ﷺ) differed about cases in positive law and every practice has taken effect as they dispersed to all the regions. Harūn replied, "May God grant you success, O Abū 'Abd Allāh!" Al-Suyūṭī related this.

[The Mālikī School]

Mālik was the most reliable of them in relating the hadiths that the Medinans reported from the Messenger of God (ﷺ), the most trustworthy of them concerning the chain of transmitters, and the most knowledgeable of them concerning the judgments of 'Umar and the opinions of 'Abd Allāh ibn 'Umar and 'Ā'isha and their associates among the seven jurists.[13] Through him and other scholars like him the disciplines of hadith transmission and giving juristic opinions was established. Once he became the established authority he taught hadith, gave legal opinions, benefitted the people and distinguished himself. This saying of the Prophet (ﷺ), "Soon people will travel great distances seeking knowledge, but they will find none more knowledgeable than the scholar of Medina,"[14] truly applies to him (Imām Mālik). This hadith was narrated by Ibn 'Uyayna and 'Abd al-Razzāq—and the word of these two should be sufficient.

---

13. The seven early jurists of Medina who are particularly distinguished are Sa'īd ibn Musayyab, 'Urwah ibn Zubayr, Qāsim ibn Muḥammad ibn Abī Bakr al-Ṣiddiq, Abū Bakr ibn 'Abd al-Raḥmān Makrūmī, Kharijah Zayd ibn Thābit, 'Ubayd Allāh ibn 'Abd Allāh ibn 'Utba Ma'sūdī, Sulaymān ibn Yassār Hilālī.

14. Tirmidhī, *'Ilm* #18 vol V, 48, Ibn Ḥanbal.

Then Mālik's associates collected his reports and preferred opinions and summarized them, edited them, explained them, derived rulings on issues from them and discussed their principles and proofs. They (eventually) dispersed to northwest Africa and to other reaches of the world so that through them God brought great benefit to His people. If you would like to verify what we have said concerning the origin of Mālik's school then consult the book *al-Muwaṭṭa'* and you will find it to be as we have related here.

[The Ḥanafī School]

Abū Ḥanīfa (ﷺ) was the closest adherent (among the school founders) to the way of Ibrāhīm (al-Nakha'ī) and his contemporaries and he very rarely departed from his teachings. He was extremely competent in making legal derivations based on Ibrāhīm's school and was a precise inquirer into the meanings of the derivations. In addition, he gave the fullest attention to positive law (*al-furū'*). If you wish to verify the truth of what we have said then go over the statements of Ibrāhīm and his contemporaries in the book *al-Āthār* of Muḥammad (Abū Yūsuf) (ﷺ) and the *Jāmi'* of 'Abd al-Razzāq (827),[15] and the *Muṣannaf* of Abū Bakr ibn Abī Shayba,[16] then compare these with his school. You will find that he did not diverge from their procedure except on insignificant instances and that even on these minor occasions he did not deviate from views held by the Kufan jurists.

The most well-known of his students was Abū Yūsuf (ﷺ) (731/2-798). He held the post of chief-judge during the reign of Harūn al-Rashīd and thus he was instrumental in the emergence of Abū Ḥanīfa's school and in judgments being based on it spreading throughout the regions of Irāq, Khurasan, and Transoxiana. The best compiler and most assiduous student among the Ḥanafīs was Muḥammad ibn al-Ḥasan (al-Shaybānī, 805). It is reported that he studied law with Abū Ḥanīfa and Abū Yūsuf and then went to Medina where he studied the *Muwaṭṭa'* with Mālik. After that he went over it on his own and correlated the school of his associates with the *Muwaṭṭā'*, issue by issue, whenever they could be harmonized.

If they could not be harmonized in this way and he saw that a group of the Companions and the Followers held the same opinions as his associates, then he accepted this as his position. However, if he found the jurists using a weak analogy or a feeble derivation that disagreed with a sound hadith or that was opposed by the practice of most of the scholars, then he abandoned it in favor of one of the opinions of the pious ancestors that he found preferable. These two (Abū Yūsuf and Muḥammad ibn Ḥasan al-Shaybānī)

15. 'Abd al-Razzāq ibn Hammām al-San'ānī (744-827) *Muṣannaf* (Beirut, 1970-72).

16. 'Abd Allāh ibn Muḥammad ibn Abī Shayba, 775/6-849, a Ḥanafī traditionalist and historian. Ibn Māja was his pupil.

followed the way of Ibrāhīm al-Nakha'ī and his colleagues in so far as they were able, just as Abū Ḥanīfa (ﷺ) had done.

Juristic disagreement (among these three Ḥanafī jurists) would arise in one of two ways. Either in some cases the two students disagreed with a derivation which Abū Ḥanīfa had made based on Ibrāhīm's opinion, or the opinions held by Ibrāhīm and his peers would be at variance and the two students disagreed with Abū Ḥanīfa concerning which opinion they found to be preferable over the others. Muḥammad (ibn Ḥasan) (ﷺ) compiled and gathered the opinions of these three (Ibrāhīm, Abū Ḥanīfa, and Abū Yūsuf) and this benefitted many people.

The followers of Abū Ḥanīfa (ﷺ) devoted themselves to these compilations by abridging them, simplifying them, writing commentaries on them, making derivations from them, or by establishing fundamental principles and making deductions. Later they dispersed to Khurasan and Transoxiana and this became known as the legal school of Abū Ḥanīfa.

The school of Abū Ḥanīfa is considered the same as that of Abū Yūsuf and Muḥammad (Ibn Ḥasan), despite the fact that these two were "absolute *mujtahids*"[17] in their own right and although their disagreements with him concerning both theoretical and applied jurisprudence are significant, due to their fundamental agreement and due to the fact that their opinions are recorded jointly in *al-Mabṣūṭ* and *al-Jāmi' al-Kabīr.*[18]

[The Shāfi'ī School]

Al-Shāfi'ī came on the scene during the early emergence of these other two (Malikī and Ḥanafī) schools and at a time when their legal theory and positive law had begun to be systematized. He examined the method of the earliest figures and found in it certain elements that kept him from following their procedure. This he discusses at the beginning of his *Kitāb al-Umm.*[19]

1) Among these elements is that he found that they accepted hadiths that were not connected to the Prophet directly through a Companion (*mursal*) and otherwise interrupted (*munqaṭi'*) hadiths and that these two types of hadith in many cases were defective. When he collated the chains of transmission of the hadiths it became evident that many of the (*mursal*) hadiths not transmitted directly by a Companion from the Prophet were baseless, and many conflicted with those hadiths that were uninterruptedly transmitted (*musnad*). Therefore, he decided not to accept *mursal* hadiths unless certain conditions were fulfilled, and

17. The levels of *ijtihād* are discussed in Chapter Four of this text.
18. These are authoritative collections of Ḥanafī *fiqh*. This paragraph is not found in *Ḥujjat Allāh al-Bāligha.*
19. While some recent available printed texts of *Kitāb al-Umm* begin with the book on Purity, manuscripts and earlier editions often contained al-Shāfi'ī's treatise, *al-Risāla,* which contains this theoretical material.

these are mentioned in the books of juristic theory.[20]

2) A second factor that dissuaded him from following their procedure was that the rules for reconciling conflicts had not been rendered precise by the earlier figures, so that due to this, defects had entered into their *ijtihāds*. Therefore al-Shāfi'ī established principles for doing this and recorded them in a book[21] that was the first recording made of the theory of jurisprudence (*uṣūl al-fiqh*). An example of this is what we have heard concerning al-Shāfi'ī, i.e., that he went over to inquire directly from Muḥammad ibn al-Ḥasan while the latter was disparaging the scholars of Medina for their giving a judgement concerning (the sufficiency of) one witness for giving an oath. Ibn al-Ḥasan held that this practice was not justified by the Qur'ān.[22] Al-Shāfi'ī said, "Is it affirmed by you that it is not permitted to go beyond what the Qur'ān says on the basis of the report of a single individual?" He replied, "Yes." Al-Shāfi'ī said, "Then why do you hold that the will in favor of an heir is not permitted on the basis of the Prophet's (ﷺ) saying, "Know that there is no will in favor of an heir"[23] while God (ﷻ) said, in the qur'ānic verse "It is prescribed for you that if death is drawing near to one of you. . ."[24] [that if some property is to be left a will should be made in favor of parents and relatives].[25] He raised a number of objections of this sort to him so that Muḥammad ibn al-Ḥasan was silenced.

3) A third element is that some of the sound hadiths were not known to the *'ulamā'* among the cohort of the Followers who were charged with delivering legal opinions, so that they performed independent reasoning based on their personal opinions, made generalizations, or fol-

---

20. For example, in his *al-Risāla*, 279-284.

21. al-Shāfi'ī's *al-Risāla.*

22. Qur'ān 2:282 which requires two witnesses. See Ibn Rushd, *Bidāyat al-mujtahid* ll (trans.), 562-3. The Ḥanafī's do not allow a singly transmitted hadith to augment the Qur'ān. A *khabar wāhid* (individual narration) is always only probable (*ẓannī*), not certain, in the Ḥanafite system. Thus, even if it is specific it cannot restrict a general pronouncement of the Qur'ān. Imran Ali Khan Nyazee, *Theories of Islamic Law*, (Islamabad: Islamic Research Institute, 1994), 164 ff.

23. Bukhārī Waṣāyā 6, Abū Dāwūd, Tirmidhī, Nasā'ī, Ibn Māja, al-Dārimī, Ibn Ḥanbal.

24. "...if he bequeath wealth, that he bequeath unto parents and near relatives in kindness. (This is) a duty for those who ward off (evil)." (Qur'ān 2:180)

25. al-Shāfi'ī, *al-Risāla,* 142-144 considers that bequests to parents are invalid since their right to inherit certain shares was confirmed elsewhere in the Qur'ān. Bequests to others valued up to one-third of the estate were allowed in certain cases. In the case of this hadith, the Ḥanafī's hold that it is not singly but rather, multiply, transmitted. Ibn Rushd, *Distinguished Jurist's Primer ll* (trans. Nyazee), 405-6.

lowed one of the deceased Companions, delivering legal opinions on this basis. Then, when these sound hadith reports later became known in the third generation, they were not implemented by them out of the supposition that these conflicted with the practice and custom of the people of their city to which they had all agreed, and that this constituted a reason for rejecting these hadith and was a case for not taking them into consideration. Or (in some cases) these hadith did not come to light in the third generation, but only after that. By this period the hadith scholars had deeply investigated the chains of transmission and traveled to all corners of the earth seeking them out from the bearers of traditional knowledge. Also by this time the body of those hadiths that had only been transmitted by one or two persons among the Companions, and then passed on from them by only one or two persons, had proliferated, and things had continued in this vein. Thus these hadiths had not been known to the juristic theorists (*ahl al-fiqh*) and only came to light in the time of the memorizers of tradition who collated the chains of many of the hadith, for example, those transmitted by the people of Baṣra, although residents of other regions were ignorant of them. Al-Shāfi'ī explained that knowledgeable people in the cohorts of the Companions and Followers never ceased seeking out the hadith reports relative to an issue, and if they didn't find any then they would seize on to some other means of deduction (*istidlāl*). Then if they later became aware of such a hadith they would revoke their answer based on *ijtihād* in favor of the hadith. Therefore, if this were the case, their (the Companions') failure to have (previously) adhered to the hadith did not constitute a reason for rejecting it, never indeed—unless they explained the reason behind this rejection.

An illustration of this is the hadith about the two large jars,[26] for this is a sound hadith transmitted by many chains, the majority of them going back to Abū al-Walīd ibn Kathīr from Muḥammad ibn Ja'far ibn al-Zubayr from 'Abd Allāh—or from Muḥammad ibn 'Ibād ibn Ja'far from 'Ubayd Allāh ibn 'Abd Allāh—both of these from Ibn 'Umar. Then after that the chains of transmission branched out further. These two hadith transmitters (Muḥammad ibn Ja'far and Muḥammad ibn 'Ibād), although they are considered to be reliable, are not among those who were authorized to give legal opinions, nor did people consider them reliable. This hadith (of the two jars) did not come to light in the period of Sa'īd ibn Musayyab, nor in the time of al-Zuhrī, and neither the Mālikīs nor the Ḥanafīs proceeded according to it, so they did not

---

26. That if an amount of water reaches an amount that could be held in two large jars it remains ritually pure for the purposes of major ablution (*ghusl*). Abū Dāwūd, Sunan I, Ṭahāra 33, 17 #65. Tirmidhī, Nasā'ī, Ibn Māja, al-Dārimī, Ibn Ḥanbal.

implement it whereas al-Shāfi'ī did.[27] Similar is the case of the hadith about sales contracts remaining open as long as the parties are in each other's company (*khiyār al-majlis*), for it is a sound hadith,[28] transmitted by many chains of reporters. Among the Companions Ibn 'Umar implemented it and so did Abū Ḥurayra but it was not known among the seven jurists and their contemporaries so they did not uphold it. Mālik and Abū Ḥanīfa held this to be a reason for rejecting the hadith while al-Shāfi'ī implemented it.

4) The fourth (reason for al-Shāfi'ī's developing his own procedure) is that the opinions of the Companions were collected at his time, so that these came to proliferate, disagree with one another, and branch out, and he observed that many of them opposed sound hadiths since the Companions had not been aware of those hadiths. Al-Shāfi'ī saw that the pious ancestors had never ceased giving preference to the hadith in such cases so he abandoned rigid adherence to their opinions when they did not agree (with hadith) saying, "They are (only) human beings and so are we."

5) The fifth factor is that al-Shāfi'ī observed that a group of the jurists combined personal opinion, which the divine law did not sanction; with analogical reasoning, which it affirmed; so that they did not distinguish one from the other. They sometimes termed this procedure *istiḥsān*.[29] What I mean by personal opinion (*ra'y*) is that they ascribe the expected occurrence of some hardship or benefit as the reason (*'illa*) behind the ruling. Qiyās, however, requires that they derive the reason for the ruling from the transmitted text, and that then they issue the ruling based on this rationale.

Al-Shāfi'ī completely nullified this type of personal opinion (*ra'y*), saying, "Whoever performs *istiḥsān* wants to become the lawgiver." Ibn al-Ḥājib related this in *Mukhtaṣar al-Uṣūl*.[30] An example of this is the ruling concerning reaching puberty or attaining legal maturity in the

---

27. Discussed in Ibn Rushd, *Distinguished Jurist's Primer* 1 (trans. Nyazee), 21-24. Shāh Walī Allāh mentions this hadith again in Ch. 5, p. 71.

28. Bukhārī Buyū' 19, 20, 42, 43, 44, 46, 47; Muslim, Abū Dawūd, Tirmidhī, Nasā'ī, Ibn Māja, al-Dārimī, *Muwaṭṭa'*, Ibn Ḥanbal. al-Shāfi'ī, *al-Risāla*, 227-8. Ibn Rushd, *Distinguished Jurist's Primer* ll, 204-5.

29. *Istiḥsān*. That a less apparent analogical conclusion (*qiyās*) may be preferred to other more obvious ones if it fulfills the general purpose of the sharī'a better. Likewise in other cases where the result of the *qiyās* process is passed over in favor of other results from the sources of Islamic law (Qur'ān, Sunna, or consensus) or due to necessity or the force of customary practice.

30. *Mukhtaṣar al-Muntahā al-Uṣūlī* II, (Beirut: Dār al-'Ilmiyya, 1983), 288 with slightly different wording "*qāla al-Shāfi'ī man istaḥsana fa-qad shara'a.*" "The one who performs *istiḥsān* has made his own law (based on his own opinion)."

> case of an orphan, which is a covert matter. Therefore they established the expected time of maturity as having reached the age of twenty-five years in its place, saying, "When an orphan attains this age his property should be remitted to him." They opined that this was *istiḥsān*, while the derivation based on analogy is that it should not be remitted to him.[31]

In sum, since al-Shāfi'ī found things like this among the procedure of the preceding figures he reconstructed jurisprudence by setting out its theoretical foundations, drawing out their practical ramifications, and compiling books that distinguished his reputation and benefitted humanity. The jurists concurred with him and devoted themselves to summarizing, commenting on, deducing, and deriving rulings from his books. Then they dispersed to the various cities so that this developed into the Shāfi'ī school, and God knows better.

---

31. Some of the Ḥanafīs, including Abū Ḥanīfa set the age of maturity at twenty-five years, on the attainment of which the orphaned person's property should be put at his disposal irrespective of his mental capacity or judgement. Abū Yusuf disagreed and preferred analogy on the basis that incompetence or stupidity constituted a reason that property should not be remitted, despite the age of the person. 'Abd al-Raḥmān al-Jazīrī, *Al-Fiqh 'alā Madhāhib al-Arbā'a.* Vol. II, (Beirut: Dār al-Fikr, 1986) 350-352. Chafik Chehata in *Études de Droit Musumane* I, (Paris: Presses Universitaires de France, 1971), 77-155 devotes a chapter, "*La notion d'incapacité en droit hanèfite*" to this issue.

# Chapter 3
# Causes for the Disagreement Between the People of the Hadith and Scholars Who Exercise Personal Opinion

You ought to know that there were among the *'ulamā'* at the time of Sa'īd ibn al-Musayyab, Ibrāhīm, and al-Zuhrī[1] and in the time of Mālik and Sufyān, and (even) after that, a group who despised engaging in the use of personal opinion (*ra'y*). They feared giving fatwas and making deductions except in cases of unavoidable need. Their greatest concern was for transmitting the reports of the Prophet of God (ﷺ).

'Abd Allāh ibn Mas'ūd was once asked about a matter and he said, "I would hate to permit for you something that God had forbidden to you, or that I should forbid a thing which God had permitted you."[2] Mu'ādh ibn Jabal said, "O People, don't hasten to calamity before it has struck, for there will always remain among the Muslims those who, if asked, will respond with many details."[3] Similar statements were reported from 'Umar, 'Alī, Ibn 'Abbās, and Ibn Mas'ūd concerning the dislike of speculative discussion of matters which had not been revealed. Ibn 'Umar said to Jābir ibn Zayd,[4] "You are one of the jurists of Basra so don't give legal opinions unless they are based on a conclusive qur'ānic injunction or an established prophetic practice, for if you do otherwise you will perish and cause the ruin of others."[5]

Abū al-Naṣr said, "When Abū Salama arrived at Basra, Ḥasan (al-Baṣrī) and I went to see him. He asked Ḥasan, 'Are you Ḥasan? There is no one in Basra whom I would rather meet than you. This is because I heard that you give fatwas on the basis of your personal opinion. (In the future) don't give fatwas based on your personal opinion unless it is (based on) a *sunna* from the Prophet (ﷺ) or a revealed qur'ānic verse.'"[6]

Ibn al-Munkadir said, "The scholar stands in the middle between God and His servants—so he had better find a way out."[7]

Al-Sha'bī was asked, "What did you do when you were asked (about legal matters)?" He replied, "You have asked the expert. If when any per-

1. Muḥammad ibn Muslim al-Zuhrī, d. 742
2. al-Dārimī I, 55.
3. al-Dārimī I, 49.
4. Jābir ibn Zayd, 642-c. 721. A famous Basran jurist affiliated with the Ibāḍī sect.
5. al-Dārimī I, 59.
6. al-Dārimī I, 58-59.
7. al-Dārimī I, 53.

son were asked about an issue, he would say to his associate, 'you give the fatwa on the question,' then in the very same way this would go on from one to another until it wound up back up at the first person." Al-Sha'bī said, "Accept whatever these ones reported to you from the Messenger of God (ﷺ), and whatever they said on the basis of their own opinion, throw in the trash."[8] Al-Dārimī related all these reports.

Then the recording of the Prophet's hadith and reports from the Companions spread in the Islamic regions as did the writing of compilations and manuscripts. Eventually there remained very few hadith transmitters who did not have a recorded copy, a collation, or a manuscript due to their need of this in important situations.

The great scholars of that time circulated among the regions of the Hijaz, Syria, Iraq, Egypt, Yemen, and Khurasan and collected the books, studied the manuscripts, and carefully scrutinized the less known and rare hadiths. Through the great endeavors of these people hadiths and reports were collected that no one had ever gathered before, so that they could accomplish what had never been possible previously. Many chains of hadith transmission became known to them, so much so that some hadiths were available to them transmitted through over one hundred or more lines. Some of the chains illuminated what had been obscure about certain others and the hadith scholars recognized the status of each hadith as being transmitted by a single person or by a wide variety of transmitters. They were enabled to investigate the hadiths that were reinforced (*mutābi'āt*)[9] and supported by other accounts (*shawāhid*).[10] Many sound hadiths came to light for them that had not been known to the people giving legal opinions previously. Al-Shāfi'ī said to Aḥmad (ibn Ḥanbal), "You are more knowledgeable about the hadiths than I, so if there exists a sound report, please inform me so that I can follow it, whether it is Kufan, Basran, or Syrian." Ibn al-Humām related this.

This is because a few sound hadiths were only related by the people of a particular locale such as individual Syrians or Iraqis or by the members of a particular family such as the manuscript of Barīd transmitted from Abū Burda from Abū Mūsā,[11] and the manuscript of 'Amr ibn Shu'ayb (736)

---

8. al-Dārimī I, 67.

9. Mutabi' pl. Mutābi'āt are hadiths that are supported or corroborated on the basis of multiple transmissions from persons further down along their chain of reporters.

10. *Shahīd*, pl. *Shawāhid* are hadiths which agree on a matter or have the same meaning while they come down through differing chains of transmission. *Kashshāf*, 34. 'Abd al-Ḥaqq Muḥaddith Dihlavī, *Muqaddima fī Uṣūl al-Ḥadīth*, (Lukhnow: Dār al-'Ulūm, 1984), 57-59.

11. This manuscript had been passed down to Barīd from his grandfather, Abū Burda (d. c. 722), who was named as a judge in Kufa and noted as a hadith trans-

transmitted from his father and from his grandfather.[12] In other cases a certain Companion might have been of minor influence and relative obscurity so that only a small group of hadiths were passed on from him. Thus most of the people giving legal opinions were unaware of these types of hadiths.

This generation of scholars had available to them the reports of the jurists of each city who had been Companions and Followers, for before their time a person had only been able to collect the hadiths of his own city or associates. Those before them had relied on the situational and circumstantial evidence available to them for knowing the names of the transmitters and the degree of their reliability. This generation (of scholars) went deeply into this discipline (of biography) and made it a distinct field for recording and investigation. They debated the rulings of hadith soundness, and so on. Through this process of putting into writing and debate, things that had been previously unknown were disclosed to them in terms of whether a hadith went back uninterruptedly to the Prophet or was interrupted. Sufyān, Wakī' and ones like them had made the greatest efforts but had only been able to find less than one thousand hadiths going back uninterrupted to the Prophet, as Abū Dāwūd al-Sijistānī mentioned in his treatise addressed to the people of Mecca. In contrast, the people of this generation transmitted about forty thousand hadiths.

It is true that al-Bukhārī condensed his *Ṣaḥīḥ* to six thousand hadiths and that Abū Dāwūd limited his *Sunan* to five thousand, and that Aḥmad made his *Musnad* a standard by which to recognize the hadith of the Messenger of God (ﷺ). Thus, whichever hadith is found in the *Musnad*, even if reported by one chain could be valid, and if not, it would have no validity.

The chief hadith scholars of this generation were 'Abd al-Raḥmān ibn Mahdī (813), Yaḥyā ibn Sa'īd al-Qaṭṭān (813), Yazīd ibn Harūn (736), 'Abd al-Razzāq (827), Abū Bakr ibn Abī Shayba (849), Musaddad [ibn Musarhad (843)], Hannād [ibn al-Sarīd, (857)], Aḥmad ibn Ḥanbal (855), Isḥāq ibn Rāhawayh (852/3), al-Faḍl ibn Dakayn (748), 'Ali al-Madīnī (849), and their peers. This generation was an excellent model for the subsequent generations of hadith scholars.

The researchers among them, after consolidating the discipline of hadith transmission and recognizing the ranking of hadith, next turned to jurisprudence. They didn't hold the opinion that people should agree to perform *taqlīd*[13] of any previous scholar due to the fact that they observed that each of

mitter. Abū Burda was the son of Abū Mūsā al-Ash'arī (c. 614-663) who was a Companion of the Prophet, and governor of Basra. The hadith scholars differ about its reliability.

12. This transmission was said to go back to 'Abd Allāh ibn 'Amr ibn al-'Aṣ (682/3), great-grandfather of 'Amr ibn Shu'ayb.

13. *Taqlīd*—to accept or follow a previous ruling or judgement as the "binding authority" of a legal school or scholar, as opposed to reinvestigating the sources

these schools contained contradictory hadiths and reports. Thus they took up evaluating the Prophet's hadith and the reports of the Companions, Followers and mujtahids according to rules which they themselves established—and I will explain to you in a few words what these principles are.

[Principles of the Research Oriented Jurists]

1) They held that if a conclusive qur'ānic verse pertained to an issue, it was not permitted to abandon this in favor of something else.

2) If the Qur'ān could support various interpretations then the Sunna would rule on the issue.

3) If they didn't find a response in the Divine Book, they implemented a sunna of the Messenger of God (ﷺ) whether it was abundantly reported, current among the jurists, or known only to the people of a certain region or family, or reported through a particular chain of transmission, and whether the Companions and jurists had implemented it or they did not.

4) In the case where there existed a hadith from the Prophet about the issue, they wouldn't follow any report from the Companions or any *ijtihād* of a scholar which opposed it.

5) Once they had concluded their efforts in tracing the hadiths and had not found any hadith relevant to the matter, they would accept the opinions of a group of the Companions and Followers. In doing so they would not restrict themselves to one group at the exclusion of another or one region at the exclusion of another, as those before them had done.

6) If the majority of the Caliphs and jurists had agreed on something, they accepted this, and

7) If they (the Caliphs and jurists) disagreed, they would accept the opinion of the one who was the most knowledgeable and pious, or the most accurate or the most renowned.

8) If they found a matter in which two opinions held equal force, this was considered an issue in which both views could be valid.

9) If they were unable to do even this, then they would look attentively into what could be generalized on the basis of the Qur'ān and the Sunna, their referents by way of allusion, and what they logically entail. They would bring parallel cases to bear in responding to the issue in instances when the two cases were obviously close to each other.

In doing this they did not rely on principles of legal theory but rather on what could be arrived at through pure human understanding and what would assure the heart, just as the standard of multiple reporting (*tawātur*) for hadith traditions is not the number of transmitters, nor their status, but rather the certainty in the hearts of people that follows hearing the report,

through independent reasoning (*ijtihād*).

as we have previously recounted concerning the status of the Companions of the Prophet.[14]

These principles were derived on the basis of the practice of the first scholars and their clear pronouncements. It is reported from Maymūn ibn Mihrān (734) that he said, "Whenever a dispute (between two parties) was laid before Abū Bakr he used to consult the Book of God, and if he found something in it by which to adjudicate among them he judged by it. If it wasn't in the Qur'ān and he knew of a sunna from the Messenger of God (ﷺ) pertaining to the matter, he judged by it. If he failed in this he would go out and ask the Muslims saying, "Such and such a case has been referred to me, so do you know if the Messenger of God (ﷺ) had made any judgement on this?" Thus sometimes a whole group of people would gather around him mentioning a judgement from the Messenger of God (ﷺ) about this situation. Then Abū Bakr would say, "Praise be to God, who put among us those who have preserved reports of our Prophet." If he failed to find a sunna of the Prophet (ﷺ) pertaining to the case he would gather the pious and reliable people and the best among them and he would consult them. Then if their opinion concurred on a soluton he would judge according to this.

It is reported from Shurayḥ that 'Umar ibn al-Khaṭṭāb wrote to him, "If you find something in God's book, judge according to it and don't let others divert you from this. If something arises which is not in God's book, then look at the practice (*sunna*) of the Prophet (ﷺ) on it and judge on the basis of this. If there arises something which is not in God's book and neither is there a sunna of the Prophet (ﷺ) about it, then consider what people have concurred on, and act on this. If there arises something which is not in God's book, nor covered by any sunna of the Prophet (ﷺ) nor has anyone before you discussed it—then choose either of two courses of action. If you wish to perform independent reasoning (*ijtihād*) based on your own opinion and proceed in that manner, then proceed. If you wish to delay, then delay and I consider the delay as nothing but good for you."[15]

It is reported that 'Abd Allāh ibn Mas'ūd said, "There was a time when we did not judge, nor were we capable of judging. God has decreed that we should arrive at this (situation) which you see. Thus, from now on whoever is presented with a case to judge should rule on the case based on what is in the book of God (ﷻ). If something comes up which is not found in the book of God, then he should rule on it based on what the Prophet (ﷺ) ruled. If something comes up which is neither in God's Book, nor legislated by the Prophet (ﷺ), then he should judge according to what the righteous ones did (i.e., by *ijmā'*). He should not say, 'I am afraid' or 'I hold the opinion,'

14. In Ch. 1, p. 8. For a discussion of the standards for abundant transmission (*tawātur*) see Wael Hallaq, *A History of Islamic Legal Theories: An Introduction to Sunni uṣūl al-fiqh* (Cambridge: Cambridge University Press, 1997), 60-62.
15. al-Dārimi, Muqaddima, 60. Also Nasā'ī.

for, 'the forbidden is clear and the permitted is clear, and between them are ambiguous matters—so leave aside what you are dubious about in favor of that about which you have no doubt.'"[16]

Ibn 'Abbās, when asked about a matter, provided an answer about it: if it was found in the Qur'ān, and if it was not in the Qur'ān but was ruled on by the Prophet (ﷺ), he related this. If not—then he related what Abū Bakr and 'Umar had ruled. If none of these resources was available, then he gave his own opinion about the case.[17]

It is reported from Ibn 'Abbās, "Don't you fear that you will be punished or made to sink into the ground for saying, 'The Prophet (ﷺ) of God said such and such, and some other person said....'"[18] Qatāda said, "Ibn Sīrīn recounted to a man a hadith from the Prophet (ﷺ), then that man said, 'so and so said such and such a thing.'" Then Ibn Sīrīn said, "I tell you a hadith from the Prophet (ﷺ) and you said, 'so and so said such and such a thing!'"[19] Al-Awzā'ī[20] said, "'Umar ibn 'Abd al-'Azīz gave orders that no one could give personal opinions about what was in the Qur'ān. Only the leaders of the legal schools could give valid opinions concerning things which the Qur'ān had not revealed, nor had a sunna of the Prophet been transmitted about them. Nor could anyone hold their own personal opinion above a matter for which a sunna of the Prophet existed. Al-A'mash[21] said, "Ibrāhīm (al-Nakha'ī) used to say that the *muqtaḍī*[22] should stand on the left (of the prayer leader). Then I related to him a hadith from Samī' al-Ziyāt from Ibn 'Abbās, that the Prophet (ﷺ) had made (Ibn 'Abbās) stand on his right side, so Ibrāhīm adopted this."

Al-Sha'bī reported that a man had come to him asking about an issue so he replied that Ibn Mas'ūd had given a certain opinion about it. The man then said, "Tell me your opinion about it." Al-Sha'bī said, "Aren't you amazed at this person, I told him what Ibn Mas'ūd had said and he asked about my opinion. My religion is more important to me than that! By God,

16. This report in found in al-Dārimī I , 59. The quotation is a hadith of the Prophet found in al-Bukhārī Īmān 39, Buyū' 2, Muslim, Abū Dāwūd, Tirmidhī, Nasā'ī, Ibn Māja, al-Dārimī, Ibn Ḥanbal.
17. al-Dārimī I, 59.
18. For raising some other person's opinion on par with a statement of the Prophet.
19. al-Dārimī I, 117.
20. 'Abd al-Raḥmān ibn 'Amr al-Awzā'ī (d. 774), a Syrian jurist.
21. Sulaymān ibn Mihrān al-A'mash, c. 680-765. Traditionalist and Qur'ān reader who studied with Mālik.
22. The *Muqtaḍī* is an individual who follows a prayer leader *(imām)*. Ibn 'Abbās's hadith is in Khan's translation of al-Bukhārī I, 377.

I would rather burst into song than inform you on the basis of my own opinion."[23] Al-Dārimī gathered all of these reports.

Al-Tirmidhī reported from Abū al-Sā'ib who said, "We were with Wakī' and he said to one of those persons who favored giving his own personal opinion, 'the Prophet of God (ﷺ) used to practice branding (*ish'ār*).[24] Did Abū Ḥanīfa hold that branding (*ish'ār*) is a form of mutilation (*mathla*)?'[25] The man said, 'It had been reported that Ibrāhīm al-Nakha'ī said, "Branding is the same as mutilation."'" Then (Abū Sā'ib) related, "I saw Wakī' get very angry and he said, 'I tell you that "the Prophet of God (ﷺ) said" and you say, "Ibrāhīm said." It's better that you should be imprisoned and not set free until you repudiate what you have just said.'"[26]

It is reported that 'Abd Allāh ibn 'Abbās, 'Aṭā, Mujāhid and Mālik ibn Anas (ﷺ) used to hold that, "Except for the Prophet of God (ﷺ), everyone else's speech may either be accepted or rejected."

In summary, once (the scholars) had laid out jurisprudence according to these principles there remained no issue among those that had been discussed by their predecessors or had come up in their own era but that they had found a hadith pertaining to it, whether this hadith went back uninterruptedly to the Prophet (*marfū'*), or had all its transmitters mentioned (*muttaṣil*), or was interrupted at the level of a Companion (*mursal*), or was the statement of a Companion (*manqūl*), or whether it was sound, good, or worthy of being considered. Otherwise they found a statement of Abū Bakr or 'Umar, or the other caliphs or the judges of the early Islamic garrison cities and the legists of the (early) regions or made an inference (*istinbāṭ*) through a generalization, allusion, or entailment (of the revealed text) that would pertain to the case. In this way, God (ﷻ) facilitated implementing the Sunna for them.

The highest of the scholars in stature, and the one who transmitted hadith most extensively, the most knowledgeable of the ranking of hadiths, and the most astute in jurisprudence was Aḥmad ibn Ḥanbal, then after him Isḥāq ibn Rāhawayh (852).[27]

The systematization of jurisprudence along these lines depended on collecting a great number of hadiths and reports to the point that Aḥmad

---

23. al-Dārimī I, 47.

24. *Ish'ār* was a practice of branding a camel vowing it as a sacrifice for Allāh's sake. Abū Hanīfa disapproved of *Ish'ār* in the case that the animal was tortured or harmed by it. *Ṣaḥīḥ Muslim*, (Siddique trans.) Hadith #2865 and note, p. 632.

25. *Mathla* is mutilation that defaces the appearance. For the classification of Abū Ḥanīfa's opinion as *istiḥsān* or *ra'y* see Schacht, J. *The Origins of Muhammadan Jurisprudence* (Oxford: Oxford University Press, 1950), 112.

26. Tirmidhī, *Sunan* II, 195. Hajj Ch. 66 #908.

27. A traditionalist contemporary of Aḥmad ibn Ḥanbal who was also hostile to the people of personal opinion (*ra'y*).

was asked if (knowing) 100,000 hadiths would suffice a person to be able to give a legal opinion. He replied, "No," until the number of 500,000 hadiths was suggested. Then he said, "I hope that this will be the limit."[28] He meant that this basis (would suffice for) giving legal opinions.

God later brought forth a generation who observed that their predecessors had spared them the trouble of gathering hadiths and laying out jurisprudence on their foundation. They therefore were free to turn their attention to other disciplines such as isolating those sound hadiths concurred on by the great masters of the hadith scholars such as Zayd ibn Harūn,[29] Yaḥyā ibn Sa'īd al-Qaṭṭān, Aḥmad, Isḥāq and ones like them. Secondly, they collected the legislative hadith upon which the jurists of the early Islamic cities and the *'ulamā* of the early regions had built their legal schools. Thirdly, they ruled on each hadith according to its merits such as the irregular (*shādhdha*)[30] and singly transmitted (*fādhdha*) hadiths that the earlier reporters had not transmitted. Fourthly, they followed up their lines of transmission that earlier scholars had not traced in which there might be found a chain reaching back directly to the Prophet or an uninterrupted chain of transmission. They also studied the line of transmission from one juristic expert to another jurist or from one hadith memorizer to another and so on with this type of technical topic.

These traditionalist scholars are al-Bukhārī, Muslim, Abū Dāwūd, 'Abd ibn Ḥumayd (863), al-Dārimī, Ibn Māja, Abū Ya'lā (1066),[31] al-Tirmidhī, al-Nāsā'ī, al-Dāraquṭnī, al-Ḥākim, al-Bayhaqī, al-Khāṭib, al-Daylamī, and Ibn 'Abd al-Barr (1070)[32] and their like.

[Hadith Scholars]

In my opinion, the ones among them who are the most famous, the most knowledgeable, and whose writings are the most useful, are four, who were approximately contemporary to one another.

The first of them is Abū 'Abd Allāh al-Bukhārī (870) whose goal was to sort out the sound, abundantly transmitted hadith that went directly back to the Prophet from the others, and to derive from them jurisprudence, the Prophet's biography and Qur'ān interpretation. Thus he compiled his collection *al-Ṣaḥīḥ*, remaining faithful to his own conditions. We heard that a pious man saw the Prophet of God (ﷺ) in a dream and he said, "What's wrong with you that you have become preoccupied with the jurisprudence

---

28. Some other versions of this report mention 300,000 hadiths as the number, for example Abū Ṭālib al-Makkī in *Qūt al-Qulūb* I (Cairo: Muṣṭafā al-Bābī al-Ḥalabī, 1961), 300.

29. Zayd in the text has been corrected to Yazīd.

30. A *shādhdh* hadith is one reported by a trustworthy person but which goes against the narration of a person who is more reliable.

31. Abū Ya'la Muhammad ibn al-Husayn ibn al-Farra, 990-1066.

32. Ibn 'Abd al Barr, 978-1070. A scholar distinguished in *fiqh* and genealogy.

of Muḥammad ibn Idrīs (al-Shāfi'ī) and gotten away from my book." He asked, "O Prophet of God, what then is your book?" He replied, "*Ṣaḥīḥ al-Bukhārī*." By my life, this book has achieved fame and acceptance to a degree beyond which none could possibly aspire.[33]

The second of them is Muslim al-Nīsāpūrī (875), who aimed to isolate those sound, elevated, connected hadith which the hadith scholars had agreed upon, and from which the prophetic Sunna could be inferred. He wished to popularize them and facilitate the inference of jurisprudence from them. Thus he did an excellent job of organizing them, assembling the chains of transmission of each hadith in one place in order to clarify as fully as possible textual variants and the branches of the lines of transmission. He also correlated the variants so that there remains no excuse for the person who is cognizant of the Arabic language in turning away from the Sunna to something else.

The third of them is Abū Dāwūd al-Sijistānī (889) whose concern was with collecting the hadiths in which jurists found the indicants (*istadalla*) for rulings and which were current among them and upon which were founded the rulings of the *'ulamā'* of the early cities. To this end he compiled his *Sunan* collecting in it the sound, good, without defect (*līn*), and worthy of being implemented (*sāliḥ l-il 'amal*) hadith. Abū Dāwūd said, "I did not cite in my book any hadith which people had agreed to leave aside." He exposed the weakness of any weak hadiths and in the case of deficient hadiths he explained the deficiency in a way that the expert in hadith studies would understand. He explained in the case of each hadith whatever (ruling) a scholar had deduced from it, or whatever opinion a knowledgeable person had based on it. Therefore al-Ghazālī and others stated that his book would suffice the legal scholar undertaking independent reasoning (*mujtahid*).

The fourth of them is Abū 'Isā al-Tirmidhī (892). It's as if he perfected the method of the two shaykhs (Bukhārī and Muslim) in so far as they clarified and left no ambiguity, and the method of Abū Dāwūd in so far as he collected everything on which an opinion had been given. Consequently, al-Tirmidhī combined each of the two methods and added to them the explanation of the views of the Companions, Followers, and jurists of the early Islamic cities. He compiled a comprehensive book and elegantly abridged the hadith chains. Thus he would cite one chain while pointing out what he had omitted. He explained the status of each hadith in its being sound, good, weak, or undetermined, giving the reason for defectiveness so that the student of hadith would be informed concerning its status and rec-

33. Shāh Walī Allāh wrote on al-Bukhārī's methodology in a separate treatise, *Sharḥ Tarājim Abwāb Ṣaḥīḥ al-Bukhārī* (Hyderabad, India: Dā'ira al-Ma'ārif al-Uthmāniyya, 1949), 1-6. One of his letters in the collection *Kalimāt al-Ṭayyibāt* (Delhi: Mujtabā'ī, 1309 A.H.) also addresses the role of al-Bukhārī. Nadvī, *Arā'*, 110.

ognize those hadiths which could properly be taken into consideration from those which could not. He also indicated whether a hadith was transmitted by a variety of persons or by a single narrator. He cited the schools of the Companions and Jurists of the early Islamic cities, providing the first and last names[34] for individuals who needed identification and he did not omit anything about persons of knowledge. Therefore it is said that his book suffices the *mujtahid* and is more than enough for the *muqallid*.[35]

[The Jurists]

In contrast to these persons, another group of scholars during and after Mālik and Sufyān's time were not reluctant to delve into juristic issues, nor did they fear giving legal opinions. They held that jurisprudence was the foundation of religion so that it must become disseminated. They rather feared the transmission of prophetic hadith that were being made to reach back to him. For example, al-Sha'bī said, "We prefer (a hadith) going back to someone other than the Prophet (ﷺ) for if there should be any addition or deletion from it, that would involve someone other than the Prophet (ﷺ)."

Ibrāhīm (Nakha'ī) said, "I prefer to say, that 'Abd Allāh said,' and 'Alqama said.'" When Ibn Mas'ūd related hadith reports that he had heard from the Prophet his face became pale and he used to say, "(The Prophet said) exactly this or something along these lines, and so on."[36]

'Umar said when he sent a group of the Anṣār to Kufa, "You are going to Kufa to a people who weep when they recite the Qur'ān. They will come to you saying, 'The Companions of Muhammad have arrived, the Companions of Muhammad have arrived'. Then they will come to you and ask you about hadith so try to be sparing in giving reports from God's Messenger (ﷺ)."[37] Ibn 'Aun (933) said, "When al-Sha'bī was presented with an issue he was cautious, while Ibrāhīm used to expound on it at great length."[38] Al-Dārimī reported these accounts.

Their recording of hadith, jurisprudence, and specific legal issues took place due to their need for another approach. This was because they didn't have enough hadith reports and accounts from the Companions to suffice in inferring (*istinbāṭ*) jurisprudence according to the principles which the People of the Hadith had chosen. They were not enthusiastic about studying the pronouncements of the religious scholars of the (various) regions, collecting and investigating them, for they considered this to be a dubious

34. *Kunya* is the patronymic element of a name, i.e., Abū (father of) or Umm (mother of) plus a name.

35. *Muqallid*, a person who does imitation or follows (*taqlīd*) the previous rulings of a legal scholar.

36. al-Dārimī I, 84.

37. al-Dārimī I, 85.

38. al-Dārimī I, 52.

method. They believed, however, that their leaders (Imams) were at the highest level of inquiry and they were very much biased toward their colleagues. 'Alqama said, "Was anyone among them (the Companions) more reliable than 'Abd Allāh (ibn Mas'ūd)?" Abū Hanīfa said, "Ibrāhīm has more legal acumen than Sālim, and if not for the virtue of being a Companion I would have said, "'Alqama has more legal acumen than Ibn 'Umar."[39] They were astute, intuitive, and quick in shifting the intellect from one thing to another. This enabled them to deduce the answer to issues based on the pronouncements of their associates.

As the Qur'ān says, "For everyone will find it easy to do that for which he was created."[40] And, "Each sect rejoicing in its own tenets."[41]

[Principles of Derivation]

Thus the scholars laid out jurisprudence according to the principle of derivation (*takhrīj*), which are as follows:

> Each jurist memorizes the book of the one who was the spokesman for his associates and the most knowledgeable about the group's pronouncements and the most correct in examining its preferred opinion (*tarjīḥ*). In each case he takes into consideration the reason for the ruling. Whenever he is asked about a matter, or needs some further information, he will look into the pronouncements of his associates that he had memorized. In the case that he finds the answer there, it is settled. If not:
>
> 1) He may examine the general pattern of their rulings so as to make the matter conform to this form,
>
> 2) He will take into account an indication implicit in the statement so that he can infer the response on the basis of this.
>
> 3) Sometimes there may be an allusion (*īmā'*) or *iqtidā* (logical entailment) of certain statements (of a scholars) from which the intent can be understood.
>
> 4) Sometimes the stated issue may have a precedent parallel instance to which it may be referred.
>
> 5) Sometimes the scholars may investigate the rationale for legislation (*'illa*) of the declared ruling through derivation (*takhrīj*), simplification, or ellipsis so that its ruling can be applied to a case other than the one that had originally been pronounced upon.
>
> 6) Sometimes a jurist may have two rulings (made by scholars) about a case that, if combined according to the format of a conjunctive

---

39. Recounted in detail in Chapter 1 on pages 14-15.

40. The hadith. As in al-Bukhārī Tauḥīd, 54. Muslim, Abū Dāwūd, Tirmidhī, Ibn Māja, Ibn Ḥanbal.

41. Qur'ān 30:32.

syllogism (*qiyās iqtirānī*)[42] or hypothetical (*sharṭī*) syllogism,[43] will produce the answer to the issue.

7) Sometimes there would be in the jurists' statements a thing known through pattern and category but not through a comprehensive exclusive definition. Here they would have recourse to the expert linguists and take pains to establish the essential properties (of the statement), in order to determine its comprehensive exclusive definition,[44] settle its ambiguities, and distinguish its problematic aspects.

8) Sometimes their sayings might have two possible interpretations so they would attend to establishing a preference for one of the possibilities.

9) Sometimes the mode of argumentation of the proofs (*taqrīb al-dalā'il*) for the cases would be obscure so that they would clarify this.

10) Sometimes certain scholars had recourse to using derivation, would make deductions on the basis of the founders of their school having acted in a certain way, or upon their remaining silent, and so on.

This methodology is known as derivation (*takhrīj*). It may be said about it that "the opinion derived from such and such a person is thus," or "it is said according to the opinion of so and so," or "according to the principle of so and so," or "according to the opinion of so and so—the response to the question is such and such."

Those scholars (who derive in this way) are called persons exercising independent legal reasoning (*mujtahids*) within a legal school. What is meant by *ijtihād* according to this principle is that whoever memorizes the *Mabṣūt*[45] is a *mujtahid*, even if he has no knowledge at all about hadith transmission, nor even knowledge of a single hadith.

In this manner the process of derivation took hold in every legal school, and proliferated. The school that had famous members who became judges

42. A conjunctive syllogism is of the type that if the two initial premises are true then a third may be deduced. If all A's are B and all B's are C then all A's are C. In Islamic legal reasoning an example would be: All intoxicants are forbidden, wine is intoxicating. Therefore wine is forbidden.

43. A hypothetical or disjunctive syllogism is of the form, "If A then B. A is true, therefore B is true." A good discussion of these logical issues is found in the notes to Wael Hallaq, *Ibn Taimiyya's Refutation of Greek Logic* (Oxford University Press, 1994).

44. *Al-ḥadd al-jāmi' al-māni'* is a definition that applies to all members of the set and excludes all the non-members. See R. Brunschvig, "Jami' mani'" in *Etudes D'Islamologie* I, ed. A. M. Turki pp. 355-7 and al-Thahanawī, *al-Kashshāf fī-iṣṭilāḥāt al-funūn* 1, 905-906.

45. *Kitāb al-Mabsūṭ* of Muḥammad ibn Aḥmad al-Sarakhsī, 11th C. A basic book in the Ḥanafī school.

and givers of legal opinions, whose writings became authoritative among people and who taught publically spread to all regions of the world, and still continues to spread. The school which had undistinguished members who were not entrusted to judge and give fatwas, and who were not sought after by the public, died out after a time.[46]

Know that both making derivations (*takhrīj*) from the statements of the jurists, and following the literal meaning of the hadith, have a fundamental basis in the religion. In each age researchers among the *'ulamā'* have employed each of them. Among them there have been those who minimized one of them and emphasized the other, and vice versa. Thus it is not suitable to neglect one of them entirely as did most of the members of the two factions. Rather what is absolutely right is to correlate one with the other and to compensate for the defects of each through the other. This is the opinion of Ḥasan al-Baṣrī, "Your practice, by God, besides whom there is no other God, should lie between the two—between the excessive and the deficient."

Thus, he who is one of the People of the Hadith must subject what he selects to critical examination and uphold it against the opinion of the *mujtahids* among the Followers and those who succeeded them, while whoever is among those jurists using derivation (*takhrīj*) must acquire enough knowledge of the Sunna to prevent him from opposing a sound, obvious hadith, and to protect himself from speaking out of personal opinion in a case about which there exists a hadith or report from a Companion, in so far as he is able. The hadith scholar (*muḥaddith*) should not be over-scrupulous about principles established by his associates for which there are no textual stipulations of the lawgiver, so that through this he would reject a sound hadith or analogy, such as rejecting hadiths that have the slightest flaw in reaching back to the Prophet or in being transmitted uninterruptedly. Ibn Ḥazm did this when he rejected the hadith forbidding musical instruments due to a suspicion of a break in the transmission of al-Bukhārī, despite the fact that on its own the hadith was soundly connected to the Prophet.[47] Rather, one should have recourse to something like this only in cases where there is another conflicting report. Another case (of excessive fastidiousness) is when the hadith scholars say, "So and so preserved more hadiths of a certain person than someone else, so we prefer his version to the version of the hadith reported by some other person for this reason"—even if there were one thousand reasons for preferring the other's version.

---

46. This concludes the third of the chapters of *al-Inṣāf* that are also found in *Ḥujjat Allāh*, I. The following paragraphs are duplicated in the final chapter of *Ḥujjat Allāh*, I.

47. Bukhārī VII, 345. Ibn Ḥazm claimed that the chain of reporters was broken between al-Bukhārī and Hishām. This hadith is referred to in *Ḥujjat Allāh al-Bāligha* II, Chapter "Clothes, Adornments, Utensils, etc."

The concern of the majority of hadith reporters when narrating the meaning of hadith was with conveying the essentials of the meanings, not with (precise) expressions which are recognized by experts in the Arabic language. Such experts might draw inferences from things like the "*fa*" (but) or the "*waw*" (and) and a certain word preceding or coming after another and other sorts of hair-splitting. Often another transmitter will have relayed this same account, putting one word or letter in place of another. The truth is that whatever the transmitter reports should be taken as being the apparent meaning of the statement of the Prophet (ﷺ); then if another hadith or piece of evidence comes to light it must also be taken into account.

The person using deductive methods should not deduce a meaning that his peers would not find plausibly conveyed by the same expression and which neither native speakers nor scholars of the language would understand from it. Nor for no apparent cause should he derive an opinion based on identifying the reason (*takhrīj al-manāṭ*) for legislation in a case where judgement has been pronounced, or should he apply a parallel case to it about which the authorities in the legal school (*ahl al-wujūh*) disagree and about which there are conflicting opinions. For if his associates had been asked about this case, perhaps they would have drawn a parallel to a parallel instance that would exclude it, or perhaps they would have cited a reason for legislation (*'illa*) other than that which he himself derived.

In fact, derivation is only permitted because it is a form of following (*taqlīd*) a *mujtahid* and it is only executed based on what may be understood from his opinion. A jurist must not reject a hadith or report of a Companion on which Muslims have agreed in favor of a principle that he himself or his peers derived such as occurred in the case of the hadith of the milk-giving camels,[48] or like the annulment of the inheritance share of relatives.[49] Indeed, adhering to the hadith is more necessary than caring about this derived principle. This is what al-Shāfi'ī meant when he said, "What-

48. This refers to the practice of leaving camels or cattle unmilked or tying up their udders some days before they are sold to make them appear more productive. In this case the hadith says that the buyer should have a purchase option of three days and then if he gives the animal back he should give a *ṣā'* of dates. The debate concerns the approving of the purchaser's option and remittance of this set amount of food which is allowed according to al-Shāfi'ī and not allowed according to Abū Ḥanīfa because the amount of dates is fixed while the amount and type of milk may vary. This conflicts with the answer one would arrive at by analogy. *Kasfshāf*, p. 52. He returns to this issue in *HA* 2 "Forbidden Sales" in *Muṣaffā* 1, p. 367. Some hadiths on this topic are Bukhārī Buyū' 23, 26, 28, Shurūt 11, Muslim, Abū Dāwūd, Tirmidhī, Nasā'ī, Ibn Māja, al-Dārimī. Shāh Walî Allāh again mentions this issue in Ch. 5, p. 60.

49. This refers to a share of 1/25 of the spoils of war being distributed to members of the Banū Hāshim clan of Banū Muṭṭalib by the Prophet and early Caliphs. Later the juristic schools disagreed about whether this practice should be continued or

ever I have said or established as a principle, if there should later come to your attention some saying of the Prophet (ﷺ) conflicting with what I said, then what he (ﷺ) said must be upheld."[50]

Among the testimonies to the situation in which we find ourselves is what the Imām Abū Sulaymān al-Khaṭṭābī (931-996) wrote in the introduction to his book, *Ma'ālim al-Sunan* (Signposts on the Paths of the Prophet),[51] when he said,

> I have observed that the people of knowledge in our time have become two parties and divided into two factions: the proponents of reports from the Prophet and the Companions, and the proponents of jurisprudence and speculative thinking (*naẓar*). Each one of these factions is not distinguished from the other in its concern, and is not independent from the other in achieving its object or intent.
>
> For the hadith is in the position of the foundation that is the root while jurisprudence is in the position of the structure that is like a branch of this (root). Any structure not laid on the base of a foundation will be destroyed and any foundation devoid of a structure or building is desolate and a ruin.
>
> I find these two groups, despite the things that draw them together, to be at two ends of the spectrum; and despite the things drawing them near to one another, to hold opposing views. Despite their common need for each other, which includes the dire need of each of them for his fellow, I find them to be estranged brothers who in the path of truth require mutual support and genuine cooperation, without competing with one another.
>
> As for that group who are the proponents of hadith and reports from the Companions, most of them only work with these sayings; collating the lines of transmission, seeking the rare and anomalous hadiths of which the majority are fabricated or mixed up. They do not take care for the text or comprehending the sense nor do they dig out the (hadiths') precious treasures or derive their juristic import. At times they censure the jurists and discuss them disparagingly, accusing them of being opposed to the prophetic traditions. They don't realize that they are lacking the range of knowledge that they have been given, and that they are mistaken in their speaking badly of them.

---

whether it terminated with the Prophet's death. *Kashshāf* p. 52. Abū Dāwūd III pp. 145-147. Ibn Rushd, *Distinguished Jurist's Primer* ll, 466-7.

50. This concludes the paragraphs found in the final chapter of *Ḥujjat Allāh,* Volume 1. The following section is only found in the treatise *al-Inṣāf.*

51. A commentary on the *Sunan* of Abū Dāwūd (Beirut: al-Maktaba al-'Ilmiyya, 1981), 3-5. I compared the two printed texts and found a small number of variants. I have followed the Beirut edition of al-Khaṭṭābī where the sense seemed more appropriate and so indicated in the notes.

As for the other group, the people of jurisprudence and speculative thinking, most of them are rarely inclined towards the hadith and they can scarcely distinguish the sound from the faulty, and they don't recognize the excellent hadiths from those hadiths of poor quality. They don't give imprtance about what they might come to know about a hadith when they use it to argue against their opponents if it favors the legal schools to which they belong, and agrees with the opinions that they hold.

They adopt an arrangement among themselves to accept a weak report or a hadith that does not reach back to the Prophet uninterruptedly if this has become well-attested among them, and their spokesmen have taken turns in passing it along among themselves without there existing any confirmation or certain knowledge about it, so that this becomes misjudgement and cheating,[52] may God help us and them.

They are the very ones who, if there is recounted to them an opinion of one of the heads of their *madhhabs* or the leaders of their sects that he formed based on his own *ijtihād*', will seek to establish its reliability and try to establish a guarantee for it. Thus we find the followers of Mālik only depending in their *madhhab* on the reports of Ibn Qāsim, and Ashhab[53], and others of their type among his distinguished followers. Then if a recension of 'Abd Allāh ibn 'Abd al-Hakim[54] and his sort comes up it will not be of any force according to them.

You see the followers of Abū Hanīfa (ﷺ) only accepting reports from him through Muḥammad ibn al-Ḥasan, the most prominent of his associates, or his most important students. Thus if they heard a statement from al-Ḥasan ibn Ziyād al-Lū'lū'ī (868) or those lesser than him in rank that opposed the former opinion, they would not accept it or accord it any confidence.

Likewise you will find the followers of al-Shāfi'ī in their school only taking into account the reports of al-Muzanī (878) and al-Rabī' ibn Sulaymān al-Murādī (884), so that if a report of Harmala or al-Jarmī[55] or their like came up, they would not take it into consideration nor make use of it in their opinions. This is the custom of every group of the *'ulamā'* with regard to the rulings of the schools of their founders and teachers.

52. In rendering this phrase I have preferred the reading of the Beirut edition of al-Khaṭṭabī.

53. 'Abd al-Raḥman ibn Qasim al-'Utaqī (806) and 'Amr Ashhab ibn 'Abd al-'Azīz (819) who were prominent students of Mālik.

54. He studied with Ashhab and al-Shāfi'ī..

55. The Beirut edition of al-Khaṭṭābī's text has the names Harmala and al-Jīzī, and the Lahore and Delhi editions of Walī Allāh, Harmala and al-Buḥtarī. Harmala was (ibn Yaḥyā al-Tujibī), a 10th C. Egyptian scholar.

If such is their persistent tendency and they are not satisfied in the case of these applied rulings in positive law (*furū'*) and their being transmitted from these shaykhs except through sure method and confirmation, how could it be possible for them to be negligent about important cases and major declarations and to trust each other in reporting and transmitting from the leader of the Imams and the Prophet of the Lord of Power (s) whose ruling carries the force of obligation, who must be obeyed, and whose command we must accept, and whose order we must follow without finding in ourselves any feelings of objection to what he decreed. We must wholeheartedly accept whatever he said and ordered.

What would you think about a person who was negligent about his own affairs and indulgent in the cases of those who acted against his interest so that he accepted falseness from them and overlooked any shortcomings in them. Would it be permissible for him to do that in the case of someone else's rights if he were that person's representative such as the guardian of the feeble person, the caretaker of the orphan, and the trustee of the absent person? Wouldn't this be on his part, if he should do it, a betrayal of promise and a breach of trust? Indeed it is so, whether you see it with your own eyes or by means of an example.[56]

Possibly some groups found the road of the truth to be rugged, and they found that it was taking too long to get their share. They loved hasty gain so that they abbreviated the path of knowledge, and were satisfied with a measly amount and some words pulled out from the concepts of theoretical jurisprudence (*uṣūl al-fiqh*) that they called reasons for legislation. They raised these as banners for themselves in entering the lists of knowledge, and took them as a shield when they encountered their opponents and assumed them as a target[57] of discussion and disputation, debating about them and exchanging blows over them. When they broke off, the winner was judged on acumen and excellence and he became the jurist renowned in his time, and the leader glorified in his region and city. It was as if the devil had suggested a subtle ruse to them and taught them a penetrating artifice for he said to them, "What you have at your disposal is scant knowledge and paltry wares which is an insufficient amount to do the job or meet the need. Seek some support from theological argumentation (*kalām*) and join to it some fragments of this and that and have recourse to the principles of the theologians which will enlarge for people the scope of discussion and the range of speculative investigation. "Thus Iblis proved true his

56. Here I have preferred the reading of the Beirut edition. The Lahore and Delhi editions have *'ayyar mathal*, "measuring by an example."

57. Here the reading of the Beirut and Lahore editions is *dar'iyya* (target) as opposed to the Cairo *dhariyya* (means).

calculation about them and many of them obeyed him and followed him, except for a group of the believers."[58] What a calamity for people and minds is the place where Iblis is taking them! How far is the devil going to divert their fortune and guidance. Allah is the One to turn to for help.

This ends the quotation from al-Khaṭṭabī.

58. Qur'ān 34:20.

# Chapter 4
# An Account of the Situation Before the Fourth Islamic Century together with an Explanation of the Levels of *Ijtihād*

This chapter contains an explanation of the cause of juristic disagreement between the earlier scholars and the later ones regarding the requirement that a jurist be affiliated with or unaffiliated with one of the legal schools. It also features an explanation of how the religious scholars differ about the status of practitioners of absolute *ijtihād* and practitioners of *ijtihād* within a legal school and what is the distinction between these two statuses.

You ought to know that during the first and second centuries people did not concur about the need to perform *taqlīd* within one specific *madhhab* only. Abū Ṭālib al Makkī (d. 996) said in his *Qūt al-Qulūb*, "Books and compilations are all later phenomena, as is holding to statements that people have made, issuing legal opinions based on the school of a single individual, holding to his opinion, emulating him in every thing, and conducting jurisprudence according to his school. This was not the practice of the people who preceded us in the first and second centuries."[1]

Rather, at that time people were at two levels, the religious scholars and the common people. In cases involving issues of consensus about which there was no disagreement among the Muslims and the majority of the *mujtahids*, the common people performed *taqlīd* of the master of legislation (the Prophet). They used to learn the manner of ablution, full bath, prayer, *zakāt* and so on from their forefathers or the teachers of their cities—and they practiced according to this. If some uncommon situation arose they would ask for a legal opinion about it from whichever muftī they found without specifying a legal school.

Ibn al-Humām (1457) said at the end of his book *al-Taḥrīr,*[2] "On one occasion they would ask one person for a legal opinion and on another occasion they would ask someone else without restricting themselves to one muftī."

As for the religious scholars, they were at two levels. Among them were ones deeply involved in researching the Qur'ān, the Sunna, and the reports of the Companions until potentially they acquired the capacity to be appointed as muftis among the people. They would respond to their

1. *Qūt al-Qulūb* I (Cairo: Muṣṭafā al-Bābī al-Ḥalabī, 1961), 324. Shāh Walī Allāh quotes this same passage in a similar context in *al-Tafhīmāt al-Ilāhiyya* 1:206.
2. Ibn al-Humām, *al-Taḥrīr fi Uṣūl al-Fiqh* (Cairo: Muṣṭafā al-Bābī al-Ḥalabī, 1932).

questions in most cases in such a way that their responses achieved broad acceptance and they became designated as "*mujtahids*."

This ability [of being a *mujtahid*] was sometimes achieved through jurists' exerting their utmost efforts in collecting hadith reports, for many of the (*shar'ī*) rulings are found in the hadiths, and many in the sayings of the Companions, Followers, and Successors to the Followers, along with what the intelligent person who is cognizant of the (Arabic) language will not fail to perceive as being the contexts of the utterances. The scholar who has mastered the discipline of hadith will recognize the methods for reconciling any disparities, systematizing the proofs, and so on. This was the case of the two exemplary Imams, Aḥmad ibn al-Ḥanbal and Isḥāq ibn Rāhawayh.

Sometimes (this ability for *ijtihād* was attained) through mastering the rules of derivation and accuracy in the principles that were transmitted in each field from the masters of jurisprudence. These principles pertain to the rules and regulations (of *takhrīj*). In addition, such a scholar must have mastered a sound body of prophetic hadiths and reports from Companions, as in the case of the exemplary Imams Abū Yūsuf and Muḥammad ibn al-Ḥasan.

Among *mujtahids* are those who have acquired enough knowledge of the Qur'ān and the Sunna to enable them to know the chief points of jurisprudence and the basic issues through their detailed proofs (*adilla*). They can arrive at the probable opinion in some of the other issues through their proofs. In some of them they hesitate and need to consult other religious scholars, since they have not perfected the tools and skills as they are perfected by the absolute *mujtahid* (*al-mujtahid al-muṭlaq*).[3] Thus such jurists can function as *mujtahids* in some cases and not in others.

It is abundantly reported that whenever a hadith reached the Companions and the Followers, they implemented it without considering any condition. After the second century, scholars began to coalesce into legal schools based around the *mujtahids* themselves. People who did not depend on the *madhhab* of an individual *mujtahid* became scarce, and this became the requisite practice at this time.

The reason for this development is that being involved in jurisprudence is never devoid of two conditions.

1) One of them is that the scholar's greatest concern should be with

3. Within the discussion of *ijtihād* among Muslim scholars, some have used the terms *muṭlaq* and *mustaqill* as being synonymous in meaning "independent." Among these scholars are Ibn Taymiyya (1254) and Ibn al-Ṣalāḥ (1245). For others one or the other of these terms may refer to a higher degree of *ijtihād* practiced by the eponyms of the legal schools only. There is however, some variation as to which term should refer to this higher level. On this see Wael Hallaq, "Was the gate of *ijtihād* closed?" *International Journal of Middle Eastern Studies* 16, 1984, 17, 25, 27.

knowing the cases to which the *mujtahids* had responded to previously in terms of their detailed proofs, the criticism of these, reviewing their sources, and giving some of them preference over others.

This is a weighty endeavor which a person will not accomplish except through an Imam whom he can take as a model, who has sufficiently covered the range of the cases and presented the proofs in subcategories, so that he can have recourse to his precedents. Then he can proceed independently with critiquing and adjudging preference (*tarjīḥ*), and if not for that Imam, this would be difficult for him. There is no sense in doing things the hard way when it is possible to simplify the matter.

It is inevitable that this follower will deem correct a certain number of the precedents of his Imam in the legal school and rectify a certain proportion of others. If his rectifications are fewer than his concurrences he will be counted as one of the authorities (*aṣḥāb al-wujūh*) within the legal school. If his rectifications are more numerous than his distinctive opinions, such a scholar will not be considered authoritative within the legal school. Despite this, such a jurist is still considered to be overall affiliated with the founder of the legal school, as distinct from a scholar who takes another founder as a model for imitation in many of the principles of his legal school and its applied rulings. There will be found in the case of such a jurist certain rulings based on *ijtihāds* which had not been previously answered, since new circumstances keep on coming up and the gate (of *ijtihād*) is open. Thus he will take them from the Qur'ān, the Sunna, and the reports of the predecessors without depending on his Imam. However, these will be few in comparison to issues in which there are precedents. This scholar is called an absolute *mujtahid* who operates within the boundaries of a legal school (*al-mujtahid al-muṭlaq al-muntasib*).[4]

2) The second of these conditions is that a person's greatest concern should be to recognize the issues not addressed by the preceding scholars among those on which muftis are asked to give legal opinions. His need for an Imam to imitate in the principles set out for each topic is greater than that of the former person. This is because the issues of jurisprudence are interdependent and involved, and the rules in the new cases will depend upon those of the original cases. If this person begins all over again to criticize their opinions and reexamine their pronouncements, he will have become committed to something which he cannot

4. These categories follow those established by al-Nawawī (1233-77) in the Shāfi'ī *madhhab*. "This theory recognized the possibility that there were still absolute *mujtahids* without however compromising the superiority of the founders of the *madhhabs*." Rudolph Peters "Idjtihad and Taqlīd in 18th and 19th Century Islam" in *Die Welt des Islams* 20 (1980), 137.

master and which he will not be able to finish within a whole lifetime. There is no way for him in what concerns him except to apply the results of the precedents and thus be free to apply this to the new cases.

Such a jurist may make rectifications to what his Imam said about the Qur'ān, the Sunna, the reports of the ancestors, and analogical reasoning, but these will be few in comparison to his agreements. This person is termed the *mujtahid* within the boundaries of a legal school (*al-mujtahid fī-l-madhhab*).

3) As for the third condition,[5] it is that a scholar as a priority makes every effort to know the proofs (*adilla*) that had applied in precedent cases. Then he should secondarily exert his efforts in applying these to new cases according to what he has preferred and deemed correct. This is a status which is remote and no longer extant due to the distance of this (our) age from the era of the revelation, and the need of every scholar to have knowledge of much that is essential from the past. This knowledge consists of hadiths transmitted in many recensions and chains of reporters. He must know the statuses of the hadith transmitters and the classifications of the soundness and weakness of the hadith. He must be able to reconcile the discrepancies in the hadiths and reports of the Companions, and expose the sources of jurisprudence in them. He must know the obscure words, the roots of jurisprudence, and about the cases that have already been discussed by the preceding scholars despite their extensively vast quantity, their variations and their differences. He must direct his thoughts to distinguishing among these reports and relating them to the proofs.

If he has spent his life in attaining this degree of knowledge, how will he ever be able to do justice to dealing with all of the ramifications for positive law on top of this? The human soul—even when it is pure—has a recognized limitation beyond which it cannot reach. Even if this (exceptional achievement) was facilitated for the first group of *mujtahids* when the era (of the Prophet) was near and the disciplines of religious knowledge were not so complex, still it was not easy except for rare individuals. In spite of that even they imitated their teachers and were reliant on them. However, due to their great expenditure of effort for the sake of knowledge these scholars attained the status of independent (*mustaqill*) [*ijtihād*].[6]

---

5. The type of absolute unaffiliated *mujtahid* which is no longer extant.

6. In his treatise *'Iqd al-jīd fī aḥkām al-ijtihād wa-l-taqlīd*, Shāh Walī Allāh cites the classifications of the scholars al-Rafi'ī and al-Nawawī that there are within the category of absolute *ijtihād* (*ijtihād mutlaq*) two levels—independent (*mustaqill*) and affiliated (*muntasib*) *ijtihād* (p. 5). Below this are further rankings—the *mujtahid* within the boundaries of a legal school (*mujtahid fi-l-madhhab*); the *mujtahid al-fatayā* or *mujtahid* who can give legal opinions since he is well acquainted with

In summary, adhering to the legal schools of the *mujtahids* and agreeing to follow them is an inner inclination with which God (ﷻ) inspired religious scholars whether they are aware of it or not.

Among the testimonies to what we have mentioned is the statement of the jurist Ibn Ziyād al-Shāfi'ī al-Yamanī (1568) in his *Fatāwā*. He was asked about two cases in which al-Bulqīnī (1403) had answered at variance with the school of al-Shāfi'ī. Ibn Ziyād said in response,

> You do not recognize the level of distinction of what al-Bulqīnī said so long as you have not recognized his level of knowledge (of jurisprudence), for he is an Imam and an absolute (*muṭlaq*) *mujtahid* who is affiliated to a legal school and not independent (*mustaqill*) who is capable of performing derivation (*takhrīj*) and judging preference (*tarjīḥ*). I mean by 'absolute affiliated,' a jurist who has (the right) of selecting and preferring something which opposes the preponderant opinion within the legal school of the Imam to which he is affiliated. This is the case of many of the brilliant minds among the greatest of the Shāfi'ī scholars both in earlier and recent times, and citing them and setting out their ranking will follow.
>
> Among those who classified al-Bulqīnī in the ranks of absolute *mujtahids* affiliated to legal schools was his student, al-Walī Abū Zar'a (1423) who said,
>
> > Once I said to my teacher, Imām al-Bulqīnī, "What is the shortcoming of Shaykh Tāqī al-Dīn al-Subkī (1370) in practicing *ijtihād*? Since he fulfilled all the conditions for it, how could he then perform *taqlīd*?" He said, "I did not bring up his name—i.e., that of his teacher, Shaykh al-Bulqīnī's—out of embarrassment before him due to what I understood to be the consequences of this (not carrying out *ijtihād*)." Then he fell silent so I said, "What I think is that the only barrier to that is that official posts are assigned to jurists according to the four legal schools. Any scholar who goes outside of them and performs *ijtihād* will not get anything out of this and will be prevented from succeeding to a judgeship. People avoid asking him for legal opinions, and innovation (*bid'a*) will be attributed to him." Then he smiled, and agreed with me in this.
>
> I (Ibn Ziyād) say, "As for me, I do not believe that what prevented them from practicing *ijtihād* was what he indicated. Their high position is far from this! If they were to abandon *ijtihād*, despite their ability to do it, out of desire for a judgeship or other causes, this would be something impossible to believe about them, for it has already been stated that the preponderant opinion among the majority is the incumbency of *ijtihād*

---

the literature of a school (*mutabaḥḥir fi-madhhab imāmihi*), and finally the common person who must follow the legal opinion which he is given.

upon such a person. How could al-Walī Abū Zar'a have accepted to impute this to them and to say that al-Bulqīnī agreed with him about this?"

Al-Jalāl al-Suyūṭī (1445-1505) said in his *Sharḥ al-Tanbīh* in the chapter on divorce,

> Whatever disagreement occurred among the Imams was due to their *ijtihāds* changing, for they are correct in every instance at the time in which they practice their *ijtihād*. The author, i.e., the author of *al-Tanbīh,*[7] had an undeniable standing in *ijtihād*. More than one of the Imams held that he, Ibn al-Sabbāgh (1084), Imām al-Ḥaramayn (al-Juwayni,1085), and al-Ghazālī (1111) had reached the rank of absolute (*muṭlaq*) *ijtihād*. What is found in the *Fatāwā* of Ibn al-Ṣalāḥ (1245) i.e., that they had reached the rank of *ijtihād* within a legal school but not that of the absolute (*muṭlaq*) *mujtahid*, refers to the fact that they had reached the rank of affiliated *ijtihād* rather than independent (*mustaqill*) *ijtihād*.

Absolute (*muṭlaq*) *ijtihād* as he (Ibn al-Ṣalāḥ) himself and [the commentator] al-Nawawī (1233-1277) had determined in his book *Sharḥ al-Muhadhdhab,*[8] is of two types:

> (1) "Independent" (*mustaqill*) which had been defunct since the beginning of the fourth century, and is no longer extant, and (2) "affiliated" which will remain until the conditions of the final great Hour have come. The second type may not be discontinued according to the divine law since it is a religious duty incumbent on at least some of the Muslims (*farḍ kifāya*). When the people of an age are negligent of this duty so that they abandon it, then they have all sinned and disobeyed. The (Shāfi'ī) masters clearly stated this, among them al-Māwardī (1058) in *al-Ḥāwī,*[9] al-Ruyānī (1108) in *al-Baḥr*[10], and al-Baghawī (929) in *al-Tahdhīb,*[11] and other scholars. This duty is not carried out through dependent (*muqayyad*) *ijtihād* as Ibn al-Ṣalāḥ[12] had stated and al-Nawawī

7. Abū Isḥāq al-Shirāzī (d. 1054), one of the greatest Shāfi'ī scholars. Author of *Kitāb al-Tanbīh*, French translation by G. H. Bousquet (Alger: Maison des Livres, 1949).

8. al-Nawawī, *al-Majmū' sharḥ al-Muhadhdhab* (Cairo: Maṭba'a al-'āṣima, 1966-9).

9. *al-Hawī al-Kabīr*, cited in al-Suyūṭī, *al-Radd 'alā man akhlada ilā al-'arḍ wa jahila anna al-ijtihād fi kulli 'aṣr farḍ* edited by Shaykh Khalīl Al-Mais (Beirut: Dār al-Kutub al-'Ilmiyya, 1983), 68.

10. 'Abd al-Waḥīd al-Ruyānī, a Shāfi'ī jurist who wrote *al-Baḥr al-Madhhab.* Cited in al-Suyūṭī, *al-Radd*, 68.

11. Cited in al-Suyūṭī, al-*Radd*, 69.

12. Cited in al-Suyūṭī, *al-Radd*, 75-76.

in *Sharḥ al-Muhadhdhab.*[13] The issue is treated extensively in our (al-Suyūṭī's) book called *al-Radd 'alā man akhlada ilā al-'arḍ wa jahila anna al-ijtihād fī kulli 'aṣr farḍ*[14] (The rebuttal of the base person[15] who is ignorant of the fact that in every age *ijtihād* is a religious duty).

These jurists (mentioned above) were excluded from the category of absolute affiliated *ijtihād* due to their being Shāfi'īs as al-Nawawī declared and Ibn al-Ṣalāḥ in the *Ṭabāqāt* and al-Subkī agreed with him. Therefore they compiled books on their legal schools, gave legal opinions, deliberated among themselves, and assumed the posts of the Shāfi'īs. For example, the compiler (of the *Tanbīh* i.e., al-Shīrāzī) and Ibn al-Sabbāgh took up teaching in the Niẓāmiyya in Baghdad and Imām al-Ḥaramayn and al-Ghazālī held teaching posts at the Niẓāmiyya in Nishapur, and Ibn ('Abd) al-Sallām taught at the Ḥibbāniyya[16] and the Ẓāhiriyya in Cairo and Ibn Daqīq al-'Īd (1302)[17] held the post at the Ṣalāḥiyya near the tomb of our Imam, al-Shāfi'ī (ﷺ) and at the Fāḍiliyya and the Kāmiliyya as well as other places.

As for the scholar who reaches the rank of independent *ijtihād*, through that he ceases to be a Shāfi'ī and his opinions will not be transmitted in the books of the legal school. I don't know of any one of the affiliates of the Shāfi'ī school who reached that rank except Abū Ja'far ibn Jarīr al-Ṭabirī (921) for he had been a Shāfi'ī and then become unaffiliated with any school. For this reason al-Rāfi'ī (1226) and others have said that his individual opinions do not represent the authoritative doctrine of the school.

In my view this (opinion of al-Suyūṭī) is preferable to the course of al-Walī Abū Zar'a (ﷺ) except that his statement entails that Ibn Jarīr may not be counted as a Shāfi'ī. This is refuted by what al-Rafi'ī said at the beginning of his commentary on the book on Zakāt, i.e., "The individual opinion of Ibn Jarīr is not considered to represent the authoritative doctrine of our school, even if he is to be counted in the ranks of the followers of al-Shāfi'ī."

Al-Nawawī said in the *Tahdhīb*[18] that Abū 'Āṣim al-'Abbādī (1066) mentioned al-Tabarī in his *Ṭabaqāt al-Fuqahā' al-Shāfi'iyya* (Biographical Compendium of Shāfi'ī Scholars) saying, "He is among our unique (*afrād*)

---

13. Cited in al-Suyūṭī, al-*Radd*, 76-77.

14. Published in edited form by Shaykh Khalīl Al-Mais, (Beirut: Dār al-Kutub al-'Ilmiyya, 1983).

15. Literally "one who clings to the earth" as in Qur'ān VII: 176.

16. The Lahore and Delhi editions have al-Jābiyya. Ibn al-Sallām claimed the right of *ijtihād* within the Shāfi'ī school. al-Subkī, *Ṭabaqāt* V, 93, 95 cited in Wael Hallaq, "Was the Gate of Ijtihād Closed," 38, 39.

17. Subkī maintained that Ibn Daqīq was a *mujaddid* as well as a *mujtahid muṭlaq*. *Ṭabaqāt* VI, 2, 3, 6. Cited in Wael Hallaq, "Was the Gate of Ijtihād Closed," 39.

18. al-Nawawī, *Tahdhīb al-asmā' wa-l-lughat* (Cairo: Idārat al-Ṭibā'a al-Munīriyya, 1927).

scholars. He learned Shāfi'ī *fiqh* from al-Rabī' al-Murādī (884) and al-Ḥasan al-Za'farānī (874)." He [al-Tabarī] is affiliated with al-Shāfi'ī in the sense that he followed his methodology in *ijtihād*, investigating the indicants and organizing them with respect to one another, and he agreed with his *ijtihād*. If on occasion he differed, his differing was not paid attention to and he did not depart from his way except in certain cases and this does not preclude his inclusion in the Shāfi'ī *madhhab*.

Of this type is Muḥammad ibn Ismā'īl al-Bukhārī, for he in considered within the ranks of the Shāfi'īs. Among the ones who mentioned him in the Shāfi'ī biographical compendia is al-Shaykh Tāj al-Dīn al-Subkī. He said, "He studied jurisprudence with al-Ḥumaydī (834) and al-Ḥumaydī studied jurisprudence with al-Shāfi'ī." Our learned shaykh deduced al-Bukharī's being included among the Shāfi'īs by his being mentioned in their biographical compendia, and the statement of al-Nawawī that we cited attests to this.

In his *Ṭabaqāt*[19] Shaykh Tāj al-Dīn al-Subkī said, "In the case of every derivation (*takhrīj*) that the scholar deriving applies unrestrictedly,[20] should be considered in terms of whether that scholar doing the deriving is a person who predominantly follows his legal school and performs *taqlīd*—such as Shaykh Abū Ḥāmid [al-Isfarāyīnī] (1016) and al-Qaffāl (948). If so, then the opinion should be counted within his legal school. If he is a scholar whose going outside (of his legal school) preponderates such as the case of the four Muḥammads—I mean Muḥammad ibn Jarīr (al-Ṭabarī), Muḥammad ibn Khuzayma (923), Muḥammad ibn Nasr al-Marwazī (906), and Muḥammad ibn al-Mundhir (930)—then it is not considered (within the school). As for al-Muzanī and after him Ibn Surayj (918), they are between the two degrees. They didn't go as far outside as the Muḥammads and they didn't restrict themselves to the school as closely as the Iraqis and the Khurasanis."

Al-Subkī mentioned Shaykh Abū al-Ḥasan al-Ash'arī (945), the Imam of the People of the Sunna and Community in his *Ṭabāqāt*, saying, "He is numbered among the Shafi'īs for he carried out jurisprudence according to the Shaykh Abū Isḥāq al-Marwazī (951/2)."

Further testimony to what we have mentioned is what is found in the *Kitāb al-Anwār*[21] when the author says,

People affiliated with the *madhhabs* of al-Shāfi'ī, Abū Hanīfa, Mālik,

---

19. al-'Abbādī, *Ṭabaqāt al-Shāfi'iyah al-Kubrā* (Cairo: Maṭba'a al-Ḥusainiyya, 1327-1370 A.H.).
20. That is he adopts the *takhrīj* of the school.
21. *Kitāb al-Anwār* is a commentary on al-Nasafī's *al-Manār* by Aḥmad ibn Abī Sa'īd Jiwān (1637-1717). Published as *Nūr al-Anwār* (Delhi: Kutubkhāna Rāshidiyya, 1946).

and Aḥmad (Ibn Ḥanbal) are of various types.

One of them consists of the general public, and their practicing *taqlīd* of al-Shāfi'ī branches out from their performing *taqlīd* of a *mujtahid* affiliated (*al-muntasib*) (to his school). The second are those scholars who have reached the rank of *ijtihād*. Mujtahids do not perform *taqlīd* of another *mujtahid*, but rather they become affiliated with him due to their proceeding according to his methodology in *ijtihād* and following his use of the indicants and ordering them in relationship to others. The third are in an intermediate position. These are scholars who have not attained the rank of *ijtihād* but depend on the methodological principles of an Imam, and they are able to draw analogies based on what he ruled in cases in which they find no clear rulings reported from him. These scholars perform *taqlīd* of an Imam, and so do the lay people who accept their opinions. It is generally thought that such scholars are not practicing *taqlīd* because they are followed by others.

Then if you said, "How can something that is not obligatory at one time be required at another time despite the fact that there is one divine law?"

Your statement, "Following an independent (*mustaqill*) *mujtahid* was not obligatory and then it became obligatory," is nothing but a self-contradictory proposition that cancels itself out.

I say, "The primary obligation was that there always be among the Muslim community someone who could recognize the rulings in specific cases from their detailed indicants, and the people of truth have concurred on this, and the premise of its being obligatory is a requirement. Thus if there are numerous ways to fulfill the obligation, what is required is that one of these ways be achieved without specification. If only one way was specified for fulfilling the obligation, that way in particular would be required.

If a man were extremely hungry so that he was afraid of starving, and there existed various ways to eliminate his hunger such as buying food, gathering fruit from the wild, and trapping something to eat, it would be necessary to accomplish one of these ways without specification. However, if he found himself in a place with neither game nor fruit, he would have to spend money to purchase food.

Likewise the pious ancestors had at their disposal various ways of fulfilling this obligatory thing, and what was required was fulfilling any one, without specification, of these ways. Then all of these ways became blocked except for one, so that this way, specifically, became obligatory.

Our pious forebears did not write down hadith, then the recording of the hadith became obligatory since there is no means for the transmission of hadith today except through knowing these books. Our pious predecessors did not concern themselves with grammar and vocabulary, for their native language was Arabic and they had no need for these disciplines. Now in our times the knowledge of the Arabic language has become obligatory due to the distance of our era from the time of the first Arabs, and the examples corroborating what we hold are extremely copious.

According to this example an analogy to the case of following a particular Imam must be drawn, for this may be obligatory or it may not be required. Thus, if there is an ignorant person in India or Transoxiana where there is no Shāfi'ī, Mālikī, or Ḥanbalī scholar, nor any books of these schools; it is necessary that he should practice *taqlīd* of the school of Abū Hanīfa. He is forbidden to depart from his school since in that instance he would be casting off the constraint of the sharī'a and remain useless and negligent.

This is in contrast to what would be the case if he were in Mecca and Medina. There it would be easy for him to be acquainted with all of the legal schools, and it would not be sufficient for him to act on conjecture without verification, nor to take up the practice of the general public, nor to act on books which are not authoritative. All of this has been mentioned in the book, *al-Nahr al-Fā'iq sharḥ Kanz al-Daqā'iq*.[22]

You should know that the absolute (*muṭlaq*) *mujtahid* is a person whose knowledge encompasses five disciplines. Al-Nawawī says in the *Minhāj (al-Ṭālibīn)*:

> The condition for the judge is that he be Muslim, of an age liable to perform religious duties, free, male, just, with sound hearing, sight, and speech, competent, and a *mujtahid*. This means that he should know:
>
> 1) the Qur'ān and the Sunna in so far as their language is particular, general, equivalent and explicit. He should also know the abrogated and abrogating texts.
>
> 2) the abundantly transmitted aspects of the Sunna as well as the others and the hadiths going back to the Prophet, those which are interrupted at the level of a Companion (*mursal*), and the status of the transmitters whether strong or weak and
>
> 3) the Arabic language—vocabulary and grammar, and
>
> 4) the statements of the scholars among the Companions and later, which constitute consensus or disagreement and
>
> 5) analogy in its various forms.[23]

---

22. Sirāj al-Dīn Abū'l Barakāt (1596) wrote a commentary entitled *al-Nahr al-Fā'iq* on *Kanz al-Daqā'iq fi'l-Furū*' by al-Nasafī, 'Abd Allāh ibn Muḥammad (1310). *al-Bahr al-Rā'iq* is a commentary by Ibn Nujaym.

23. al-Nawawī, *Minhāj al-Ṭālibīn*. (Beirut: Dār al-Ma'rifa, 1978), 148. French translation by L. W. C. van den Berg (Batavia: Imprimerie du Gouvernement, 1882-84). English translation based on the French by E. C. Howard (London: Thacker, 1914).

[Conditions for Absolute Ijtihād]

Then know that this (absolute) *mujtahid* may be independent (*mustaqill*) or may be affiliated to an independent one.

The independent *mujtahid* is distinguished from the rest by three traits, as we clearly see in the case of al-Shāfi'ī: [24]

1) One of them is that he works with the roots and principles from which jurisprudence is deduced. He (al-Shāfi'ī) mentioned in the first part of his book *al-Umm* when he enumerated the practice of the first scholars in their making deductions and he set up a system based on them.[25]

Our Shaykh, Abū Ṭāhir Muḥammad ibn Ibrāhīm al-Madanī[26] (al-Kurdī d. 1145/1733), transmitted from his two Meccan Shaykhs, al-Shaykh Ḥasan ibn 'Alī al-'Ujaymī (1113/1702)[27] and Shaykh Aḥmad al-Nakhlī (1130/1718)[28] from Shaykh Muḥammad ibn al-'Alā al-Bābilī (1077 A.H.-1666/7)[29] from Ibrāhīm ibn Ibrāhīm al-Laqqānī (1041 A. H.

---

24. According to the biographical notice which Shāh Walī Allāh included in *Anfas al-'Ārifīn* he was a master of hadith, and a Ḥanafī but not a *muqallid*. Details about his personal appearance and style of teaching may be found in *Anfas al-'ārifīn*, Urdu trans. by Sayyid Muḥammad al-Fārūqī al-Qādirī, (Lahore: al-Ma'āriif, 1974), 389-392.

25. As discussed at the end of Chapter Two.

26. Shāh Walī Allāh's main teacher (al-Kurdī) in the Hijaz. His father was the noted Ibrāhīm ibn Ḥasan Kūrānī al-Kurdī (d. 1690). The following list of names represents Shāh Walī Allāh's links of transmission back to al-Shāfi'ī himself. He speaks of some of these teachers and the transmission of hadith in *al-Irshād 'alā Muhimmat 'Ilm al-Isnād* (Lahore: Sajjād Publishers, 1960). For the dates and vocalizations of these names I have used the notes prepared by Muḥammad 'Aṭā Allāh Ḥanīf for Shāh Walī Allāh, *Ittiḥāf al-Nabīh fī mā yuḥtaju ilaihi al-muḥaddith wa-l-faqīh* (Lahore: al-Maktaba al-Salafiyya, 1969). His biographical notice, which indicates his tolerance in matters of *fiqh* and Sufism is given in *Anfas al-'Ārifīn*, 396-400.

27. A famous Ḥanafī scholar and Sufi who lived in Mecca. There is some disagreement as to the proper vocalization with Kahāllah *Mu'jam al-Mu'allifīn* III, (Damascus: Maktaba , 1957-61), 264) and others prefering the rendering "*al-'Ujaymī.*" Links between Ibrāhīm b. Ḥasan al-Kurānī al-Kurdī, al-'Ujaymī and Muḥammad ibn al-Wahhāb, Shāh Walī Allāh, al-Sanūsī, and al-Shawkānī have been pointed out by R. Peters, "Idjtihād," 144-145 and John Voll, "Muḥammad Ḥayya al-Sindī and Muḥammad ibn 'Abd al-Wahhāb: An Analysis of an intellectual group in eighteenth century Madīna," *Bulletin of the School of Oriental and Asian Studies* 38 (1975), 32-39.

28. Was both a hadith scholar and Sufi noted in *Anfas al-'Ārifīn*, 392-394. Kahāllah, *Mu'jam* II, 73 vocalizes the name thus.

29. Shaykh Shams al-Dīn Muḥammad ibn al-'Alā Bābilī, whose biographical notice is given by Shāh Walī Allāh in *Anfas al-'Ārifīn*, 382-384. He was a noted hadith scholar of Egyptian origin.

1631/2)[30] from 'Abd al-Ra'ūf al-Ṭablāwī from Jalāl Abī Faḍl al-Suyūṭī (911/1505) from Abū Faḍl al-Marjānī with permission from Abū al-Faraj al-Ghazzī from Yūnus ibn Ibrāhīm al-Dabūsī from Abū Ḥasan ibn al-Muqīr from al-Faḍl ibn Sahl Isfarāyīnī from al-Ḥāfiẓ al-Ḥujja Abū Bakr Aḥmad ibn 'Ali al-Khaṭīb, saying, "Abū Nu'aym al-Ḥafiẓ told us that he heard from Abū Muḥammad 'Abd Allāh ibn Muḥammad ibn Ja'far ibn Ḥibbān[31] (965) that he heard from 'Abd Allah ibn Muḥammad ibn Ya'qūb that he heard from Abū Ḥātim—i.e., al-Rāzī (890)—that Yūnus ibn 'Abd al-A'lā (877) told me saying, 'Muḥammad ibn Idrīs al-Shāfi'ī said, "The foundation is the Qur'ān and the Sunna, and if there is nothing available there, then analogy may be drawn based on them. If there is an uninterrupted hadith from the Prophet of God (ﷺ) and its chain is sound, then it has the status of being a sunna. Consensus is of greater weight than a singly narrated report. A hadith should be interpreted according to its literal meaning, and if multiple interpretations are conceivable then the one that seems to be the closest to the literal meaning should be given priority. If there are a number of hadiths on par then the one with the soundest chain of narration (*isnād*) should be given priority. The interrupted hadith has no status except ones transmitted by Ibn al-Musayyab. The first term of a syllogism should not be derived from another first term by analogy. One does not ask 'why' or 'how' of a first term for one can only ask 'why' of a case which is an instantiation (*far'*) of the basic first term. If his analogical deduction is done soundly on the basis of the basic first term (*aṣl*), then it (the instantiation of a new case-*far'*) will be sound and constitute a proof.""'"

2) The second characteristic is that the independent *mujtahid* collects the hadith and the reports from the Companions so that he learns their rulings and becomes aware of how to conduct jurisprudence with them. He reconciles their variants and is able to prefer some over others and determine some of their probable meanings. This is close to two thirds of the science of al-Shāfi'ī in our opinion, and God knows best.

3) The third characteristic is that he deduces from the ramifications of cases so as to give responses in new cases presented to him that were not previously responded to in the early centuries.

In summary, the indepenedent *mujtahid* should be very active in these traits, superior to his contemporaries, preeminent among his rivals, outstanding in his field.

A fourth trait follows upon these. This is that an acceptance from the heavens should descend upon him so that groups of scholars whether Qur'ān interpreters, hadith experts, theorists of jurisprudence, or memorizers of the books of law will devote themselves to his knowl-

30. An Egyptian Maliki scholar. Some give his date as 1078/1667.

31. The Pakistan edition has Ibn Ḥiddān which seems to be an error.

edge, and long centuries will pass in this acceptance and devotion until this takes in people's hearts.

[The Absolute Affiliated Mujtahid and the Mujtahid within a Legal School]

The absolute *mujtahid* affilitated with a legal school is the scholar who follows a jurist and who accepts what he did under the first trait mentioned above, and follows his practice in the second trait.

The *mujtahid* within the boundaries of a legal school is the scholar who is sound in the first and the second traits and who, in addition, follows another scholar's course in deriving the responses in new cases (*tafrī'*) according to the methodology of his (Imam's) results in secondary cases.

Let us give an example of this. Anyone who wants to practice medicine in these recent times either follows the Greek doctors or the doctors of India and he is at the level of the independent (*mustaqill*) *mujtahid.* If this aspirant to medical practice came to know the properties of medicines, the types of illnesses and how to formulate the potions and treatments within his own mind, he would have become aware of this through their instructions until he became confident on his own without imitation (*taqlīd*). Then he would be able to do what they had done, so that he would know the properties of remedies that had not been discussed previously, and be able to explain the causes of ailments, their symptoms, and cures that had not been observed by the previous doctors. He would then rival the first ones in some of the things they had spoken of, whether in a few or many cases. Thus he would be in the position of the absolute affiliated *mujtahid.*

If he rather learned this from them without attaining complete certainty and usually was concerned with producing potions and remedies based on these principles that had already been set out, similar to the state of most of the medical practitioners of these recent times, then he would be in the position of a *mujtahid* within the boundaries of a legal school.

Likewise is the case of whoever composes poetry in these times. Either he takes as a model for this the poetry of the Arabs and chooses their prosody, rhyme schemes, and the styles of their *qāṣīdas*; or he imitates the poetry of the Persians and such persons are at the position of the independent *mujtahid* (*mustaqill*).[32] Then if this poet makes up types of *ghazals*, *tashbīb*,[33] panegyric, satire, and verses of admonishment and brings forth the most wondrous metaphors, poetic devices, and so on, the like of which are unprecedented, still he must have become aware of how to do this on the basis of certain of their works. He therefore drew a parallel and made an analogy of one thing to another, and was able to invent a new meter that no one had ever spoken of before, as well as new poetic forms such as the

32. Again reading 'they' for 'he'.

33. *Tashbīb*-ornate openings to poems which traditonally exalted love and youth.

composition of the mathnawī, the ruba'ī, and hypermeter—that is a separate word which is repeated in every verse after the rhyme scheme. Thus he is at the level of the absolute (*muṭlaq*) *mujtahid*. If he is not original but merely follows their ways he will be at the level of the *mujtahid* within a legal school. The situation is similar in Qur'ān interpretation, Sufism, and fields of knowledge other than these two.[34]

If you say, "What is the reason that the first ones did not speak very much about the roots of jurisprudence, and then when al-Shāfi'ī came on the scene he spoke about them unequivocally and achieved useful and excellent results?"

I say, "The reason for this is that in the case of the preceding ones, each of them used to collect the hadiths and reports of his city, and the hadiths from all the countries were not compiled. Thus if the indicants found in the hadith of his city were in conflict with one another he ruled on this discrepancy with a sort of intuition according to the best of his ability. Later, during the time of al-Shāfi'ī the hadiths of all the regions were collected so that incompatibility came to be found both among the hadiths of the various regions and the preferences of their legal scholars, from two aspects.

One incompatibility concerned the hadiths of one city and the hadiths of another, and the second involved the incompatibility of the hadiths of a single city with each other. As a result each person sided with[35] his teacher in terms of what he had judged according to intuition. The ruptures widened and the divergences multiplied, and innumerable disagreements assailed the people from all sides. Thus they remained bewildered and astounded, unable to take any course until assistance came to them from their Lord. al-Shāfi'ī was (divinely) inspired with the principles of accommodating these divergences and he opened a door for the ones who follow him, and what a door it is!"

[Comparison of Ijtihād among the Four Sunni Schools]

The absolute affiliated *mujtahid* within the school of Abū Ḥanīfa died out after the third century. This is because such a *mujtahid* must be a brilliant[36] hadith scholar and their (the Ḥanafīs') devotion to the discipline of hadith studies has been minimal, formerly and currently. In this school there were only found *mujtahids* within the school and this (type of) *ijtihād* is what the

---

34. Shāh Walī Allāh suggests that four levels of competency are general to all such fields of intellectual endeavor and uses the same two analogies to medicine and poetry in his *Intibāh fī Salāsil Awliyā' Allāh* published as *Ittiḥāf al-Nabīh* (Lahore: al-Maktaba al-Salafiyya, 1969), 106-107.

35. Lahore "*intaṣara*" as opposed to "*iqtaṣara*" in Cairo.

36. Reading Lahore and Delhi '*jahbadh*' (brilliant) and not following the Cairo '*jahira*' (outwardly).

person was referring to who said, "The minimum condition for the *mujtahid* is memorization of the *Mabsūṭ*."[37]

The affiliated *mujtahids* in the school of Mālik are few. Whoever was one of them did not have his individual rulings counted as an authoritative point of view within the school such as Abu 'Umar who is known as Ibn 'Abd al-Barr (1070) and the Qāḍī Abū Bakr ibn al-'Arabī (1148).

As for the legal school of Aḥmad [ibn al-Ḥanbal], its members were few, formerly and currently, and *mujtahids* have been found in it, generation after generation, until it became moribund in the ninth century and the school vanished in most regions except for a few persons in Egypt and Baghdad. The position of the school of Aḥmad with respect to the school of al-Shāfi'ī is comparable to the position of the school of Abū Yūsuf and Muḥammad in the school of Abū Hanīfa except that his (Aḥmad's) school is not combined in being recorded with the school of al-Shāfi'ī while their opinions are recorded together with the school of Abū Ḥanīfa. For this reason these two should not be considered as a single school, according to what we think, and God knows best. However, recording (the Ḥanbalī school) together with al-Shāfi'ī's school is not a problem[38] for a person who has studied both of them in a correct manner.

As for the *madhhab* of al-Shāfi'ī, it is the legal school possessing the most absolute *mujtahids* and *mujtahids* within the school. It is also the school with the most developed legal theory and theology and the one which has provided the most Qur'ān interpretation and commentary on the hadith. It is the strongest in (establishing) chains of hadith reporters and transmission, the most accomplished in verifying the statements of the founder, the strongest in distinguishing between the opinions of the founder and the points of view of his associates, and the most scrupulous when giving certain opinions and points of view of prominent scholars' preference over others. All of this will not be concealed from scholars who are involved in the legal schools and study them.

The first group of al-Shāfi'ī's students were *mujtahids* in the absolute sense and none among them followed him in all of his derivations based on *ijtihād* until Ibn Surayj came along and established the principles of *taqlīd* and derivation. Then his students began to follow his way and imitate his procedure and for this reason he (al-Shāfi'ī) is numbered as one of the Renewers (*mujaddidūn*)[39] coming at the beginning of the centuries, and God knows best.

---

37. A manual of Ḥanafī law by Muḥammad ibn Aḥmad al- Sarakhsī (1096).

38. Following Lahore '*'asīr*' vs. Cairo '*tamayyuz*'.

39. Renewers or renovators-*mujaddidun*- the concept in Islamic tradition that there will be a renewer (*mujaddid*) of the religion who will arise at the beginning of every century. This is based on the hadith, "God sends at the beginning of each century a man who renovates for this community the matters of its religion." Lists

It also will not be concealed from the scholar well-versed in the legal schools that in the Shāfi'ī school the corpus of hadiths and reports are recorded, authoritative, and current and nothing like this takes place in the other schools. Among the corpus of his school is the book *al-Muwaṭṭa'*. Even if it preceded al-Shāfi'ī, still al-Shāfi'ī built upon it. Also included are the *Ṣaḥīḥ* of al-Bukhārī and the *Ṣaḥīḥ* of Muslim and the books of Abū Dāwūd, al-Tirmidhī, Ibn Māja, and al-Dārimī, next the *Musnad* of al-Shāfi'ī, the *Sunan* of al-Nasā'ī, the *Sunan* of al-Dāraquṭnī, the *Sunan* of al-Bayhaqī and the *Sharḥ al-Sunna* of al-Baghawī.

As for al-Bukhārī, even if he was affiliated with al-Shāfi'ī and agreed with him in many of his jurisprudential activities, still he also disagreed with him on many points, and therefore his individual opinions on certain cases are not counted within the school of al-Shāfi'ī. As for Abū Dāwūd and al-Tirmidhī, they were *mujtahids* affiliated to Aḥmad and Isḥāq (ibn Rāhawayh) and likewise al-Dārimī and Ibn Māja as far as we can tell, and God knows best. As for Muslim and al-'Abbās al-Aṣamm (860) who compiled the *Musnad* of al-Shāfi'ī, and those whom we mentioned after the *Musnad,* they are distinct from the school of al-Shāfi'ī, and use others besides him as a basis.

If you have comprehended what we said then it should be clear to you that whoever opposes the school of al-Shāfi'ī is excluded from the rank of absolute *ijtihād* and that the discipline of hadith studies precludes taking counsel with scholars who did not try to learn from al-Shāfi'ī and his students (رضي الله عنهم).

Politely become their companion,
For I don't see any Shāfi'ī[40] lacking good manners.

---

of these renewers may vary somewhat, but almost all of the jurist renovators have been Shāfi'īs. Ibn Surayj (305 A.H. (917/18)) is viewed as the renewer of the fourth century. The Cairo edition has Ibn Shurayḥ instead of Ibn Surayj, but this seems to be an error.

40. There is a pun here on 'Shāfi'ī' meaning 'a petitioner or intercessor' and 'a member of the Shāfi'ī school'.

# Chapter 5
# Account of the Developments that Took Place after the Fourth Century

Following the first four centuries scholars went off in all directions and many new developments occurred.

Among these developments were disputation and disagreement in the science of jurisprudence. The elaboration of this, based on what al-Ghazālī said, is that when the era of the Rightly Guided Caliphs came to an end the Caliphate passed to people who held it illegitimately. They were not self-reliant in the science of giving fatwas and making (*sharī'a*) rulings, thus they were forced to ask assistance from jurists and to associate with them in all circumstances.

A remnant of the scholars stayed faithful to the original mode and held to the purity of the religion. If they were sought after they fled and shunned (the sultans). Thus the people of those times saw the greatness of the scholars and the interest of the leaders in them despite their avoidance of them (the rulers). Later, the scholars abandoned (this) refusal and pursued knowledge in order to gain access to achieving honors and attaining high rank. The jurists went from being sought after to becoming the seekers, and they went from having been dignified by their avoiding the sultans to being despicable in their running after them, except those ones whom God made successful (in their resolve).

Even before them, persons had compiled works in theology and multiplied the (scholastic) questioning and answering, objecting and responding, and laying the groundwork of argumentation. This had already taken place among them before the time when some of the officials and kings became disposed toward debates about jurisprudence and determining priority between the schools of al-Shāfi'ī and Abū Ḥanīfa (رضي الله عنهما). Jurists abandoned theology and the disciplines of knowledge of the religious sources (*'ilm*) and became interested instead in contentious issues, in particular those between al-Shāfi'ī and Abū Ḥanīfa (رضي الله عنهما). At the same time they were tolerant of the disagreements among Mālik, Sufyān, Aḥmad ibn Ḥanbal and others.

They claimed that their goal was deducing the finer points of the religious law, determining the reasons for legislation according to the legal schools, and laying out the principles of legal opinions. Thus they multiplied the compilations and deductions concerning this and they schematized the types of disputations and classifications and they persist in this until today. We don't know what God (تعالى) will decree in later times.

(End of the gist of what al-Ghazālī said)[1]

---

1. al-Ghazālī, *Iḥyā' 'Ulūm al-Dīn* I (Beirut: Dār al-Ma'rifa, 1982), 41-42.

You should know that I have found most of them (the later scholars) claiming that the basis of the disagreement between Abū Ḥanīfa and al-Shāfiʿī (☙) is founded on those principles which are mentioned in the book of al-Pazdawī[2] and other similar ones. Rather, the truth is that most of these controversial issues are principles derived on the basis of their (these later scholars') opinions.

According to my view, the controversial claims that:

A) the specific pronouncement (*khāṣṣ*) is clear and it needs no explanation,

B) the augmenting statement can carry (the force) to abrogate[3],

C) a general statement (*ʿāmm*) is as definitive as a particular one (*khāṣṣ*),[4]

D) there is no preference given (to a hadith) due to a greater number of transmitters,

E) no recourse should be had to the hadith narrated by a non-legal expert when resorting to the use of personal opinion is not possible,

F) particularizing a general statement by the linguistic implication of a condition (*mafhūm al-sharṭī*)[5] or a quality[6] is absolutely out of the question

G) the imperative form always entails obligation.[7]

Other issues like these are principles derived from the statements of

---

2. Al-Pazdawī (1089) a Ḥanafī jurist and author of *Kanz al-wuṣul ilā maʿrifat al-uṣūl.*

3. That is, when a text particularizes another text, the particularized text would have some parts of it rendered ineffective, and these parts are deemed by some jurists to have become abrogated.

4. The majority of jurists would argue that a general statement yields conjecture (*ẓann*), not certainty (*yaqīn*).

5. The *mafhūm* is what is understood from the language of a statement without being explicitly stated. In terms of legal interpretation, words with clear linguistic implications are considered clear and thus legally binding. See Wael Hallaq, *A History of Islamic Legal Theories: An Introduction to Sunni Uṣūl al-Fiqh* (Cambridge: Cambridge University Press, 1997), 43-44.

6. Quality (*waṣf*) is one of the type of allusions (*īmāʾāt*) in which the meaning must be inferred from a statement. Quality (*waṣf*) is not relevant in the statement's legal force unless it functions as the reason for the ruling. Thus it may become clear from a sequence of cases which element is critical to the ruling. For example, the Prophet refused to enter a house where there was a dog but entered it when there was a cat, explaining that the cat was not ritually impure. Robert Brunschwig "*Raisonnement par analogie d'après al-Ghazālī,*" *Studia Islamica* 34 (1971), 65-67. al-Ghazālī, *Mustaṣfā* (Cairo: Maṭbaʿa al-Amīriyya, 1334 A.H.) II, 74.

7. That is, it is not a recommendation or one of the other five forms. This is discussed in al-Ghazzali, *al-Mankhūl min Taʿlīqāt al-Uṣūl* (Damascus, 1970), 104 ff.

the founders (of the legal schools). These are not soundly transmitted from Abū Ḥanīfa and his two associates. Persisting in them and taking trouble to refute what contravenes them, as part of the deductive methodology of the scholars as al-Pazdawī and others did, is not more correct than holding what opposes these and responding with what refutes them.

[Discussion of Some of these Controversial Issues in Juristic Methodology]

[Examples of Type A]

An example is that they (the Ḥanafīs) established a principle that the specific expression (*khāṣṣ*) is clarified (*mubayyan*), and no further explanation should be joined to it. They derived this based on what the earlier jurists had said about the qur'ānic verses, "Bow down and prostrate yourselves"[8] and the Prophet's (ﷺ) saying, "The prayer of a person is not rewarded unless he holds his back straight in the bow and the prostration." This was in so far as they did not hold that keeping the back straight (during the bow and prostration) to be obligatory,[9] nor did they consider that the hadith was in explanation of the qur'ānic verse. So there was raised as an objection to what the earlier ones had made of His (ﷻ) saying, "Rub your hands over your heads."[10] and the Prophet's (ﷺ) rubbing the face up to his forelock, in so far as they (the earlier scholars) had made the *sunna* an explanation.[11] [Other examples are] the qur'ānic verses, "The male fornicator and the female fornicator, scourge each of them."[12] and "Cut off the hand of the thief, male or female."[13] and His (ﷻ) saying, "Until she marries a husband other

8. Qur'ān 22:77.

9. The Shāfi'īs consider this obligatory, most Ḥanafī's do not since they hold that the qur'ānic wording "bow down" and "prostrate" is already specific and cannot be further specified by a hadith. *Muṣaffā* I, 114. Ibn Rushd, *The Distinguished Jurist's Primer* l, 148-9. Pālanpūrī 2:762.

10. Qur'ān 5:6.

11. That is, during the ablution (*wuḍū'*) preceding the ritual prayer some Ḥanafīs state that the qur'ānic injunction cannot be further specified, while some do take the hadith into account. Some of these cases are cited in the article by Robert Brunschwig, "*Raisonnement par analogi*e," *Studia Islamica* 34 (1971), 65-66.

12. Qur'ān 24:2. Free, married, adulterers could be stoned to death as a punishment while unmarried persons or female slaves were only to be scourged based on hadith reports. al-Shāfi'ī, *al-Risāla*, 105-6.

13. Qur'ān 5:38. The category of "theft" is considered in jurisprudence to be specified by further conditions mentioned in hadith, including that the stolen goods are worth more than 10 dirhems, etc. al-Shāfi'ī , *al-Risāla,* 105, Pālanpūrī 2:762.

than him,"[14] and those things which had been appended to these (specific verses) as explanations after that, so that they had to take great pains in responding to criticism as is mentioned in their books.

[Examples of Type B]

They formulated the principle that the general statement (*'āmm*) is as (legally) definitive as the particular one (*khāṣṣ*). They derived it on the basis of what the preceding scholars had done in interpreting the qur'ānic verse, "Recite of the Qur'ān what is easy for you."[15] and the Prophet's (ﷺ) saying, "No prayer is valid without the opening chapter (al-Fātiḥa) of the Book."[16] in so far as they had not considered it (the Prophet's report) to be a specification.[17] Another example is the Prophet's (ﷺ) saying, "There is a one-tenth *zakāt* (*'ushr*) due on spring-watered land."[18] and his (ﷺ) saying. "There is no *ṣadaqa* (alms tax) due on what is below five *Awāq* (of silver)."[19] in so far as they didn't consider the first[20] hadith to be specified by the second,

---

14. Qur'ān 2:230. A woman cannot remarry a man who has divorced her until she marries another man and the marriage has been consummated. al-Shāfi'ī , *al-Risāla*, 149-151. All of the above qur'ānic verses are considered by legal scholars to contain specific (*khaṣṣ*) injunctions. They are, however, considered by some if not all schools to be further explained by hadith or early practice. This contravenes the principle that a specific injunction does not require further explanation.

15. Qur'ān 73:30.

16. Close to the hadith *"Lā ṣalāt illā bi (qirā'a) fātiḥa al-kitāb."* Tirmidhī Taḥrīm al-Ṣalāt. There are a number of variants of this hadith including Abū Dāwūd Ṣalāt 36. Vol. II #822 *"Lā ṣalāt li man lā yaqra' bi.... "*. Al-Shāfi'ī considers this a pillar of the prayer while the Ḥanafīs do not. Discussed in detail in al-Marghinānī, *Ḥidāya* I, with the *Mi'rāj al-Darāyah* of Muḥammad Muḥyī al-Dīn 'Abd al-Ḥamīd (Cairo: Muḥammad 'Alī Ṣubayḥ, 1966), 97-98.

17. The Arabic word *'mā'* "what is easy" in the Qur'ān verse is considered to be general (*'āmm*) and thus should not be specified by the hadith. *Kashhāf*, 74.

18. In Arabic this phrase also contains the general word "*mā*"—"what is watered by springs." Bukhārī Zakāt 55. Muslim, Abū Dāwūd, Tirmidhī, Nasā'ī, Ibn Māja, al-Dārimī, *Muwaṭṭa'*, Ibn Hanbal.

19. Bukhārī Zakāt 32, 42, 56. Muslim, Abū Dāwūd, Tirmidhī, Nasā'ī, Ibn Māja, al-Dārimī, *Muwaṭṭa'*, Ibn Hanbal. al-Bukhārī, III. 328. One ūqiyya equals forty Ḥijāzī dirhems.·

20. *Saḥīḥ al-Bukhārī*, Vol. 3, p. 328. The issue here is whether a general and specific injunction are in conflict. Most jurists combine the two hadiths in this case and hold that there is one-tenth *zakat* (*'ushr*) payable if the land production exceeds a minimum. Abū Hanīfa disagrees and holds that 1/10 is due on any quantity of agricultural produce since the measures stated in the hadiths are used in the grain trade (*wasq*) or in terms of money (*awāq*), and not in terms of other produce. Shāh Walī Allāh discusses this issue in *Ḥujjat Allāh al-Bāligha* II "Amounts Stipulated for Zakāt."

and so on with other subjects. Then the objection was presented to them that the qur'ānic verse, "Such a sacrifice offering as can be afforded."[21] (which is general [*'āmm*]) to (specified as) being a female sheep or something that is worth more, according to the explanation made by the Prophet (ﷺ),[22] so that they were reluctant to answer this (criticism).

[Examples of Type F]

They made a principle that there should be no consideration (in particularizing a command) of what could be understood from a statement without its having being explicitly stated (*mafhūm*) concerning a condition or a quality. They derived this based on what the earlier ones had done when interpreting the qur'ānic verse, "If anyone among you does not have the capacity."[23] Then many objections were raised to them based on the other rulings such as his (ﷺ) saying, "There is *zakāt* due on the camel which is a pasture animal."[24] so that they had to make a lot of efforts to respond to these criticisms.

[Examples of Type E]

They made a principle that the hadith narrated by a non-jurist does not need to be implemented if recourse to personal opinion[25] would be blocked by it. Then they transgressed their own principle in rejecting the hadith about the female animals that are sold without being milked for some time.[26] Then

21. Qur'ān 2:196.
22. That is during the Hajj al-Tamattu' when the state of consecration [*iḥrām*] is broken by one who performs the 'Umra before the Hajj. The sacrifice should be at least a sheep. *Muṣaffā* 1, 280-281. Bukhārī Hajj 102. The general qur'ānic injunction is thus specified by a hadith.
23. Qur'ān 4:25. In this qur'ānic verse, the context refers to a man's having the resources to marry a Muslim lady of respectable family. If a person does not fulfill a condition, i.e., having resources, he is encouraged to marry a slave woman. If one held the condition to be intrinsic to the force of the order, then it would imply that a person able to marry a free woman should not marry a slave or captive.
24. This is a case of "*mafhūm ṣifa*," i.e., the intended object of a descriptive characteristic, in this case "pasturing." From it might be understood that there is no *zakāt* on "stall-fed" (*ma'lūfa*) animals. Ibn Ḥājib, *Mukhtaṣar al-Muntahā*, II, 173-174. The Shāfi'īs consider the condition and description to be taken as specifying a particular case while the Ḥanafīs do not.
25. Here (*ra'y*) personal opinion, refers to the results of analogical reasoning (*qiyās*).
26. *Maṣarrāt*. Walī Allāh prefers the judgement of al-Shāfi'ī, *al-Risāla*, 330-1, who decides that the milk is the property of the buyer as is the analogy to the case of young born to animals after they are purchased. This opinion follows a hadith that states that a fixed compensation will be paid to the seller for such milk. The buyer may also return the animal if the milk given does not meet expectations. This opinion was rejected by the Ḥanafīs who considered the fact that the value of the

there was raised to them an objection regarding their treatment of the hadith about laughing aloud (during prayer),[27] and the hadith about the fast not being invalidated by eating out of forgetfulness,[28] so they were reluctant to respond.

Cases of what we have just mentioned are many, not hidden from the one who investigates while the person who does not investigate will not be sufficed by prolixity any more than from having this briefly pointed out. The opinion of the research scholars should suffice you as proof about this issue, i.e., that it is not necessary to implement the tradition narrated by a person who is known for accuracy and justice but not for legal acumen in cases where the option of using personal opinion would be blocked. An example is the case of the hadith about the female animals that are sold without having been milked for some time. This is the opinion of 'Īsā ibn Ibān[29] and many of the later jurists preferred this. However, al-Karkhī[30] was followed by many of the *'ulamā'* in holding that the condition that the *hadith* transmitter must have legal acumen does not hold here due to the precedence of a hadith report over an analogy. They maintained that this opinion was not transmitted from our predecesors, rather what was transmitted from them is that a singly transmitted hadith report (*khabar wāḥid*) has precedence over any analogy. Don't you see that they implemented the report of Abū Ḥurayra concerning the fasting person who eats or drinks out of forgetfulness, even if this opposes analogy. Abū Ḥanīfa (ﷺ) said, "If not for this hadith report I would have held the analogy (to be correct)."[31]

---

milk would vary to be problematic and thus appear to reject the hadith. A further issue is whether the seller is at fault and the animal defective. *Muṣaffā* I, 367. Discussed in I. Nyazee, *Theories of Islamic Law*, 171.

27. Abū Ḥanīfa and some of the Ḥanafites accept a mursal hadith report holding that laughing aloud invalidates the ritual prayer, while other schools hold this hadith to be weak. Al-Ghazzali, *al-Mankhūl*, 376. Al-Sarakhsī, *Kitāb al-Mabsūt* (Cairo: Maṭba'a al-sa'āda, 1324 A.Ḥ [1907/8]), 172-73. Ibn Rushd, *Bidāyat al-nihāya* 1, 39-40. Shāh Walī Allāh comments on this in *Ḥujjat Allāh al-Bāligha* II in the chapter on "Things Which Make Ablution Necessary." These hadiths, which are accepted despite the fact that they conflict with analogical cases, were transmitted by non-jurists.

28. The crucial consideration in *qiyās* is that food has entered the fasting person's body. In this case *qiyās* was abandoned on the basis of a prophetic report declaring the fast to remain valid in this case. See Hallaq, *A History of Islamic Legal Theories*, 108.

29. A Basran Ḥanafī d. 221 A. H. *al-Jawāhir al-Mudiya fī ṭabaqāt al-ḥanafiyya*, II (Cairo: Maṭba'a 'Īsā al-Bābī al-Ḥalabī, 1978), 678-680.

30. Abū al-Ḥasan (d. 951/2). A Ḥanafite jurist and author of *Risāla fī'l uṣūl*.

31. By analogy to other ritual actions, an omission due to forgetting would violate their validity.

You may also be guided to what is correct by the disagreement of scholars over many of the deductions that they inferred based on their (the earlier scholars') actions and their refutations of one another.

[Other Claims of Later Scholars]

I found some of the legal scholars claiming that everything that is found in these voluminous commentaries and thick tomes of legal opinions are the opinions of Abū Ḥanīfa and his associates; so that they do not make a distinction between the derived statements and the original. They do not make any discrimination considering that the meaning of jurists' statements are based on a certain derivation of al-Karkhī being thus, and according to the derivation of al-Ṭahawī thus. Nor do they make a distinction between their saying, "Abū Ḥanīfa said thus," and their saying, "the response to this case according to the view of Abū Ḥanīfa is thus," or "based on the principle of Abū Ḥanīfa is thus." Neither do they heed what the Ḥanafī scholars like Ibn al-Ḥumām and Ibn Nujaym said about the case of ten by ten (water)[32] and similarly the case of the condition of having to be a mile distant from water in order to be able to perform the ablution with sand, and other cases like these—i.e., that these are derivations done by members (of a legal school) and not, in fact, an essential part of the school.

I have found some of them claiming that the legal school is founded upon these polemical disputes mentioned in the *Mabsūṭ* of al-Sarakhsī,[33] the *Hidāya*,[34] the *Tabyīn*,[35] and other works like these. They don't realize that the first ones among whom these disputations appeared were the Mu'tazila, and that their legal school is not founded upon these. Then the subsequent scholars liked using these disputes for expanding and honing the minds of the students, and if for some other reason than that, then God knows best. Many of these ambiguities and doubts may be resolved through what we set out in this book.

I have found some of them claiming that there are only two groups with no third—"Literalists" (*Ẓāhiriyya*) and "People of Personal Opinion" (*ahl*

32. The size of a pond whose water may be considered pure for the ritual bath. See *Ḥujjat Allāh al-Bāligha* II, "Rules About Water."

33. The *Mabsūṭ* is a commentary on the *al-Kāfī* of al-Ḥākim al-Shahīd by Ibn Sahl al-Sarakhsī d. 1090, a Ḥanafī scholar

34. Of al-Marghīnānī, (d. 1197), translated into English by Charles Hamilton, (New Delhi: Islamic Book Trust, 1982) and used by the British in India as a model of Islamic Law. An annotated Arabic edition is (Cairo: Muḥammad 'Ali Ṣubayḥ, 1966).

35. *Tabyīn al-Ḥaqā'iq* (Cairo: Bulāq, 1895-97) of al-Zayla'ī d. 1342. A work on Ḥanafī law which is a commentary on Nasafī's *Kanz al-Ḥaqā'iq*. It examines in detail the differences with al-Shāfi'ī and refutes his arguments from the Ḥanafī viewpoint.

*al-ra'y*)—and that whoever uses analogy or deduction is one of the people of personal opinion—no, by God! On the contrary, isn't what is meant by using personal opinion the same as using understanding and reason? This is not foreign to any scholar. Nor is this the type of personal opinion that is absolutely not based on the Sunna, for certainly no Muslim would claim to be doing this. Nor is what is meant (by *ra'y* in this case) the ability to make deductions and use analogy (*qiyās*), for Aḥmad, Isḥāq, and even al-Shāfi'ī too, unanimously were not "People of Personal Opinion," while they used inferential methods and analogical reasoning. Rather, what is meant by "People of Personal Opinion" is a group of scholars who reopen for derivation issues agreed on among the Muslims or among the majority of them, using the principles of one of the early scholars. Thus what they do in most cases is to relate parallel precedents to other cases, and to refer to one of the theoretical principles (of jurisprudence) without consulting the hadiths and reports.

The Ẓāhirī (literalist) is a scholar such as Dāwūd Ibn Ḥazm,[36] who neither accepts using analogies nor accepts using the reports of the Companions and Followers. Between the two groups are research scholars among the People of the Sunna such as Aḥmad ibn Ḥanbal and Isḥāq (ibn Rahwaya).

[The Rise of Taqlīd]

Among them (new developments of later times) is that people have come to depend on *taqlīd*, and this *taqlīd* slowly crept into their hearts while they remained unaware of it.

The reason for this was that competition among the jurists and their disputing among themselves reached the point that whoever gave a fatwa about something found himself contradicted about that fatwa. He would then respond to this so that the discussion was not brought to a conclusion except through recourse to the pronouncement of one of the early scholars who had set precedents in the issue.

An additional reason for *taqlīd* becoming widespread was the injustice of the judges, for once most of the judges had become unjust and were no longer reliable, only something about which the common people had no doubt was accepted from them, i.e., something which had previously been established.

An additional reason was the ignorance of the leaders, and people's asking for fatwas from those with neither knowledge of the hadith nor the method of juristic derivation (*takhrīj*) as you may observe apparent in most of the recent scholars. Ibn al-Humām and others warned about this. At that

36. Ibn Ḥazm 994-1064. Andalusian jurist, theologian, poet, and historian. Codifier of the literalist (*Ẓāhirī*) doctrine which approaches the sources of the religion through their literal meaning.

time non-*mujtahids* began to be called jurists, and at that time people became confirmed in intolerance.

[Preference for One Legal Opinion rather than Another]

The truth is that most instances of disagreement among jurists, especially in cases where sayings of the Companions could support two sides, such as the *takbīrs* (pronouncing Allāhu Akbar) of the Days of Tashrīq,[37] the number of takbīrs of the two ʻĪd prayers,[38] the marriage of one in Iḥrām[39] (the special sanctified state of one on the Hajj pilgrimage), the manner of performing tashahhud of Ibn ʻAbbās and Ibn Maʻsūd,[40] whether to silently (or loudly) pronounce the *Bismillāh* and the *Āmīn*,[41] reciting the formula of the call to prayers twice or once during the *Iqāma*,[42] and this type of thing—have to do with giving preference to one of the two opinions. The pious ancestors did not disagree on the essential legality on all of these opinions, but rather their disagreement concerned which was the more correct of the two things.

---

37. The three days after the ʻĪd of Sacrifice, when "*Allahu Akbar*" is said aloud in various litanies. The Hanbalīs and Shafi'īs consider this practice *sunna* (established as recommended), the Ḥanafīs consider it obligatory, and the Mālikīs recommended (*mandūb*). *al-Fiqh ʻalā al-Madhāhib al-Arbaʻa* Vol. 1, 355-357.
38. On the occasion of the ʻĪd prayers the Kufans used to increase the *takbīr* (saying *Allāhū Akbar*) to three times in each prayer cycle (*raka'*) and the Medinans to seven takbirs in the first *raka'* and five in the second. *Muṣaffa*1,178. This is examined in *Ḥujjat Allāh al-Bāligha* II, Chapter "The Two ʻĪds." Also, al-Shāfiʻī says that the *takbīr* should be pronounced loudly on ʻĪd al-Fiṭr, Abū Ḥanīfa does not.
39. This is invalid according to al-Shāfiʻī and most others but Abū Ḥanīfa allows it due to his belief that Prophet Muḥammad married Maimūna at this time. *Muṣaffā* 1, 289-290. Shāh Walī Allāh prefers that one should not marry. *Ḥujjat Allāh al-Bāligha* II "Characteristics of the Hajj Observances."
40. *Tashahhud* (bearing witness) is a litany recited silently during the ritual prayer and each school varies slightly in the exact wording of the litany, position of the feet, etc. Walī Allāh prefers al-Shāfiʻī who follows the wording of Ibn ʻAbbās. See *Muṣaffa* 1, 115-116. al-Shāfiʻī, *al-Risāla*, 206-208. Ibn Rushd, *The Distinguished Jurist's Primer* l, 142-44.
41. Discussed in *Ḥujjat Allāh al-Bāligha* II, Chapter on "Recitations During the Prayers." See also Ibn Rushd, *The Distinguished Jurist's Primer l*, 136-8.
42. *Iqāma* is the second call to prayer given inside the mosque. The Ḥanafīs repeat the formula twice as in the call to prayer (*ādhān*) while other schools say them only once except for the phrase "*qad qāmat aṣ-ṣalāt*." (Prayer has begun). *Muṣaffā* 1, 83. An article discussing some aspects of this is I. K. A. Howard, "The Development of the *ādhān* and *Iqāma* of the Ṣalāt in Early Islam" in *Journal of Semitic Studies* XXVI/2, Autumn 1981: 219-228.

A parallel to this is the differing of Qur'ān reciters on the (acceptability of) variant modes of reading of the Qur'ān.[43]

Scholars usually explained this matter by saying that the Companions differed although they were all correctly guided. Therefore the *'ulamā'* continue to endorse the legal opinions of the muftis in issues involving independent reasoning, and to accept the judgement of the judges, and on some occasions to act at variance with their legal schools. In these situations you will see the leaders of the legal schools holding each opinion to be valid. They used to deal with disagreement of opinion by saying, "This is the more prudent, this is the preferred view, and I like this opinion better," or the scholar might say, "We only know about this opinion." These sorts of examples are often found in the *Mabsūṭ*, the *Āthār* of Muḥammad (Abū Yūsuf) (ﷺ) and the discussions of al-Shāfi'ī (ﷺ).

Later a group of scholars succeeded them who abbreviated the discussions of the jurists in such a way that they emphasized the disagreement and maintained the preferences of their leaders contending that whatever was reported from the pious ancestors reinforced remaining within the legal school of their associates and not going outside of it under any circumstance. This attitude may be either due to human nature, for every person likes what his peers and nation have chosen even in dress and cuisine, or due to some arbitrary leap arising in considering the proof, or due to other reasons of this sort. Some took up this fanaticism in religion, but they (the early scholars) were completely free from this.

Among the Companions and Followers and those who succeeded them there were those who recited the *basmala* and those who did not; and those who pronounced it aloud and those who did not;[44] and those who performed the *Qunūt*[45] prayers at the time of the dawn prayer and those who did not; and those who performed the ablution after have blood drawn by leeches, nosebleeds, and vomiting, and those who did not; and those who believed

---

43. That is, each one of the recognized variant readings of the Qur'ān is sound and acceptable and no preference is stipulated. al-Shāfi'ī, *al-Risāla,* 208-210.

44. That is, whether the Imam pronounces the formula, "In the name of Allah" before the Fātiḥa and whether he says it aloud. Ibn Rushd, *The Distinguished Jurist's Primer l*, 136-138.

45. *Qunūt* refers to an extra supplication made during the *witr* or other prayers, especially when Muslims are struck by a calamity. There are various types: (a) *Qunūt nāzila*. This is made at a time of calamity and may be offered with any prayer but preferably at morning, sunset, or night; (b) *Qunūt Witr*. The Ḥanafīs offer this during the final *rak'a* of the *witr* prayer after the night prayer and do not do it during the *fajr* (morning) prayer. The Shāfi'is only pray the *qunūt* prayer as part of the *witr* prayer during Ramaḍān, but do pray it at morning prayer. Shāh Walī Allāh refers to this in *Ḥujjat Allāh al-Bāligha* II, Chapter "Recitations During the Prayers" and *Muṣaffā* I, 112. See also Ibn Rushd, *The Distinguished Jurist's Primer* l, 145-6.

that performing ablution was required after touching a woman out of lust or touching the male member, and those who did not. Among them were those who did ablution after eating things cooked in fire and those who did not; and those who performed ablution after eating camel's meat and those who did not.[46]

In spite of these differences, they used to pray behind each other, as did Abū Ḥanīfa or his associates; and al-Shāfi'ī and others (ﷺ) used to pray behind the Imams from Madīna who were Mālikīs and others even if they neither recited the basmala silently nor aloud. Harūn al-Rashīd[47] led the prayer as Imam after having blood drawn by leeches and Imām Abū Yusūf prayed behind him and didn't repeat the prayer. Imām Aḥmad ibn Ḥanbal held that ablution was necessary after a nosebleed and being leeched so someone once asked him, "If the Imam had experienced a flow of blood and had not done ablution, would you pray behind him?" He replied, "How could I not pray behind Imām Mālik and Sa'īd ibn al-Musayyab?"

It is reported that Abū Yūsuf and Imām Muḥammad used to perform the two *'Īd* prayers by reciting the two *takbīrs* according to the pattern of Ibn 'Abbas[48] because Harūn al-Rashīd preferred the way of performing the *takbīr* of his ancestor. Once Al-Shāfi'ī (ﷺ) prayed (in the morning) near the grave of Abū Ḥanīfa (ﷺ) and did not perform the *Qunūt* out of respect for him.[49] He also said, "Sometimes we incline toward the 'Irāqī (Ḥanafī) school (of law)." Mālik (ﷺ) told al-Manṣūr and Harūn al-Rashīd what we have previously cited.[50] In the *Fatāwā al-Bazzāziyya*[51] it is reported that the second Imam—i.e., Abū Yusūf (ﷺ)—prayed the Friday prayer having performed the full ablution at a public bath. He led the prayer and then the congregation dispersed. After that he was informed that a dead mouse had been found in the well of the bath-house. He then said, "In this case, we will use the response of our brothers from the Medinan (Mālikī) school that if the water reaches the amount held by two large jars it will not become ritually impure."[52]

---

46. These matters are dealt with in *Ḥujjat Allāh al-Bāligha* II, Chapter "Things Which Make Ablution Necessary." *Muṣaffā* II, 36. See Ibn Rushd, *The Distinguished Jurist's Primer* l, 36-40.
47. Harūn al-Rashīd (d. 809), the Abbasid caliph.
48. That is, seven *takbīrs* in the first *rak'a* and five in the second.
49. This was respectful since the followers of Abū Hanīfa do not perform the *Qunūt* supplication in the morning prayer.
50. See Chapter 1, 16-17.
51. A treatise of Hanifī law by Ibn al-Bazzāz, Muḥammad ibn Muḥammad . Printed on the margin of *Fatāwā 'Ālamgīrī*,IV (Beirut, 1973), 118.
52. Otherwise as a Ḥanafī, he would consider the water unusable for ablution and the ritual bath. Abū Dāwūd Ṭaḥāra 33, Vol. 1 p. 17 #65. Tirmidhī, Nasā'ī, Ibn Māja, al-Dārimī, Ibn Hanbal.

[Over-specialization]

Most of the scholars became over-specialized in each discipline. Some claimed to have laid the foundation of the discipline of knowing the biographies of the hadith transmitters (*'ilm al-rijāl*) and determining their ranks in being reliable or unreliable (*jarḥ wa ta'dīl*). Then they would go on from this to ancient and modern history. Among them were those who sought out the unusual and rare hadith reports even if they lay within the scope of fabrication. Among them were those scholars who increased the argument over the roots of jurisprudence and each deduced principles of argumentation in support of his peers, so that he posed an issue, then exhausted it, critiqued it, answered the objections, defined, classified, and edited, sometimes lengthening the discussion and at other times condensing it.

Some of the scholars began to concoct remote instances that were not worthy of the attention of a reasonable person. They liked the generalizations and allusions in the discussions of the legal interpreters and those of a lower rank, to whom neither the knowledgeable person nor the ignorant one would care to listen.

The harmfulness of this disputation, disagreement, and hair-splitting was nearly as severe as that of the first crisis (or *fitna)* within the Muslim community) when people quarreled over who should rule and people took sides. Just as the first crisis resulted in a tyrannical rulership and events of severity and folly—similarly these latter (disputes) led to ignorance, interpolations, doubts, and conjecture from which there is no hope of deliverance.

Subsequently there arose generations who relied on pure *taqlīd*, neither distinguishing the true from the false, nor distinguishing polemical argument from inference (*istinbāṭ*). The *fiqh* scholar of this time was a prattler and wind-bag who indiscriminately memorized the opinions of the jurists, whether these opinions were strong or weak, and related them in a loud-mouthed harangue. The hadith scholar (*muḥaddith*) became a person who counted up the hadiths whether sound, faulty, or nonsensical, and recited them quickly like an entertainer, flapping his jaw full-force.

I don't say that this is so in all cases, for God has a group of His worshippers unharmed by their failure, who are God's proof on His earth even if they have become rare. No time has come after that but that the crisis has increased, reliance on *taqlīd* has become more prevalent, and integrity has become more and more absent from people's hearts until they have become content to abandon involvement in religious matters saying, "We found our fathers following a community and we follow in their footsteps."[53] Our complaint may be raised to God and He is the One to turn to for help. He is reliable and our trust is in Him.

---

53. Qur'ān 43:22.

This is the end of what we wanted to present in this treatise entitled "Fairness in Explaining the Causes for Juristic Disagreement." Praise be to God in the beginning and at the end, and outwardly and inwardly.

# Qur'ānic Citations



# Hadith Citations

# Shāh Walī Allāh's
# 'Iqd al-Jīd fī Aḥkām
# al-Ijtihād wa-l-Taqlīd
# (Chaplet for the Neck concerning the Rules of Ijtihād and Taqlīd)

# Shāh Walī Allāh's Preface

All praise be to Allah who sent our master Muḥammad (ﷺ) to the Arabs and non-Arabs in order to illuminate them in the darkness (of ignorance), so that through him those endowed with the highest levels of religious and spiritual zeal might attain the most noble stations. I testify that there is no God but God, Unique, and that Muḥammad is His bondservant and His messenger and that there will be no Prophet after him, may the peace and blessings of God be on him and his family and Companions.

This humble person who is in need of his noble Lord's mercy, Walī Allāh, son of 'Abd al-Raḥīm, may God protect his affairs and render virtuous his mind, situation, and status, says, "This is a treatise that I entitled 'The Chaplet for the Neck concerning the Rules of Ijtihād and Taqlīd.'" I was led to compose it due to the questioning of certain colleagues concerning important issues within that topic (of *ijtihād* and *taqlīd*).

# Chapter 1
# The Definition of *Ijtihād* and its Prerequisites and Types

According to what may be understood from the discussions of the scholars, the definition of *ijtihād* is making utmost effort (*juhd*)[1] in order to discern the applied *sharīʿa* rulings on the basis of detailed evidence for them that goes back in its entirety to four categories: the Qur'ān, the Sunna, consensus, and analogical reasoning.[2]

From this it can be understood that *ijtihād* is broader than (a scholar's) making the utmost effort to discern whether a ruling has previously been discussed by earlier scholars or not, and whether he agrees with them about this or not. It is also broader than accomplishing this *ijtihād* through seeking aid from certain scholars in being made aware of the source of the rulings in detailed evidence, or through not seeking aid from them. It should not be thought that a scholar who agrees with his shaykh about most issues—but who recognizes a proof for every ruling and is fully satisfied by this proof and assured by it—is not a *mujtahid.* This would be a false conjecture. Similarly, the idea that no *mujtahid* exists in these times, which is based on the first conjecture, is also false due to its restng on a false supposition.

The prerequisite for being a *mujtahid* is that a scholar must have knowledge of the Qur'ān and Sunna in whatever bears on legal rulings, including the matters about which there is consensus, the prerequisites of analogical reasoning, the manner of establishing parallel forms (*naẓar*), knowledge of Arabic grammar, (knowledge of) the abrogating and the abrogated texts, and the status of the hadith transmitters. There is no necessity of knowing scholastic theology or (theoretical) jurisprudence (*fiqh*).

Al-Ghazālī said, "*Ijtihād* in our times is only arrived at through the practice of jurisprudence, and this is the means for knowing how to perform it in this age, although this was not the method in the era of the Companions."

My opinion is that this refers to the (level) of absolute affiliated *ijtihād* which is not fulfilled except through knowing the pronouncements of the independent *mujtahid.* Similarly, the independent *mujtahid* must be knowledgable about the discussions of those who passed before; Companions, Followers, and Successors, and those who came after them, regarding the various topics of jurisprudence. This is what we have mentioned above concerning the conditions for *ijtihād* that are laid out in the books about the

1. Thus derived from the same Arabic root j-h-d.

2. The basic roots of Sunni jurisprudence.

principles of jurisprudence. There is no harm in quoting from al-Baghawī[3] concerning this subject:

> A *mujtahid* is someone who combines in himself five types of knowledge: (1) knowledge of the Book of God, exalted and majestic; (2) knowledge of the Sunna of the Prophet (ﷺ); (3) knowledge of the statements of the scholars of earlier times recording their consensus of opinion and their difference of opinion; (4) linguistic competence; and (5) knowledge of analogical reasoning, which is the method for inferring the ruling from the Qur'ān or the Hadith if something is not stated explicitly in a text from the revealed book, the hadith, or as a consensus of opinion.
>
> In terms of the qur'ānic sciences, the *mujtahid* should know the abrogating and the abrogated passages, the ambigous (*mujmal*) and the clarified (*mufassar*) expressions, the specific and the general ordinances, the unequivocal (*muḥkam*) and the unclear verses, as well as (the legal categories) of disliked, forbidden, neutral, recommended, and obligatory.
>
> In (terms of) hadith (Sunna) studies he must have knowledge about the sound and the weak prophetic traditions, the ones supported by complete chains of narrators going back to the Prophet (*musnad*), and the ones in which the chains lack a link at the level of the Companion who transmitted the traditions (*mursal*). He must know how to apply the Sunna to the Qur'ān and the Qur'ān to the Sunna, so that if he encounters a tradition whose outward meaning does not conform to (the meaning of) the Qur'ān, he will know how to properly interpret it. Indeed, the Sunna elucidates the Book, and cannot contradict it. He need only be cognizant of elements of hadith that pertain to the rulings of the divine law, not whatever goes beyond this in terms of stories, accounts of events not related by the Prophet, and pious admonitions.
>
> Similarly, he must have sufficient linguistic competence to understand what the Qur'ān and Sunna say about the legal rulings without necessarily having complete mastery of every word in the Arabic language. He should persist in the language to the level that enables him to grasp the semantic range of Arabic speech in order to indicate its meanings in various contexts and circumstances. This is because we were addressed (in the revelation) through the Arabic language and the person who does not know it will not understand the meaning intended by the lawgiver. He must be cognizant of what the Companions and the Followers of the Companions said about the rulings, and most of the legal opinions given by the jurists of the Muslim community so that his ruling does not contravene theirs, thereby introducing dissonance into the (jurists') consensus of opinion (*ijmāʿ*).

---

3. Abū Muhammad Ḥusayn al-Baghawī (d. 510/1117).

Once he knows the major portion of each of these types of knowledge, then he can be considered a *mujtahid*, while exhaustive knowledge of all of these is not a prerequisite. If he is lacks competence in any one of these areas, then his path should be that of a *muqallid* (i.e., not to undertake *ijtihād*), even if he is profoundly learned in the school of one of the bygone Imams. Such an individual is not allowed to be invested with a judgeship, or to be a candidate for a position in which he might issue judgements.

If a scholar masters all of these fields, and he shuns personal whims and innovations, armors himself with piety and abstains from major sins, while not persevering in minor sins, then it is allowable that he may take up the responsibility of the office of being a judge. He may also practice religious law undertaking *ijtihād* and pronouncing legal opinions. The person who does not meet all of these conditions must perform *taqlīd* of such a scholar in whatever circumstances present themselves to him.[4]

Al-Rāfi'ī[5] and Al-Nawawī[6] and innumerable other writers have made clear that the absolute *mujtahid* (*al-mujtahid al-muṭlaq*) that we discussed above may be of two types:

1) independent or unaffiliated (*mustaqill*) or
2) affiliated to a legal school (*muntasib*).

Type one: It is evident from their discussion that the independent *mujtahid* is distinguished from the other types by three qualities:

(a) his effective command of the principles of jurisprudence on which *mujtahadāt* (judgments by *ijtihād*) are based,

(b) his pursuing the qur'ānic verses, prophetic traditions and other reports in order to know the rulings that had already been answered, his being able to prefer some conflicting evidence over the rest and to explain why one interpretation should be preferred over other possibilities, and his ability to expose the source of the rulings among the various pieces of evidence.

We consider this, and God knows better, to constitute two-thirds of the knowledge possessed by al-Shāfi'ī.

(c) his being able to address new cases that have not been responded to previously using these proofs.

Type two: The affiliated *mujtahid* is the person who accepts the principles of his shaykh and who often has recourse to his discussions, in following up on (*tatabbu'*) his proofs (*adilla*) and exposing the source (*tanbīh*

4. al-Baghawī, *Sharḥ al-Sunna*, vol. 10 (Beirut: al-Maktaba al-Islāmī, 1976), 121-2.
5. al-Rāfi'ī (d. 623/1226).
6. al- Nawawī (d. 676/1277).

*al-ma'khadh*) (of the ruling). Along with this he has conviction about the validity of the rulings because of their proofs, and he is able to infer from them rulings in other cases, whether in few or many instances. However, the prerequisites mentioned previously are exclusive to the absolute *mujtahid* (*al-mujtahid al-muṭlaq*).

The next below him (the affiliated *mujtahid*) in status is "the *mujtahid* within the legal school" (*al-mujtahid fī-l-madhhab*). He performs *taqlīd* of his Imam (the founder of his school) in matters where unequivocal pronouncements (*naṣṣ*) of the founder of his school (Imam) exist. However, he also knows the principles of his Imam and the basis of his legal school, so that when a new situation arises for which he does know of any decision on the part of his Imām, he may exercise *ijtihād* about it in accordance with the school of the founder, thereby deriving the judgement from the pronouncements of his legal school's founder (Imam) and according to his methodology.

Still lower in rank is "the *mujtahid* who gives legal opinions" (*mujtahid al-futyā*). Such a scholar has profound knowledge of the legal school of his Imām and is able to prefer one verdict to another, and one opinion of the members of his legal school to another, and God knows best.

# Chapter 2
# Juristic Disagreement among *Mujtahids*

Scholars have differed about cases in applied jurisprudence where two *mujtahids* have ruled differently and there is no conclusive (*qāṭiʻ*) ruling. Is each of these *mujtahids* correct, or can only one of them be correct?

The former opinion is held by Shaykh Abū al-Ḥasan al-Ashʻarī, Qāḍī Abū Bakr, Abū Yūsuf, Muḥammad ibn al-Ḥasan, and Ibn Shurayḥ, and is also held by the majority of Ashʻarī and Muʻtazilite theologians. In the *Kitāb a-Kharāj* of Abū Yūsuf there are hints at this which are almost tantamount to an explicit endorsement.

The second opinion is held by the majority of jurists and is also held by the four founders of the legal schools. Ibn al-Samʻānī said in *Kitāb al-Qawāṭiʻ*[1] that this is the clear position of the Shāfiʻī school.

Al-Bayḍāwī said in *al-Minhāj*:

> The disagreement over whether each of two *mujtahids* exercising *ijtihād* can be correct is based on the argument that for every case there is only one specified verdict (whether) supported by a definitive or a conjectural proof. The preferable view is the one correctly asserted from al-Shāfiʻī, i.e., that in every instance there is a determined verdict about which there is an indicative sign (*amāra*). Whichever *mujtahid* finds that sign is correct and whichever fails to find it, errs, although he is not sinful on that account. His not being considered sinful is due to the fact that *ijtihād* is preceded by evidence since *ijtihād* consists of seeking for evidence before the ruling is given. The proof (turning out to be in error) is subsequent to the ruling. If the two (differing) *ijtihād*s were each deemed to be true, then this would entail the concurrence of two mutually contradictory elements.[2]
>
> (The erring *mujtahid* is also not a sinner) because the Prophet (ﷺ) said, "The *mujtahid* who is correct will receive two rewards and the one who errs will still receive one reward."[3]
>
> It has been objected, "If the ruling were determined and the person disagreeing with it did not rule according to what God had revealed, then he would be a sinner due to God's (ﷻ) saying, "The ones who do not judge according to what God revealed are the deviants." (5:47)
>
> We say (in response to this objection) that he (the *mujtahid*) pronounced a ruling on the basis of what he thought was correct even if the

---

1. Al-Samʻānī, Manṣur ibn Muḥammad, author of *Qawāṭiʻ al-adilla fī uṣūl al-fiqh.*
2. Therefore this would not be logical.
3. Muslim Book 18 #4261, also found in al-Bukhārī and other collections.

ruling erred with respect to what God had revealed.

It has been objected (to the opinion that only one *mujtahid* is correct), "If all the *mujtahids* making differing pronouncements in a particular case were not deemed correct, then the appointment of a dissenting *mujtahid* (to an office qualified by *ijtihād*) would not be allowable." (However we know that) Abū Bakr appointed Zayd[4] (in spite of their disagreement about certain rulings made on the basis of *ijtihād*).

We say in response that being appointed to a position of responsibility is not permissible in the case of a person who deliberately falsifies (*mubṭil*), while a person who errs (*mukhṭi'*) is not such a falsifier."[5]

[Shāh Walī Allāh responds to al-Bayḍāwī, disagreeing with his claim that only one *mujtahid* can be correct]:

Al-Bayḍāwī's saying, "for each given case there is (only one) determined verdict, etc."

We hold that this is imposing a ruling on the Unseen without a proof.

Al-Bayḍāwī's saying, "what has been correctly asserted by al-Shāfi'ī is that in each given case there is, etc."

We say, "What al-Shāfi'ī meant is that in any given case there will be one verdict which is more in conformity with the principles of jurisprudence (*uṣūl*), and more befitting of the modalities of *ijtihād*; and for which there is an evidentiary sign (*amāra*) found among the indicants for *ijtihād*. The *mujtahid* who finds it is correct, and whoever fails to find it, errs, but is not a sinner.

This is because al-Shāfi'ī declared in the opening of the *Kitāb al-Umm,* "When a scholar tells another scholar, 'You have erred,' he means, 'You have strayed from the correct course that scholars should follow,' and he expounded on this subject and has illustrated it with many examples. Perhaps al-Shāfi'ī meant that this occurs in a case where there is [only] one report, and whoever finds it is correct, and whoever fails to find it errs. This idea is also laid out in his *Kitāb al-Umm*."

Al-Bayḍawi said above (using rational proofs to reject the sinful status of the errant *mujtahid*), "*Ijtihād* is preceded by evidence ...."

We say, "We take it as an act of worship of Allāh (ﷻ) that we implement everything to which our *ijtihād* leads us, thus we try on the basis of what we know in a general way, to seek out what is more specific."[6]

---

4. Zayd (ibn Thābit) as a judge.

5. al-Bayḍāwī, 'Abd Allāh ibn 'Umar, 1286, *Minhāj al-Wuṣūl ilā 'ilm al-Uṣūl* in 'Abd Allāh al-Ṣiddīq al-Ghammāri, *al-Ibtihāj bi Takhrīj Aḥādīth al-Minhāj* (Beirut: 'Ālam al-kutub, 1985), 269-70.

6. The Urdu translator suggests that the core of this argument of Shāh Walī Allāh is that *ijtihād* constitutes an act of worship (*ta'abbud*) and that if a scholar makes

Al-Bayḍāwī said, "If the results of two (disagreeing) *ijtihād*s were each regarded as correct, this would entail the confluence of two mutually contradictory assertions."

We say, "These differing *ijtihād*s are like the alternative prescriptions for performing acts of expiation (*kaffāra*),[7] all of which are compulsory in legal status and (yet) are not compulsory (as individual acts)."

Al-Bayḍāwī cites the hadith, "The *mujtahid* who is correct gets two rewards and he who errs gets only one."

We hold that this quotation opposes the point that he wants to make rather than supporting it, for an error that is the cause for a reward cannot be regarded as being a sin. Thus, it follows that both the rulings had been made for the sake of Allah (ﷻ) and one of them was more meritorious than the other, just as fulfilling the regular commands of the divine law (*'azīma*) is superior to (availing oneself of) a dispensation (*rukhṣa*).[8]

The verdict that one *ijtihād* is correct and the other is not applies in the case of a legal judgement (in court). In that case only one of the two positions can be overtly ratified, either the position of the plaintiff or the position of the defendant.

When he (i.e., al-Bayḍāwī) says that, "He (the *mujtahid*) pronounced a ruling on the basis of what he thought was correct," we say that this acknowledges the correctness of what we also hold (that the *mujtahid* did not oppose the truth by making this ruling).

When he says that the erring *mujtahid* is not a deliberate falsifier (*mubṭil*), we agree with him that since such a person is not a deliberate falsifier, he is not an opponent of the truth, for every opponent of truth is a deliberate falsifier (*mubṭil*). "And what is there aside from the truth except error?" (Qur'ān 10:32)

In reality the opinion attributed to the four Imams (that only one *mujtahid*'s pronouncement on the same issue may be correct), is extrapolated from some of their statements. It is not an unequivocal ruling (*naṣṣ*) pronounced by them on this matter.

The Muslim community (*umma*) has not differed concerning the legitimacy of two *mujtahids* pronouncing (varying) judgments on matters

sincere effort, even if the *ijtihād* ultimately proves to be incorrect, the act still counts as meritorious and is not a sin. This is in analogy to a person making efforts to determine the direction of the *qibla*. If his conjecture turns out to be incorrect, still the prayer is considered valid. *Silk al-Mawārīd*, 14.

7. For example, the penalty for deliberately breaking the fast in Ramadan is either freeing a slave, fasting sixty consecutive days, or feeding sixty beggars twice in a day. Fulfilling any one, but not all, of these options is compulsory.

8. *'Aẓīmah* refers to the regular or formal commands of the law. *Rukhṣa* refers to concessions, allowances, or dispensations provided to worshippers due to hardship, for example, travelers' being allowed to shorten the prayer.

wherein there was scope for choice on the basis of an unequivocal textual pronouncement or on the basis of a consensus of juristic opinion (*ijmāʻ*). Such is the case of the seven variant recitations of the Qur'ān,[9] the formulae of invocations,[10] and the number of prostrations in *witr* prayers consisting of either seven, nine, or eleven rakʻats.[11] Likewise the *'ulamā'* should not disagree about matters where the option of choice is provided by the evidence.

In fact, there are four categories of juristic disagreement:

1) Cases in which the truth is decisively determined (*qāṭiʻ*). In these it is necessary to reject whatever disagrees because it is false at the level of certainty (*yaqīn*).

2) Cases in which the truth has been determined on the basis of the preponderant opinion and whatever is in disagreement is invalidated at the level of conjecture (*ẓann*).

(3) Cases where either of two conflicting opinions may be chosen with decisive certainty (*qāṭiʻ*).

4) Cases in which either side of the disagreement may be preferred on the basis of probable opinion (*ghālib al-ra'y*).

The detailed explanation of this is that if the case about which there is juristic disagreement is one that contravenes the ruling of the judge, in the sense that a sound pronouncement regarding it is known to have come from the Prophet, may the peace and blessings of God be upon him and his family, then every *ijtihād* that disagrees with this must be invalid. Yes, perhaps he (the *mujtahid*) may be excused due to his being unaware of the Prophet's statement until he comes to know about it and the conclusive proof is established.

In some cases the solution arrived at through *ijtihād* depends on knowing whether a particular event has actually occurred and there may be some doubt regarding this. For example, this could occur when it has not been established whether a certain individual is dead or alive. Inevitably only one of these facts is true. However, the one who errs (due to not knowing a particular fact) may be excused in his *ijtihād*.

If the *ijtihād* concerns a case that has been left up to the investigation of the *mujtahid*, and the two *mujtahids*' sources of proof are close to each other, and neither is so inconceivable that it might be thought that the one who held it was remiss and had deviated from people's common practice and their customs, then in this case both of the two

---

9. That is, on the basis of the hadith that there are seven recitations of the Qur'ān.

10. That the formulaic prayers, for example, at the beginning of the ritual prayer and in other cases may have alternate versions.

11. The *witr* prayer is a prayer performed at the end of the night prayers and may consist of varying odd numbers of prayer cycles (*rakʻats*), usually three.

*mujtahids* may be correct.

For example, take the case of two men each of whom is told by a person, "Give every poor man whom you encounter a dirhem from my wealth."

One person asks, "How would I know that he is poor?"

The response is, "If you perform *ijtihād* in tracing the circumstances that accompany poverty then you will be confident that he is poor, so give to him."

Then the two of them differ about the case of a particular person. One of them says that he is poor and the other says that he is not. The sources that each used as evidence are close to one another and plausible. Therefore both of them are correct since the command depended on concluding through investigation that the man was poor. This resulted from his (the commanded person's) investigation without any overt fault, in contrast to the case where he would have given the money to a big merchant who possesses servants and retinue. An individual who claimed him to be poor would be considered remiss, and it would not be justifiable to claim that some confusion had led him to this conclusion.

Here there are two situations, one of them concerns whether the person is poor in actuality or not. There is no doubt that only one thing is true here and that two contradictory positions can not simultaneously be upheld.

The second situation concerns whether someone who gave to a person who was not actually poor, supposing him to be in poverty, is obedient or not. There is no doubt that he is obedient and that whichever person's conjecture corresponds to the truth obtains an abundant share of reward.

If the *ijtihād* concerns making a choice in matters where choice has already been given (by the divine law) such as the (seven) variant recitations of the Qur'ān and the formulae of invocations and similar instances where the Prophet (ﷺ) offered alternatives so as to facilitate matters for people while all of the alternatives encompassed the essential benefit, then both *mujtahids* may be correct. All that we have said is clear and no one should hesitate in agreeing with this.

Most of the occasions of disagreement occurring among the jurists are of the following types:

i) A hadith had reached one *mujtahid* and not the other one. Now in this case the correct *mujtahid* is (already) determined.

ii) Each *mujtahid* (working on the same case) has access to conflicting hadiths and reports. He exercises *ijtihād* in reconciling them and in preferring some over others, and his *ijtihād* leads to a ruling so that disagreement may arise within this process.

iii) Jurists may differ in the explanation of the words used and their exclusive exhaustive definitions,[12] in recognizing the essential elements and conditions of a thing such as its being mentioned or omitted, or in deriving the anchoring point (*manāṭ*) of a rationale for legislation.[13] Otherwise they may differ about the soundness of applying what had been described in a general way to this specific case and or in extending a partial element to a totality and so on. Thus the *ijtihād* of each jurist will lead to a differing opinion.

iv) Jurists may differ about issues of principles of jurisprudence leading to a disagreement when these are applied to actual cases.

In cases under all of these categories each of two *mujtahids* may be correct provided that the sources (of their rulings) are close to one another in the sense that we have mentioned.

The truth is that the cases (of divergent rulings) mentioned in the books about the fundamentals of *fiqh* are of two types.

1) There are those that fall under the purview of knowing the subtleties of the Arabic language. Examples are questions of what is particular (*khāṣṣ*) and what is general (*'āmm*) in meaning, what is *naṣṣ* (univocal) and what is *ẓāhir* (words with two or more possible meanings, one of which is deemed, due to supporting evidence, to be superior). Other examples are the grammarians' observations such as, "'X' is a common noun (*ism al-nākira*), and 'Y' is a definite noun, and 'A' is a proper noun (*'alam*), and 'B' is a noun of category (*ismu jinsin*), or that the nominative case is indicated by the 'u' vowel marker and the accusative case by an 'a' vowel marker." There is not much disagreement about this category.

2) The second type involves ascertaining what a rational person would conclude on the basis of his good common sense (*salīqa*). The elaboration of this is as follows. Suppose you give an intelligent man an ancient book in which some letters have been altered and told him to read it. Inevitably, if something were unclear to him he would pursue the contextual material and investigate what was correct. Sometimes two intelligent persons would disagree in this sort of situation. When two courses of action present themselves to an intelligent person, how will he seek out the indications and scrutinize the benefits, and select the preferable course and the less harmful?

Similarly, when the earliest scholars encountered conflicting hadiths, they made a thorough search into the matter and then they applied their independent reasoning (*ijtihād*), ruling that certain of them were invalidated, that some of them could be reconciled on the basis of others and that some

12. "*Al-ḥadd al-jāmi' al-māni'*"—in the terminology of logic, an exhaustive, exclusive definition.

13. The *manāṭ* is the common factor that justifies the application of a primary principle from the Qur'ān or the Hadith to a derivative situation, or in application of general to particulars, etc. This is done through forms of analogy.

were to be preferred over others. Likewise, when cases arose for them that the previous scholars had not discussed, they analogized parallel cases to each other and inferred the reasons for the rulings. In summary, they developed methodologies to which they were driven by their inherent dispositions just as an intelligent person develops methods when a problem arises in his mind. Then a group of scholars desired to systematize these methods in detail in their books so as to have recourse to them during the course of their discussions. Alternatively, these methods were derived on the basis of actual cases, even if they did not articulate them. The intellectuals of later generations wholeheartedly embraced their methods since they were instinctively drawn to the same procedures. Thus these practices became established among scholars.

In a similar manner, they made exhaustive endeavors in the transmission of hadith and in discriminating the sound traditions from the defective and the abundantly transmitted traditions from the ones with a single chain of narration (*gharīb*). They also determined the status of the transmitters of the hadith, either through disparaging their integrity or establishing it, and in compiling and correcting hadith books. In these fields they relied on their instinctive intelligence. Scholars who followed them then codified these general principles.

Here you have a very useful benefit. One of the conditions laid down for implementing these general principles, is that the particular case under discussion should not be of the category where the intellectuals of earlier times have rendered a judgement disagreeing with these general precepts, since in most disputed cases there are particular extenuating circumstances that had resulted in the rulings going against the general principles. The real source of contention is persistently clinging to general principles and affirming a ruling that pure common sense ruled out (in a given case) on the grounds of the specifics of the case.

For example, suppose you see a stone and are sure that it is a stone. Then a contentious man comes and propounds the general principle that a thing is to be recognized by its color, shape, etc., and that the object before you has an appearance that is shared by many other things. Thus he counters your conviction by means of this general principle. The poor man does not know that the conviction attained in this specific case is of greater force than that achieved by following general principles.

Take care against being beguiled by such discussions from the obvious meaning of the hadith. Disagreement of this type should be resolved by research and reassuring the conscience. In summary, disagreement about most elements of the principles of jurisprudence may be resolved through reflection (*taḥarrī*), and achieving confidence through circumstantial evidence. The Prophet (ﷺ) pointed out on various occasions in his statements that matters of religious obligations could be clarified through such attempts to figure out the best answer (*taḥarrī*). On one occasion he said, "The *'Īd al-Fiṭr* (i.e., the Day of Celebrations at the end of Ramaḍān) is on the day when you cease to fast and the 'Īd of Sacrifice is on the day when you perform the sacrifice."[14]

Al-Khaṭṭābī[15] said that the meaning of this hadith (about the two *mujtahids)* is that the sin (of erring) is forgiven of people in decisions that had been arrived at on the basis of *ijtihād.* Thus, if a group of people had resorted to *ijtihād* when they did not see the 'Īd crescent moon so that they did not break their fast until they had completed thirty days of fasting, then later it was confirmed to them that the month had lasted only twenty-nine days, still their fasting and their breaking the fast would be valid and they have done nothing sinful or blameworthy. Likewise, during the Hajj if people are mistaken about which day is the Day of 'Arafat, they don't have to repeat the Hajj and they will receive the reward for their actions.[16] This is nothing other than God's leniency and kindness towards His bondservants, may He be glorified. There is another hadith of such import saying, "When the judge exercises *ijtihād* and is correct, he gets two rewards and if he errs, he receives one reward."[17]

Whoever makes a thorough study of the explicit pronouncements of the lawgiver (the Prophet) and his opinions, will derive from them a general principle. This is that the lawgiver has laid down a code regulating pious religious practices such as ablutions, the full bath, prayer, almsgiving, fasting, and pilgrimage, etc., upon which various sects of Islam are agreed. He has legislated for these practices their necessary elements (*arkān*), conditions, and the proper decorum to be observed, and has stipulated the disapproved and invalidating things that can occur in these matters and the reparations for them and has extended the discussion of these matters as appropriate.

However, he did not extensively discuss their essentials and other ele-

---

14. These two 'Īds are decided by the appearance of the new moon, which makes the exact dates unpredictable. Some scholars interpret this tradition to mean that there should be no contentious disagreement over such issues. Related by al-Tirmidhī #697. See Abū 'Iṣā Muḥammad al-Tirmidhī, *Jāmi' al-Tirmidhī* (Riyadh, Saudi Arabia: Dar al-Salaam, 1999/1420), pp. 177-178.

15. Abū Sulaymān Ḥamd ibn Muḥammad, 931-996.

16. Others, such as al-Khaṭṭābī, are of the opinion that such mistakes are only permissible in issues involving personal reasoning, such as seeing the moon on the 30th day, completing the full month, and then being informed that the moon was in fact seen on the 29th day. al-Khaṭṭabī's opinion is mentioned in Muḥammad Shams al-Ḥaqq al-'Adhim Abadī, *'Awn al-Ma'būd: Sharḥ Sunan Abī Dawūd* (Cairo: Dār al-Ḥadith, 2001/1422), 411.

17. Al-Bukhārī Volume 9, Book 92, Number 450, Muslim Book 018, Number 4261.

ments by offering exclusive exhaustive definitions of these. Whenever he was interrogated about partial verdicts relating to particular aspects of these essential elements, conditions, etc., he would direct people to their normal understandings of the words used and would guide them to resolve the particular cases by referring them back to general principles. He would not add anything more, except in very few incidental cases, due to reasons such as people's insistence, and so on.

Thus he commanded washing the four parts of the body[18] during ablutions but did not define "washing" by an exclusive exhaustive definition through which it would be known whether rubbing was essential to it or not, or whether using flowing water was part of it or not. He did not distinguish the water as being either unqualified or qualified[19] and did not explain the rules concerning well water and pond water, etc. These questions come up frequently and must have been envisioned during his time. When he (ﷺ) was asked about the case of the well of Buḍā'a[20] and the hadith about the two large pitchers[21] he did not add anything when answering beyond what people would have understood from the wording and what was their usual habit. It was in this sense that Sufyān ibn Thaurī said, "We found nothing in the case of water except accommodation."[22] When a woman asked the Prophet about a garment that had become stained with menstrual blood he did no more than say, "First scrape it off, then wash it thoroughly, then sprinkle water on it, then you can pray in it."[23] He did not add to what people were already practicing.

He commanded facing the *qibla* for prayer and did not teach us the way of ascertaining the direction of the *qibla*. The Companions used to travel a lot and they exercised individual effort (*ijtihād*) to determine the *qibla*, and therefore they had an intense need to know the way to perform *ijtihād*. All

18. The face, hands, feet, and rubbing water over the head.

19. Such as needing to come from a particular source such as a well.

20. According to a report in al-Tirmidhī (*ṭahāra* #49), Nisā'ī, and Ibn Ḥanbal, Buḍā'a was a well in Medina where dirty clothes, dog flesh and other odorous things were found. When asked whether its water could be used for ablutions the Prophet replied, "Nothing defiles water."

21. In Tirmidhī it was reported from Ibn 'Umar that he asked whether water in a forest area from which wild animals drank and in which they may have urinated would be pure for ablution. The answer of the Prophet was that it remained pure if the water was the amount that could be held in two large pitchers. The Shāfi'ī school uses this hadith to reconcile some of the different possible interpretations regarding whether water is pure for use in ablutions.

22. In the sense that the Prophet had not established extensive restrictions on what sort of water could be used to perform ablutions.

23. *Ṣaḥīḥ Muslim* Book 002, Number 0573. Abū Dāwūd Ṭahāra 130, al-Tirmidhī, Nisā'ī, al-Dārimī.

of this was done in order to entrust things like this to their opinions. Most of the Prophet's legal rulings (*fatāwā*) were in this mode as will not be obscure to a fair and reasonable person.

We have understood, after researching his judgments, that the Prophet provided a great benefit (*maṣlaḥa*) in avoiding over-meticulousness and by not excessively multiplying regulations. This (benefit) is that these issues originate in states of affairs that are customarily handled in a summary way and whose exclusive exhaustive definition cannot be known without difficulty. Sometimes establishing such a definition would require differentiating between two intricate situations through rules and regulations whose establishment would cause hardship to people. Even if these cases were to be regulated and explained, their explanation is only possible through resorting to similar states of affairs, and so on. This explanation could go on indefinitely while it could be brought to a conclusion in some cases by leaving it up to the opinion of the person affected. However, these states of affairs are not more worthy of being left up to the personal opinion of the persons who are concerned than the other instances. It was for this beneficial purpose that the Prophet left such situations up to their opinion in the first place. He was not rigid in matters about which there was disagreement in cases where the disagreement concerned something that had been left up to people, so that there was some latitude for diverse opinion.

Thus, he was not harsh with 'Umar ibn al-'Āṣ in what he understood from God's speech, "cast not yourselves by your own hands into destruction." (2:195) Thus he (ﷺ) permitted performing the major ablution using earth in the case of someone who was ritually impure if that individual was worried about becoming deathly ill due to catching cold. He was not strict on 'Umar ibn al-Khaṭṭāb in what he understood from the interpretation "or you have cohabited with women"[24], i.e., that it concerned the issue of touching a female, as opposed to (allowing earth to be used to remove) the ritual impurity resulting from sexual intercourse so that the issue of being in state of major ritual impurity (*janāba*) was not mentioned here, and ('Umar held) that the person in a state of major ritual impurity would absolutely not be allowed to perform the ablution with earth.[25]

---

24. "... and you can find no water." (4:43; 5:6) There is juristic disagreement about whether this qur'ānic verse implies that ablution is necessary (for men) after merely touching a female, or whether it pertains to the permission to perform the ablution using earth for those who have had sexual intercourse and do not have access to water for bathing.

25. There is juristic disagreement about which actions required a full ablution with water and which would suffice with *tayammum* if water were not available since the Prophet had not specified this. A fuller discussion of the jurists' positions and their rationale may be found in Ibn Rushd, *The Distinguished Jurist's Primer* I trans. Imran Ahsan Khan Nyazee (Reading, UK: Garnet, 1994), 67-71. Shāh Walī

Al-Nisā'ī reported from Ṭāriq (ibn Shihāb) that, "A man had become ritually impure (in the major sense—through emission of semen) so he did not pray. Then he came to the Prophet (ﷺ) and recounted this to him and he said, 'You have got it right'. Another man became ritually impure (*ajnaba*) then he performed the ablution with earth and then prayed. Then he came to the Prophet (ﷺ) and he (ﷺ) said something like what he had said in the first case [ i e. 'You are correct.']"[26]

He was neither harsh with those who had postponed the afternoon prayer nor with those who had performed it on time since they had all derived their interpretations on the basis of his statement, "Do not pray the afternoon prayer until you reach Banū Qurayḍa."[27]

In summary, whoever comprehends all aspects of his staements will know that the Prophet (ﷺ) left the matter up to people's judgement in those situations that are customarily handled in ambiguous ways. Similarly he left issues that needed to be reconciled with others up to people's understanding. Parallel to this is that jurists entrust many judgments to the better judgement (*taḥarrī*) of the individual concerned and to his customary practice. Thus there is no severity on their part towards any who disagree. Another parallel instance is that the whole Muslim community agreed on the use of individual effort (*ijtihād*) in determining the qibla when it is cloudy and not to be harsh on any person regarding whatever his investigation had led him to conclude. Another parallel to this beneficial purpose is the convention observed by debaters, that the premises of the proofs should not come under discussion because this would necessarily widen the scope of the argument.

Now whoever recognizes the true nature of this problem will realize:

1) that in the majority of cases of *ijtihād* the truth lies somewhere between the two extremes of difference.

2) that there is latitude in the matter.

3) that being fixated on one thing and determined to deny what the opponent says, is counter productive.

4) that formulating definitions, if this aims to make concepts accessible to every literate person, is an aid to knowledge. However, if

Allāh also refers to this instance in Chapter One of *al-Inṣaf fī Bayān Sabab al-Ikhtilāf,* 9-10.

26. *Sunan al-Nasa'ī* I (Beirut: Dār al-Qalam), 172-73, al-Ṭahāra.

27. This concerns a hadith report that at the time of the Battle of the Trench the Prophet commanded the Companions not to pray the afternoon (*'aṣr*) prayer until they reached the Banū Qurayḍa. Some understood this to mean they had to delay the prayer while others stopped on the way in order to pray in time, understanding that the Prophet meant that they should hurry in their journey. al-Bukhārī Volume 5, Book 59, Number 445. This example is often cited in the *fiqh* literature as justifying the position that two *mujtahids* can each be correct.

> these (definitions) are far-fetched and attempt to isolate the correct meaning of a multivalent (*mushkil*) term by means of concocted premises, it might possibly lead to some new *sharī'a* ruling.[28]

The accurate opinion is that articulated by 'Izz al-Dīn 'Abd al-Salām.

> He prospers who undertakes what the scholars agree to be obligatory and abstains from whatever they have agreed to be forbidden, and regards as permitted whatever scholars agree is allowed, and carries out whatever they all decree to be recommended, and avoids whatever they agree to be reprehensible.
>
> The person who takes up something about which jurists have disagreed will be in one of two situations:
>
> > 1) The matter about which they disagree may be one of those matters that contradicts a ruling of the lawgiver. There is no way to follow such a ruling because it must be absolutely in error. No ruling contravenes the *sharī'a* unless it is an error remote from the essence of divine legislation, its source, and protecting its authority.
> >
> > 2) If the matter wherein there is juristic disagreement is not something that annuls the ruling of the divine law, then there is no problem in either implementing it or in not implementing it since in this case a person is following the opinion of certain scholars.
>
> People have continued observing this practice of asking whichever scholar they met without being restricted to a legal school, and no one denied any questioner until these legal schools and their fanatic followers came on the scene. Indeed, one of such people might follow his Imam, perfoming *taqlīd* of him in whatever he rules despite the remoteness of his opinion from proofs, as if he were a prophet sent to him. This is remote from the truth and far from being correct and no person of insight accepts this.

He also said,

> Whoever follows one of the founders of the legal schools and then wishes to follow another one of them, can he do this?
>
> There is scholarly disagreement about this issue. The preferred opinion requires elaboration. If the school to which he wishes to transfer is one in which the new verdict would contradict the (previous) ruling, then he should not change to a ruling that would require such a contradiction, since it would only cause a contradiction due to its being invalid. If approaches of the respective schools are close to one another, then continuing to perform *taqlīd* of a certain legal school is allowable,

---

28. Therefore it would be a source of heretical innovation. The Arabic original did not number these clauses, but I followed the practice of the Urdu translator in including numbers for the sake of clarity.

as well as transferring to another school. This is because people have continued to follow whichever scholars they wished from the era of the Companions (🕮) until the time when the four legal schools emerged, without this being rejected by any person whose denial was worthy of consideration. Had this been invalid the scholars would have rejected it, and God knows best what is correct.[29]

Once you have verified for yourself what we explained, you will understand that every ruling that *mujtahids* treat through *ijtihād* ultimately goes back to the master of the divine law (🕮), either on the basis of his words or to a reason for legislation taken from his words. Since this is the situation, in every solution derived through *ijtihād* there are two elements that need to be assessed:

1) One of them is whether the law giver intended a certain meaning by his words or something else. In addition, did he have this reason for legislation in mind when he pronounced the textual ruling upon the case or not?

If the assessment of the possible correctness (of the opinions of two *mujtahids*) is with regard to this point, then one of the *mujtahids* can be considered to be correct without specifying that the other is necessarily in error.

2) The second aspect is that within the rules of the divine law the Prophet, may the peace of blessings of God be on him and his family, assigned to his community, either explicitly or by indication, that when they differed concerning his pronouncements or the meanings of a statement reported from him then they were commanded to perform *ijtihād* and to dedicate their effort to recognizing which of these was correct. Once something of this nature had been determined by a *mujtahid* then they were supposed to follow (*ittibāʿ*) him, as it had been enjoined on them (by the Prophet) that when the qibla was obscured for them on a dark night they were obliged to use their best judgement and to pray in the direction that their investigation indicated. The divine law makes this depend on the fact that seeking out (the *qibla*) actually took place, just as it makes the obligation to pray depend on it being the correct time (for that prayer), and as it makes a child's being held legally responsible depend on his having reached the age of legal maturity.

Therefore, if the discussion (about whether two *mujtahids* can be correct) is in regard to this point, then if the case is one in which the *ijtihād* of a second *mujtahid* would contradict a previous *mujtahid*'s being correct, then his (new) *ijtihād* is null and void with the degree of

29. ʿIzz al-Dīn ʿAbd al-Salām. *Qawāʿid al-Aḥkām fī Maṣāliḥ al-Anām* II (Cairo: Maktaba al-Kuliyyāt al-Azhariyya, 1968), 158-9.

certainty. Also if there is a sound hadith about this issue and a *mujtahid* issued a ruling that opposed it, then his *ijtihād* is invalid.

If the two *mujtahids* both follow proper procedure and they do not oppose a sound hadith, and if their disagreement is not about a matter that would annul the *ijtihād* of the judge and the *muftī* by disagreeing with it, then both of the *mujtahids* can be considered correct. This is the situation, and God knows better.

# Chapter Three
# Reinforcing staying within the four legal schools and severe stricture against abandoning them or going outside of them

Be informed that there is a great benefit in staying within these four legal schools and a great harm in deviating from them. We will explain the various reasons behind this.

Firstly, the Umma has agreed by consensus to rely on the pious ancestors in knowing the divine law. In doing this the Followers relied on the Companions, and the Successors relied on the Followers. In this way the scholars of each generation relied on those who had gone before. Reason indicates the propriety of this because the divine law is only known through transmission (*naql*) and inference (*istinbāṭ*). Sound transmission [of texts and reports] only takes place when each generation takes from whoever went before it through uninterrupted connection. In the case of inference it is incumbent that a jurist know the opinions of the predecessors in order not to deviate from their pronouncements and thereby violate juristic consensus (*ijmā'*), and in order to build upon their opinions and to take assistance from those who had gone before. This is because all of the disciplines such as composition, grammar, medicine, and poetry as well as iron smithing, copper smithing, and gold smithing are not easy for someone to master except through close association with those in the field. Any situation other than that is rare, remote, and does not occur, even though it may be rationally conceivable.

Once dependence on the pronouncements of the pious ancestors has been stipulated, it is necessary that the statements that would be relied on are related by sound chains of transmission or recorded in authoritative books. It is also necessary that these statements have been worked through so that the preferred interpretation among the plausible ones has been made clear, and that their general meanings have been specified in certain cases and their unqualified decrees (*muṭlaq*) have been qualified (*muqayyad*) in certain instances, and so that divergent opinions about them have been reconciled and the causes for the legislation underlying their rulings have been explained. If this has not been accomplished then relying upon them (these statements) is not correct.

There is no legal school that meets this criterion in these later times other than these four, unless one includes the schools of the Imāmī Shi'a and the Zaydīs, who are people of innovation whose opinions may not be considered reliable.

Secondly, the Prophet (ﷺ) said, "Follow the vast majority (*al-sawād al-a'ẓam*)."[1] Once any authentic schools other than these four died out, then following them became equivalent to following the vast majority and going outside of them was tantamount to abandoning the vast majority.

The third of them (reasons for staying within the four schools), is that once a long time had passed, the era[2] became remote and trustworthiness was lost, it is not permitted to rely on the pronouncements of the corrupt scholars among the oppressive judges and the muftis who follow their own whims. This (corruption) might reach such an extent that certain scholars would attribute their own opinions, either explicitly or by indication, to some of those pious ancestors famous for their sincerity, religiosity, and trustworthiness. Thus some pronouncement of his (such a fabricator) may have become preserved. Nor is it permitted to depend on a scholar's ruling when we do not know whether he fulfills the conditions for *ijtihād* or not.

Once we observe certain scholars to be confirmed in their fidelity to the schools of the pious ancestors then it will be possible to trust their deductions from their sayings or their inferences from the Qur'ān and the Sunna. If we don't see that on their part, then this (trust) would be out of the question.

This is what 'Umar ibn al-Khaṭṭāb (ﷺ) meant when he said, "Islam will be destroyed by the arguing of the hypocrite using the Qur'ān."[3] With respect to this (need to follow the schools) Ibn Mas'ūd said, "Whoever is a follower should follow someone from the past."

This is also what Ibn Ḥazm opined when he said,

> *Taqlīd* is forbidden. It is not permitted for anyone to follow the opinion of someone other than the Prophet of God (ﷺ) without proof, due to God's (ﷻ) saying, "Follow what was revealed to you from your Lord and do not follow guardians besides Him," (7:3) and, "If it were said to them, 'Obey what God has revealed to you,' they say, 'Rather we obey what we found our ancestors doing.'" (2:170) (God) said in praise of the ones who don't undertake *taqlīd*, "Give good news to my worshippers who hear advice and follow the best of it. Such are those whom Allāh guides, and such are those possessed of understanding." (39:17-18) And He (ﷻ) said, "If you disagree among yourselves about something, refer it to God and the

1. Hadith found in the collections of Ibn Māja (Fitan 8) and with the exact wording "follow" in the variant "*Yadu Allāh 'alā al-jamā'a, ittabi' al-sawād al-a'ẓam fa innahu man shadhdha shadhdha ilā al-nār.*" "Allah's hand is over the group, follow the largest majority, for verily whoever dissents from them departs to hell." Narrated by al-Ḥākim al-Tirmidhī and al-Tabarī from Ibn 'Abbās in *al-Sunna* and al-Ḥākim also narrated it from Ibn 'Umar.
2. Of the Prophet and the first generations.
3. al-Dārimī, Muqaddama #23.

Prophet if you believe in God and the Last Day." (4:59)

Thus God (ﷻ) did not allow recourse to any person beyond the Qur'ān and Sunna in time of dispute. In this (qur'ānic verse) He forbade referring at the time of dispute to any person's opinion because it is not the Qur'ān or Sunna. The consensus of all of the Companions, from the first of them to the last, and the consensus of the Followers, from first to last, confirmed their own refusal and their forbidding any other to blindly follow the opinion of any contemporary or preceding person, such that he would totally accept it.

Therefore, it should be known that whoever follows the totality of Abū Ḥanīfa's, Mālik's, al-Shāfi'ī's, or Aḥmad's opinions (ﷺ), and does not leave aside any opinion of a follower of theirs, or of anyone else in favor of that of someone else, and does not rely on what is in the Qur'ān and the Sunna without submitting it to the opinion of a particular person—this person has surely and indubitably opposed the consensus of the whole Muslim community from its beginning to its end. Such a person will not find any pious ancestor or person among all of the three praiseworthy first generations (to be in agreement with him). Therefore he has chosen a path other than that of the believers. We take refuge with God from this position.

In addition, all of these jurists forbade performing *taqlīd* of themselves or of anyone else. Thus, whoever blindly follows these jurists contravenes their own prohibition. Also, what is it that could make a person among them (the founders of the legal schools) or anyone else, more worthy of being blindly imitated, than say, 'Umar ibn al-Khaṭṭāb, 'Alī ibn Abū Ṭālib, Ibn Mas'ūd, Ibn 'Umar, Ibn 'Abbās or 'Ā'isha, mother of the believers (ﷺ)[4]—for if *taqlīd* were permitted then each one of these people would be more worthy of being imitated than anyone else.[5]

This statement (of Ibn Ḥazm) applies to any one who has some inkling of *ijtihād* even if only in one issue, and to whomever it is clearly apparent that the Prophet (ﷺ) commanded one thing and forbade another. This can neither be abrogated by tracing the hadiths and the opposing and concurring opinions about the case nor by finding anything that abrogates them—nor by seeing a large group of those scholars who are steeped in learning implementing it, for he sees that the person who opposes it (the Prophet's ruling) has no proof other than analogical reasoning, inference, or something like this.

In this case there would be no reason for opposing a hadith of the

4. These are known as the seven jurists of Medina.

5. Ibn Ḥazm, *al-Nabdha al-Kāfiyya fī Uṣūl Aḥkām al-Dīn* (Cairo: Dār al-Kitāb al-Maṣrī, 1991, 86-87

Prophet (ﷺ) except concealed hypocrisy or overt stupidity. This is what Shaykh ʿIzz al-Dīn ibn ʿAbd al-Salām meant when he said:

> It is one of the most amazing wonders that one of the *muqallid* jurists agrees on the weakness of something taken from his Imam, because there is found no defense against its weakness, while in spite of this he blindly imitates his decisions about it and ignores the scholar whose opinion is attested to by the Book, Sunna, and sound analogies. He remains rigid in his adherence to carrying out the *taqlīd* of his Imam. Indeed he concocts things that oppose the manifest meaning of the Book and the Sunna, and exegetes them by remote esoteric interpretations in defense of the person he is imitating.[6]

He (further) said:

> People always used to ask whichever scholar they happened to run across without being restricted to a legal school, and without rebuke to any questioner until these legal schools appeared and with them scholars practicing *taqlīd* who were prejudiced in their favor. Thus one of them would follow his Imam despite the remoteness of his opinion from evidence (*adilla*), imitating him in what he held as if he were a messenger sent from God. This is far removed from the truth and far from what is correct, unacceptable to any reasonable person.

Imām Abū Shāma said:

> It is incumbent that the scholar engaged in jurisprudence not confine himself to the school of one Imam, and that he should hold whatever is closer to the indication (*dalāla*) of the Qur'ān and the established practice of the Prophet (*sunna maḥkama*) to be correct in every case. This will be easy for him if he is well-versed in most of the traditional disciplines. Let him avoid partisanship (to a school) and the study of the recent modes of disagreement, for these are a waste of time and will disturb his serenity. It is confirmed that al-Shāfiʿī forbade performing *taqlīd* of himself or anyone else.[7]

His (al-Shāfiʿī's) associate al-Muzanī (d. 306/878) said at the beginning of his *Mukhtaṣar*:

> I summarized this book of al-Shāfiʿī's teaching and the meaning of his opinions in order to make it available to whomever wishes, while I apprise him of his (al-Shāfiʿī's) forbidding performing *taqlīd* of himself or any other. Therefore one should study it for the sake of his religion and should be cautious. I admonish whoever wishes to study alShāfiʿī's teaching, that he himself forbade performing blind imitation

6. ʿIzz al-Dīn ibn ʿAbd al-Salām, *Qawāʾid*, 159 (continuation of passage quoted in Chapter 2, p. 94).

7. Abū Shāma', ʿAbd al-Raḥmān ibn Ismāʿīl (d. 1267).

(*taqlīd*) of himself or anyone else.[8]

(Ibn Ḥazm's saying applies to) the person who is not learned and follows a particular jurist believing that a person like him could not err and that what he said must definitely be correct. Such a person has secreted in his heart not to abandon following this jurist even if evidence opposing him would come to light. Apposite here is what al-Tirmidhī reported from 'Adī ibn Ḥatim—that he said, "I heard him, i.e., the Prophet of God (ﷺ), reciting this qur'ānic verse: "They took their priests and rabbis as Lords besides Allāh." (9:31) The Prophet said, "They didn't used to worship them, rather they—if these ones permitted something for them, considered it permitted; and if they forbade a thing, they forbade it."[9]

This (statement also) applies to the one who does not allow a Ḥanafī, for example, to ask for a legal opinion from a Shāfi'ī jurist and vice versa, and does not allow a Ḥanafī to follow Imām Shāfi'ī, for example. Such a person has opposed the consensus of the early generations and contradicted the Companions and Followers.

This statement (of Ibn Ḥazm) does not apply to the one who holds himself only to the sayings of the Prophet (ﷺ) and considers permitted only what Allāh and His Prophet made permissible, and only considers forbidden what God and His Prophet have forbidden. However, when he doesn't know what the Prophet (ﷺ) said, either due to being unable to synthesize his various utterances, or being unable to infer rulings from his sayings, then he will follow a rightly-guided scholar assuming that this individual will be correct in what he says, and that obviously he will issue accurate legal opinions based overtly on the Sunna of the Prophet (ﷺ). Then, if something comes to light that conflicts with his opinion about him (the scholar) he will part company with him immediately without dispute and insistence. How can anyone condemn this, when asking for legal opinions and giving them has gone on among Muslims since the time of the Prophet (ﷺ)? There is no difference between always asking a certain person for legal opinions and asking this person on some occasions and another individual at other times, once what we mentioned has been agreed on. How can this be denied when we don't believe that a jurist, whoever he may be, received jurisprudence through Divine revelation, and that God made obeying him obligatory upon us, and that he is infallible? Thus, if we follow a jurist, this is due to our knowing that he has expertise concerning God's book and the Sunna of His Prophet, and that his opinion must either be based on a pronouncement of the Qur'ān or the Sunna or may be inferred from them through some variety of deductive apparatus.

Or the jurist knew on the basis of the contextual evidence (*qarā'in*) that

8. al-Muzanī, *al-Mukhtaṣar*, (Beirut: Dār al-Ma'rifa, n.d.), 1.

9. Tirmidhī IV, Tafsīr Sūra 9, 342. Hadith # 5093, where it is classified as gharīb.

the ruling (*ḥukm*) in a certain analogical pattern is contingent on a particular rationale for the legislation (*'illa*). His confidence about this recognition led him to draw an analogy to what was not explicitly stated in a text from something that was textually stipulated. It is as if he were saying, "I believe that the Prophet of God (ﷺ) would say, 'Whenever I find this reason for legislation (*'illa*) present then the ruling (ḥukm) in the case will be thus.'" In this way the standard for his deriving analogies became included among these sources,[10] so that this is also ascribed to the Prophet (ﷺ) although this method does entail conjectural elements (*ẓunūn*).[11]

If this were not the case then no believer would follow a *mujtahid*, since if a hadith from the infallible messenger whose obedience God made incumbent upon us reached us by a sound chain of transmission, indicating something which conflicted with his (the *mujtahid*'s) opinion and we were to ignore the hadith in favor of obeying that guesswork—who would be more evil than us? What would be our excuse on the day when people will stand before the Lord of the Worlds?

---

10. As occurs in the insertion of a particular instance into a syllogistic pattern according to the procedure of *qiyās* (analogical reasoning).

11. Therefore indicating a lower level of proof (*ẓannī*) as opposed to certainty (*qaṭ'ī*).

# Chapter 4
# Disagreements regarding following the four legal schools and the extent to which this is obligatory

Know that the followers of these legal schools are at four levels. There are explicit parameters for individuals at each of the levels.

1) The level of the absolute *mujtahid* who is affiliated (*muntasib*) to the founder of any one of these schools.

2) The level of the scholar who can derive solutions to cases (*mukharrij*) and he is a *mujtahid* within a school.

3) The level of the scholar profoundly learned in the legal school who has learned its teachings by heart and mastered them completely. He may issue legal opinions about matters wherein he has competency and about which he has memorized information from the school of his colleagues.

4) The absolute *muqallid* who asks the scholars of the legal school for legal opinions and acts on the basis of their legal opinions (fatwas).

The books of the Muslim community are replete with the conditions and rules pertaining to each level. However, some people have not distinguished among the levels and thus have become confounded by the rules and think that they are mutually contradictory. Therefore we wish to devote a subsection of this chapter to each type and to separately indicate the rules regarding each level.

## 1) The Absolute Affiliated Mujtahid

We previously presented his status[1] and therefore will not repeat it. The essence of the earlier explanation is that he (the absolute affiliated *mujtahid*) combines the discipline of hadith studies and *fiqh* as transmitted by his associates with knowledge of theoretical principles of legal methodology (*uṣūl al-fiqh*) as is the case of the great Shāfi'ī scholars. Even if such scholars exist in large numbers, still they are relatively few in comparison to those at the other levels.

The sum of their discipline according to their statements, which we have explored, is to (firstly) present the cases transmitted from Mālik, al-Shāfi'ī, Abū Ḥanīfa, al-Thaurī, and other *mujtahids* (ﷺ), whose opinions and fatwas on the *Muwaṭṭā* of Mālik and the two *Ṣaḥīḥs*[2] are accepted.

1. In Chapter One.
2. The hadith collections of al-Bukhārī and Muslim.

Next they have recourse to those (opinions) based on the hadith collections of al-Tirmidhī and Abū Dāwūd. They follow and rely upon any matter that the Sunna confirms, whether based on an explicit textual statement or on an evidentiary sign in the text. They reject any matter that the Sunna clearly opposes and desist from implementing it. In any case where the hadiths of the Prophet or reports of the Companions disagree, they employ a process of *ijtihād* in order to reconcile them, either by making the one that has clear import (*mufassar*) rule upon the more ambiguous one (*mubham*), by making each hadith be the predicate of a syllogism, or by some other means.

If the case (wherein there is disagreement) falls under the category of a Sunna or an *adab*,[3] then all instances are considered to be at the level of Sunna. If it falls within the categories of the permitted or forbidden or is from the category of a judgement, and the Companions, Followers, and *mujtahids* disagreed about it, then they state it to be a matter about which there are two or more opinions. They do not criticize the person who follows any one of these opinions and they perceive a range (of possibilities) in the affair if there are hadiths and reports attesting to each side. Next, they apply their efforts to recognizing the primary and the preferred opinion, either due to the strength of the transmission, or on the basis of its being the practice of the majority of the Companions, or due to its being the opinion of the majority of *mujtahids*, or because it agrees with an analogy and resembles parallel cases.

Then they implement that strongest opinion without rejecting anyone who upholds the alternate views. If they do not find any hadith pertaining to the issue among those two (highest) classes of hadith collections then they look for corroborating evidence (*shawāhid*)[4] supporting their opinions among the reports found in the third level of hadith collections and to what may be understood about the proofs and reasons for legislation from the discussions there. If they are satisfied by something there, they will uphold it. If they are not assured by any of their explanations but rather are convinced of something else and the issue is one in which the *ijtihād* of the *mujtahid* may be operative and wherein no previous consensus of the scholars has taken place; and according to them a clear proof has been established for the other view, then they adopt that position seeking God's help and relying upon Him.

This type is rare in occurrence, a slippery slope that is difficult to ascend, and whose treacherous aspects must be assiduously avoided. In cases where no clear proof can be determined, then follow the way of the vast

---

3. *Sunna*, "established prophetic practice" is a slightly stronger category of recommended actions of imitating the Prophet than "*adab*" (usual behavior).

4. Whereas *mutaba'a* applies to the *isnād*, i.e., other narrations from the same reporters, a narration which supports the text (meaning) of the original hadith, although it may be through a completely different *isnād*, is called a *shāhid* ("witness").

majority. In any case wherein there is no clear statement or correct derivation of its rationale from the pious ancestors, scholars must make every effort in seeking a proof text, indicant, allusion from the Qur'ān or the Sunna, or a report from the Companions or Followers. Then if they find it they must follow it. It is not for them to perform *taqlīd* of an individual scholar in everything he holds, whether they feel confident about him or not. If you have any doubts about what we have stated, then you should consult the books of al-Bayhaqī, the book *Ma'ālim al-Sunan,*[5] and the *Sharḥ al-Sunna* of al-Baghawī. This is the method of the qualified legal scholars of hadith and how few they are!

These scholars are distinct from the literalist (Ẓāhiriyya) hadith scholars who reject analogical reasoning and consensus, and other than the earliest hadith experts who did not consider the opinions of (individual) *mujtahids* at all. However, they are the group who most resemble these hadith scholars because they operate using the statements of the *mujtahids* as the latter had worked with the sayings of the Companions and Followers.

## 2) The Mujtahid within a Legal School

Three issues arise regarding this level.

### Issue #1

Know that it is incumbent upon a *mujtahid* within a school to obtain sufficient knowledge about prophetic practices (*sunnas*) and reports in order to protect himself from opposing sound hadith reports and the agreement of the pious ancestors. He should learn enough about the proofs of jurisprudence to enable himself to recognize the source that the masters of his school had used in their opinions. This is the meaning of what is stated in the *Fatāwā Sirājiyya*, "It is not appropriate for a person to issue a legal opinion unless he knows the previous rulings of the scholars, and recognizes the basis on which they ruled, and understands the daily affairs of people." If he knows the verdicts of the scholars and does not know their reasoning, then if he were to be asked about an issue and he knew that the scholars whose school he is following agreed upon it, there would be no problem in his saying, "This is permitted and this is not permitted." In this case his opinion would be in the nature of reporting (from them).

If it were an issue about which they disagreed, there would be no problem in his saying, "This is permissible according to so-and so's opinion while according to someone else's opinion it is not permitted." It is not appropriate for him to choose and respond only with the opinions of certain ones among them so long as he does not know the definitive answer.

In the *Fuṣūl al-'Imādiyya's*[6] first section it is stated that if a scholar is

5. Al-Khaṭṭābī's work, *Ma'ālim al-Sunan.*

6. Jamāl al-Dīn ibn 'Imād al-Dīn completed the *Fuṣūl al-'Imādiyya fī Furū' al-Ḥanifiyya,* a work of al-Marginānī al-Samarqandī, after the latter's death in 1253.

not capable of performing *ijtihād*, then it is not permitted for him to give a legal opinion except by way of reporting so that he should relate what he remembers about the opinions of the legal experts. It is related that Abū Yūsuf, Zufar, and 'Āfiyya ibn Zayd stated that it was not permitted for anyone to give a legal opinion on the basis of their statements as long as he did not understand the basis on which they gave them.

In the *Fuṣūl al-'Imādiyya* it is also related from some scholars that even if a jurist had memorized all the books of his masters within the legal school, it would still be necessary that he had been a student (in order to know) how to issue legal opinions, so that he would be correct in this. This is because many issues were responded to by our masters according to the custom of their regions and their usual way of dealing with things. It is therefore incumbent on every (*muftī*) to take into account the practices of the people of his region and era in so far as they do not conflict with the divine law. In '*Umda al-Aḥkām*[7] it is recounted, cited from the *Muḥīṭ,* that those capable of performing *ijtihād* should be learned in the Qur'ān and Sunna and the hadith reports and the various aspects of jurisprudence. In *al-Khāniyya*[8] it is reported from various authorities that in order to exercise *ijtihād* it is necessary to have memorized the *Mabsūṭ* and to recognize the abrogating and the abrogated and the definitive (*muḥkam*) and the words with several possible meanings (*mu'awwal*) and to know the local practices and customs. In *al-Sirājiyya* it is said that the minimal requirement for *ijtihād* is committing the *Mabsūṭ* to memory. These report were cited in *Khizānat al-Muftī'īn.*[9]

I believe that the import of these expressions is that the distinction between the *muftī* who is able to make independent derivations and the *muftī* who is profoundly learned in the legal school of his masters is that the latter issues legal opinions in the mode of reporting, not in the mode of *ijtihād.*

Issue #2

Know that it is a basic principle of research scholars of jurisprudence that cases are of four categories:

1) A category established as the most authoritative level (*ẓāhir*) by the legal school.[10] Its criterion is that the jurists accept this category in all situations whether such cases accord with the roots of jurisprudence

---

7. *Al-'Umda fī Aḥkām al-Fiqh* by Ibn Qudāma (d. 1223). A Ḥanafī book based on al-Shaybānī's jurisprudence.

8. *Fatāwā Qāḍī Khān* (d. 592/1196). A collection of Ḥanafī fatwas.

9. A work for judges collecting points from important works such as the *Hidāya*, *Nihāya* and other collections of Ḥanafī legal opinions.

10. Six books of Muḥammad ibn Ḥasan al-Shaybānī are considered to be *ẓāhir madhhab* and *ẓāhir riwāyāt* in the Ḥanafī school. They are al-*Mabsūṭ, al-Jāmi' al-Ṣaghīr, al-Jāmi' al-Kabīr*, *al-Siyar al-Kabīr*, *al-Siyar al-Ṣaghīr*, and *Ziyādāt*.

or conflict with them. Therefore you see that the author of the *Hidāya*[11] and other scholars took the trouble to explain what was the differentiating factor (*farq*) in cases falling within the same category (*tajnīs*).

2) A category that involves irregular reports[12] from Abū Ḥanīfa and his associates. The ruling here is that these are not to be accepted unless they agree with the principles of jurisprudence. Many corrections are to be found in the *Hidāya* and other books like it, made to certain irregular reports because of the proof (*dalīl*) (from *sharī'a* sources refuting them).

3) A category of derivations made by more recent scholars upon which the majority of the masters of the school concur. Its rule is that in all instances jurists should issue legal opinions on the basis of these.

4) A category that is a derivation made only by recent scholars upon which the majority of the earlier masters of the school did not agree. Its rule is that the *muftī* should present such a derived solution (*takhrīj*) according to the roots of jurisprudence and the parallel cases among the discussions of the earlier scholars. If he finds it to be in accord with these, he can accept it, and if not he should reject it.

In the *Khizāna al-Riwāyāt's*[13] chapter on "accepting reliable reporters" it is quoted from the *Bustān al-Faqīh* of the jurist Abū al-Layth[14] that, "If a person hears a hadith or hears an opinion, whose transmitter is not considered reliable then it is not allowable to accept it from him unless it is an opinion that is in conformity with the principles of jurisprudence. In this case it may be implemented and otherwise, it should not. Likewise, if he finds a hadith or a case recorded in written form, if it is in agreement with the principles of jurisprudence it is permitted to implement it, and if not, then it is not."[15]

In the *Al-Baḥr al-Rā'iq* (*The Pure Sea*) it is reported from Abū al-Layth[16] that he said:

> Abū Naṣr was asked about an issue that had been put to him. "What would you say, may God have mercy on you, if you had four books

11. al-Marghīnānī, 'Alī ibn Abī Bakr.
12. According to al-Shāfi'i, a *shādhdh* ("irregular") hadith is one which is reported by a trustworthy person but goes against the narration of a person more reliable than him. It does not include a hadith that is unique in its contents and is not narrated by someone else.
13. *Khizānat al-Riwāyāt fi-l-Furū'*, a Ḥanafi work by the Indian scholar Qāḍī Chakan d. 1514.
14. Abū al-Layth al-Samarqandī.
15. *Būstān al-'Ārifīn fī-'l ādāb al-shar'iyya* (Cairo: Dār al-Manār, 1995), 19.
16. Abū al-Layth al-Samarqandī, a Hanafī theologian and jurist of the 10th C. The *Baḥr al-Rā'iq* (Beirut: Dār al-Ma'rifa, 1993/4 from Cairo 1894) is a Ḥanafī commentary on Nasafī's *Kanz* by Zayn al-'Ābidīn ibn Nujaym al-Miṣrī (d. 1562/3).

before you—the book of Ibrāhīm ibn Rustam,[17] the *Adab al-Qāḍī* in the recension of al-Khaṣṣāf,[18] *Kitāb al-Mujarrad,*[19] and *Kitāb al-Nawādir* in the recension of Hishām?[20] First of all, would you permit us to give legal opinions based on them or not, and secondly, are these books commendable, in your opinion?"

Abū Naṣr replied, "What has been reported to be sound from our masters in the (Ḥanafī) school is a body of knowledge which is approved, appreciated, and worthy of acceptance. When it come to giving fatwas—I do not think that anyone should issue a legal opinion in a case based on something he does not understand, nor should he try to take up people's burdens. However, if the cases have become well-known, clear, and have been clarified by our master scholars, I would hope that this would permit me to rely on them in legal cases."

Issue #3

Know that in the instance of a case over which there is disagreement between Abū Ḥanīfa and his two associates, the verdict is that the *mujtahid* within the (Ḥanafī) school can either select whichever of their opinions has the strongest proof or whatever agrees most closely by analogy to the underlying cause for legislation, or he can select whichever opinion is most convenient for people. Therefore many groups of Ḥanafī *'ulamā'* issue fatwas according to the opinion of Muḥammad (ibn Ḥasan) in the case of the purity of water for use (in ablution) and according to the opinions of the two (associates) in the case of the commencement of the afternoon prayer time, the evening prayer time, and the permissibility of share cropping (*muzāra'a*). The books of the Ḥanafī jurists are replete with these cases, thereby obviating the need to present quotations here.

The case in the Shāfi'ī school is similar. Therefore it is written in the *Minhāj* and other books concerning inheritance shares that the original opinion of al-Shāfi'ī denied the rights of maternal relatives to receive anything from the estate in the absence of those mentioned in the Qur'ān (*dhū al-furūḍ*) and paternal relatives (*'usbāt*) so that the estate would revert to the treasury. Then later jurists issued fatwas that such relatives could in-

17. Ibrāhīm ibn Rustam (d. 211/826).

18. *Adab al-Qāḍī* Cairo, 1978, by al-Khaṣṣāf, Aḥmad ibn 'Umar (al-Shaybānī), a Hanafī jurist d. 874/5.

19. *al-Mujarrad* by al-Ḥasan ibn Ziyad al-Lu'lu'ī ca. 734-819.

20. *Kitāb al-Nawādir*. A number of "*nawādirs*" were composed in the Ḥanafī school. They contain reports of the three founders and others but are not considered as authoritative as the material in the six works known as the *ẓāhir al-riwāya*. Among the Nawādir works are compilations by Hishām (291/903/4) and Ibn Rustam (211/826).

herit due to the current absence of the treasury (*bayt al-māl*) system. The Yemeni jurist Ibn Ziyād (☙) reported cases in his book of *Fatāwa*, where the later jurists had issued opinions at variance with the Shāfiʿī school, among them paying the *zakāt* due on gold, silver, or trade goods in coinage. Al-Bulqīnī[21] issued a fatwa declaring that this was allowable, stating that he believed it to be permitted, although it opposed the Shāfiʿī school. In this al-Bulqīnī followed al-Bukhārī. Another case of this (differing with al-Shāfiʿī) is that of giving *zakāt* to ʿAlavī sayyids (descendants of ʿAlī but not Fāṭima). Imām Fakhr al-Dīn al-Rāzī ruled in favor of it during those times when they were forbidden their share from the community treasury (*bayt al-māl*) so that as a result some had become impoverished. Another case is selling bees in the hives along with whatever wax, etc. is present. Al-Bulqīnī issued a *fatwā* that this is permitted.

Ibn Ziyād quoted from Imām ibn ʿUjayl[22] that he had issued fatwas opposed to his legal school in three issues related to zakāt: transferring zakāt to another city, spending the *zakāt* on only one person, and spending it on only one of the prescribed categories.[23]

I hold an opinion on this topic which is that when the *muftī* from the Shāfiʿī school, whether he is a *mujtahid* within the school or one profoundly learned in it, must have recourse to something outside of his school in a specific case, then he should resort to the school of Aḥmad (ibn Ḥanbal). This is because he is one of the greatest associates of al-Shāfiʿī, in terms of knowledge and religiosity, and on investigation his school may be viewed as a branch of the Shāfiʿī school and as one of its facets, and God knows better.

### 3) The one profoundly learned in a legal school who has memorized the works of his school.

There are five issues under this topic.

Issue#1

A condition for this status is that the scholar be perspicacious; knowing the Arabic language well with its modalities of discourse and levels of preferred meanings, so as to quickly grasp the import of their discussions. In this case he usually will not fail to grasp the restrictive elements when an expression that is apparently general (*muṭlaq*) actually intends to qualify something, or he can extrapolate from what is apparently qualified, in cases

---

21. Sirāj al-Dīn al-Bulqīnī (805/1402).
22. Aḥmad ibn Muḥammad al-ʿUjayl, a Yeminī jurist.
23. According to a qurʾānic verse (9:60) *zakāt* may only be spent in nine specified ways. Since "*muʾalifat al-qulūb*" is no longer a common practice (this indicated payments to "win the hearts" of early opponents of Islam), eight types remain. According to the Shāfiʿī school money collected as *zakāt* must be spent on all eight types, spending all of the *zakāt* in the same category will not fulfill the command.

where the intended meaning is general. Ibn Nujaym alerted about this condition in the *Baḥr al-Rā'iq*.

It is obligatory that a *mujtahid* at this level never issue a fatwa except in one of two circumstances. Either he should have a reliable chain of transmission going back to the founder of his school concerning the case, or it should be a case recorded in authoritative books that circulate widely.

In al-*Nahr al-Fā'iq*[24] in the book on Judgement (it is stated that):

> There are two ways in which a *muqallid muftī* should report a *mujtahid's* statement. Either he should have a chain of transmission going back to the *mujtahid* or he should have taken it from an authoritative book that circulates widely such as the book of Muḥammad ibn Ḥasan or other books of comparable fame compiled by *mujtahids*. This is due to the fact that such books are at the level of reports that are abundantly transmitted (*mutawātir*) or authoritative (*mashhūr*).

Likewise al-Rāzī explained that according to this standard if a copy of *al-Nawādir*[25] were suddenly to come to light in our time, it should not be allowed to ascribe what is in it to Muḥammad (Ibn Ḥasan) or Abū Yūsuf (ﷺ), because these (reports) are not authoritative in our time nor in our regions nor do they widely circulate. However, if he finds something reported from "*al-Nawādir*" for example, in a book that in famous and well attested such as the *Hidāya* or the *Mabsūṭ,* then its reliability would be based on that book.

In *Fatāwā al-Qunya*[26] in the chapter "Concerning the *Muftī*" it is stated that whatever scholar's opinions and statements are found in a book that is authoritative and widely circulated may be quoted by whoever examined it in the mode of "a scholar" or "that particular person" has said, "such and such" even if he has not studied the book directly with a teacher. This is in the case of books such as those of Muḥammad ibn Ḥasan, the *Muwaṭṭā* of Imām Mālik, and so on, that have been compiled containing many topics of knowledge because these books are at the level of hadith reports that are abundantly transmitted by multiple chains so that there is no need for statements like these to include a chain of transmitters.

Issue #2

What if the profoundly learned *mujtahid* within a legal school encounters a sound hadith that opposes his school? Should he implement the hadith and

---

24. *al-Nahr al-fā'iq* is a commentary on *Kanz al-Daqā'iq* of Imām al-Nasafī by 'Umar ibn Ibrāhīm ibn Nujaym (1595/7).

25. A book by Imām Muḥammad (ibn Ḥasan) al-Shaybānī.

26. Abū al-Rajā' Najm al-Dīn Mukhtār ibn Maḥmūd al-Zāhidī (657), a Ḥanafī scholar compiled *Qunya al-Munya 'alā madhhab Abī Ḥanīfa.*

dissent with his school on this particular issue?[27]

There is a long discussion about this matter. The author of the *Khizānat al-Riwāyāt* expounded on this, quoting extensively from the "*Dastūr al-Sālikīn*"[28] and we will present his very words on this topic:

> If it is asked: If a *muqallid* who is not a *mujtahid* still is a learned scholar who can infer proofs and who knows the principles of jurisprudence and the meanings of the revealed texts and reports, is he allowed to use hadiths (in giving legal opinions)? How can this be allowed when it had been said that it is not permitted for the non-*mujtahid* to implement anything other than the transmitted material of his school and the fatwas of his Imam, and that he should not occupy himself with the meanings of the revealed texts and the reports and implementing them, as is the position of the lay person.
>
> It was replied, "This is the case with the completely lay person who is unlearned and cannot recognize the meanings of the revealed texts and the hadiths and their interpretations. As for the learned scholar who knows the texts and the reports, he is one of the people of understanding and he is able to verify these by consulting hadith scholars or on the basis of their reliable authoritative books that circulate widely. Therefore it is permitted for him to implement the hadiths even if they end up conflicting with his legal school."
>
> This view is supported by Abū Ḥanīfa, Muḥammad (Ibn Ḥasan), and al-Shāfi'ī and his associates (ﷺ), as well as being the opinion of the author of the *Hidāya*.
>
> In the *Rauḍa al-'Ulamā' Zandavastiyya*[29] in the chapter concerning the merit of the Companions of the Prophet it is related that Abū Ḥanīfa was asked, "What if you were to hold an opinion and the Book of God opposed it?" He said, "Abandon my view in favor of the Qur'ān." Then, "What if a report about Allah's Prophet opposed it? He said, "Abandon my opinion in favor of the report of the Prophet of God (ﷺ)." Then he was asked, "What if a statement of the Companions opposed it?" He said, "Abandon my opinion in favor of the

27. The rest of this subsection in its entirety appears to have been copied from the work of Muḥammad Ḥayāt al-Sindī (d. 1163/1749), a student of one of Shāh Walī Allāh's teachers in the Holy Cities, entitled, *Tuḥfa al-Anām fi-l 'Amal bi-Ḥadīth al-Nabī* (ed. Abū Bakr Ṭā Ḥā Bū Sarīḥ) (Beirut: Dār ibn Ḥazm, 1993), 18-22. The relationship between the two is not clear but al-Sindī was of a previous generation. The fact that he was also the teacher of 'Abd al-Wahhāb has led to much interest in his opinions. See Nafi, 210 ff.

28. I have been unable to find this title. The Indian editions of the text write "*Masākīn*" for "*Sālikīn*."

29. A work by Shaykh Abū 'Alī, also known as Ḥusayn al-Bukhārī al-Zandavastī al-Ḥanafī, cited in *Kashf al-Ẓunūn*.

statement from the Companions."

In *al-Iqnā'*[30] it states that al-Bayhaqī reported in his *Sunan* when he was discussing the issue of reciting the Qur'ān and transmitting his own chain of authority that the reporter had explained that al-Shāfi'ī (⸙) had commanded, "If I have issued an opinion and the Prophet (⸙) turned out to have said something that disagrees with my opinion based on a hadith that has been ruled to be sound, then give the hadith priority and do not perform *taqlīd* of me."[31]

Imām al-Ḥaramayn (al-Juvaynī) quoted al-Shāfi'ī in the *Nihāya* saying, "If you learn of a sound hadith that opposes my opinion then follow the hadith knowing that it is my opinion." It has also been reliably reported that he said, "If you have received something by way of my opinion and you have reliably confirmed a report that is in conflict with it, then be informed that my opinion will be whatever the report requires."

Al-Khaṭīb reported with its full chain of transmission that the Shāfi'ī scholar al-Dārikī[32] used to be asked for legal opinions and would sometimes give rulings outside of the schools of al-Shāfi'ī and Abū Ḥanīfa (⸙). Therefore he was told, "Is that not in conflict with their opinions?" He replied, "Shame on you, if a narrator has related a statement from a Companion going back to the Prophet (⸙), then taking the ruling from the hadith takes priority over using the two jurists' opinions when they disagree with it."

This is likewise supported by what was mentioned in *al-Hidāya* concerning the case of the fasting person who had blood drawn.[33] If a person had blood drawn and supposed that this had broken his fast, so he ate, then he should both make up the fast and pay the compensatory penalty (*kaffāra*) because the conjecture was not based on a *sharī'a* proof.

However, in the case that a jurist had given him this opinion in error, only making up the fast would be incumbent upon him, because a *fatwā* constitutes a legal proof in his case. If he comes to know about a hadith report that his fast has been broken by this action and he considers it to be reliable, still in this case Muḥammad (ibn Ḥasan) agreed that he would not be liable for making expiation (*kaffāra*) because a statement from the Prophet (⸙) could not be placed at a lower level than a ruling of the *muftī*.[34]

---

30. *al-Iqnā'* of al-Ḥujāwī al-Ḥanbalī (d. 1560).

31. Cited from Ibn 'Abd al-Barr, *al-Intiqā'* I, 82.

32. Abū Ḥassān al-Dārikī (375/956).

33. *Hijāmat*. In the Arabian context, this was usually by means of applying leeches as a medical treatment.

34. There is a sound hadith on this issue found in Abū Dāwūd and Ibn Māja from Shaddād ibn Aws. The Prophet said—whoever has leeches applied or blood drawn

In *al-Kāfī*[35] and al-Ḥumaydī[36] it says that this means that the Prophet's statement could not be at a lower level since even the opinion of a *muftī* is worthy of constituting a *sharī'a* proof, so the saying from the Prophet (ﷺ) must take precedence.

Abū Yūsuf is reported to have opposed this because the lay person must follow the jurists due to the lack, in his case, of being able to properly evaluate hadiths. Thus if he knew the interpretation[37] of this hadith, the penalty (*kaffāra*) would become obligatory on him. Al-Manāwī[38] rules about this case that there exists agreement about it within the school (*ittifāq*).

As for Abū Yūsuf's opinion that the lay person must follow the jurists, it applies purely to the layperson who is ignorant of the meanings of the hadiths and their interpretations, because this is signaled by Abū Yūsuf's mentioning his lack of ability to evaluate hadiths properly. Likewise Abū Yūsuf's statement that if the lay person were to know the interpretation of this hadith then an expiatory penalty would be obligatory for him indicates that what is meant by "the common person" is "the non-scholar." In al-Ḥumaydī it is stated that "the lay person" is someone belonging to the ignorant masses.

It is known from these indications that what Abū Yūsuf meant by the "common person" was "the ignorant one" who cannot recognize the meaning of the revealed text or its interpretation. What he cited from the opinions of Abū Ḥanīfa, al-Shāfi'ī, and Muḥammad (رحمهم الله) repudiates the view that the scholar must act on the report of his legal school which opposes a hadith or textual declaration (*naṣṣ*). (end of quote from *Khizānat*)[39]

There is yet another opinion about this issue. This is that if a scholar has not mastered the critical methodology for performing *ijtihād*, then it is not permitted for him to implement a hadith opposing his legal school because he does not know whether this hadith is abrogated, allegorical (*mu'awwal*),

---

in both cases breaks his fast. See *Fatḥ al-Qadīr*, commentary on the *Hidāya* by Ibn Humām II:96-7 (Cairo: Amīriyya, 1315).

35. Ibn 'Abd al-Barr, Yūsuf ibn 'Abd Allāh, 978 or 9-1071. *Kitāb al-Kāfī fī-l Fiqh ahl al-Madīnah al-Mālikī.*

36. al-Ḥumaydī, 'Abd Allāh ibn al-Zubayr, d. 834. Hadith scholar and student of Abū Ḥanīfa.

37. The interpretation of the Prophet's statement by experts is that if having blood drawn may excessively weaken the person it is at the degree of being "disliked" (*makrūh*), but in itself it does not break the fast, since there are sound reports that the Prophet practiced this and allowed others to practice it during Ramadan.

38. Sharaf al-Dīn al-Manāwī (757/1356).

39. End of long quotation duplicated in Muḥammad Ḥayāt al-Sindī's treatise, *Tuḥfa al-Anām*, 18-22.

or must be taken in its literal sense. Ibn Ḥājib inclined to this point of view in his *Mukhtaṣar* and so did his followers. This opinion has been rejected since if what is meant by the lack of certainty (about the status of the hadith) in eliminating these possible alternatives (the hadith being abrogated and so on), then even the *mujtahid* cannot achieve certainty about all of these things. He rather bases his *ijtihād* in most cases on the most probable conjecture (*ghālib al-ẓann*).

If the person advancing this argument meant that the scholar is not able to comprehend this through probable opinion, then we refute this by a contrast, since any scholar who is extremely learned in a legal school, who researches the sources in the books of the community and knows from memory a sound body of hadith and jurisprudence, usually will have ascertained that there is a strong probability (*ghālib al-ẓann*) that the hadith is neither abrogated nor allegorical in some way (*mu'awwal*), through an interpretation that it is obligatory for him to advance. Then the argument will concern the basis on which the learned scholar has ascertained this strong probability.

What is preferred in this instance is a third position that Ibn al-Ṣalāḥ[40] held and al-Nawawī supported by declaring it correct. Ibn al-Ṣalāḥ said that when a member of the Shāfi'ī legal school finds a hadith that opposes his school, it should be taken into consideration whether he has mastered the critical methodology for performing absolute *ijtihād* or at least perfected *ijtihād* in that specific topic and case so that he might implement the hadith independently (of his school). If he has not achieved this degree of ability but still finds opposing the hadith to be difficult, after he has researched and has not found any solution to opposing the hadith within the Shāfi'ī school, then he should implement it on the condition that some other scholar with the level of independent *ijtihād* other than al-Shāfi'ī had implemented it. This course of action would constitute an excuse for him in going outside of the school of his Imam in this situation. Al-Nawawī approved of and confirmed this position.

Issue #3

What if a person profoundly learned in a legal school wishes to oppose the school of his Imam in his practice on an issue, and to perform *taqlīd* of another Imam—will he be permitted to do this or not?

There is disagreement of the scholars about this matter. Al-Ghazālī and others forbade it. This is a weak opinion according to the majority of scholars because it is based on making a person follow a school on the basis of evidence. If this obligation were to be voided due to ignorance about the evidence, we have put belief in the superiority of his Imam in the place of evidence. Therefore it is not permitted for him to go outside of his school

40. Abū 'Amr 'Uthmān ibn al-Ṣalāḥ al-Shahrazūrī (d. 1245).

just as it is not permitted for him to oppose evidence from the *sharī'a*. This argument has been refuted on the basis that belief in the absolute superiority of his (school's founder) Imam over the other Imams is not required in order for his performing *taqlīd* to be valid. This is because the Companions and Followers believed that the best people among the Umma were Abū Bakr, then 'Umar (☙), yet still they used to follow persons other than them on many issues, thereby disagreeing with their opinions. No one has condemned that and there is consensus concerning what we have said. As for the superiority of his Imam's opinion about a specific issue—there is no way for the pure *muqallid* to recognize this—so it cannot be made a condition for performing *taqlīd*, since this would necessarily invalidate the *taqlīd* of the majority of the *muqallids*. Even if this condition were to be accepted, then in this case the argument would go against the other position rather than supporting it.

This is because in most cases where such a scholar becomes aware of a hadith that opposes the school of his Imam or he finds a strong analogy that opposes the Imam's opinion, he comes to believe that the superior view about that issue is held by someone other than this Imam. Most hold that this is permitted, among them al-Āmidī, Ibn Ḥājib, Ibn Humām, al-Nawawī and his followers such as Ibn Ḥajar and al-Ramlī, and many groups of scholars among the Ḥanbalīs and the Mālikīs, the mentioning of whose names would lead to prolixity.

This is what the *muftī*s of the four schools agreed on in later times, deriving its permissibility on the basis of the discussions of their predecessors. They have composed independent treatises about this topic. However, they have differed about the conditions under which a person may go outside of his legal school:

1) Among them are some scholars who say, "Once *taqlīd* has been performed on an issue by agreement within a school-(*ittifāq*), then it should not be reopened." Ibn al-Humām explained this saying: "This means if the ruling has been implemented." The commentators (on Ibn al-Humām) have differed regarding what he meant by these words:

    a) Some say he meant that if a specific act had been performed, (that it should not be repeated). For example, making up prayers performed according to the procedure of the previous legal school. This is so sound that no dissenting opinion has been raised against it.

    b) Other (commentators) say (that Ibn Humām meant it) generically, in the sense that types of actions performed according to the previous school should not be repeated. This opinion has been refuted on the basis that this is not established by unanimous agreement (*bi-l-ittifāq*). Rather, most of the accounts of the pious ancestors indicate that they often acted in disagreement with their school.

2) Among them are also scholars who say (that a condition for going outside of one's school) is that "allowances should not be scrounged for."

> a) Some have said that "allowances" (*rukhaṣ*) in this case means "what is easy for a person." This is refuted by the fact that the Prophet (ﷺ), when he indicated a preference between two things, would choose the milder of them as long as it was not a sin.
>
> b) Other scholars have said that the meaning of "allowance" is something that is not reinforced by proof but rather something that sound and clear proofs oppose, such as allowing temporary marriage and exchange sales.

This is a reliable opinion that I found in the book *Talkhīṣ fī Takhrīj Aḥādīth al-Rāfi'ī* "Summary of Deriving" by Ḥāfiẓ ibn Ḥajar al-'Asqilānī in the section on marriage where he quotes from al-Ḥākim's[41] book *'Ulūm al-Ḥadith* with a chain of transmission reaching back to al-Awzā'ī. He said, "Avoid or leave aside five things held permissible by the people of the Hijāz and the scholars of Iraq. The five items permitted by the Hijāzis are: listening to musical instruments, temporary marriage (*muta'*), anal intercourse, exchange sales, and combining two prayers without a valid excuse. The five opinions of the Iraqis concern: drinking *nabīdh*,[42] delaying the afternoon prayer until a shadow is four times the length of an object, holding no Friday prayer except in the seven garrison towns, fleeing from an army, and eating after dawn in Ramaḍān."

Then Ibn Ḥajar said, "'Abd al-Razzāq reported from Ma'mar, 'If someone adopts the opinion of the Medinans concerning listening to singing and anal intercourse, and the opinion of the Meccans about temporary marriage and exchange sales,[43] together with the opinion of the Kufans regarding taking intoxicants, he would become the most depraved of God's bondservants.'"[44]

3) Some scholars hold that one should not cobble together rulings from two schools because this would construct a situation deemed impossible by both of the Imams of the schools.

4) Some scholars have held that the instance of combining rulings (*talfīq*) from different legal schools that would be forbidden would be one that constructs a forbidden situation in the new combined case. An ex-

---

41. al-Ḥākim, *Ma'rifa 'Ulūm al-Ḥadīth.*

42. Apparently Ibrāhīm al-Nakha'ī allowed non-inebriating amounts of alcohol to be consumed.

43. Most jurists forbid a type of sale of the same commodity with a different weight as being a *riba* transaction. A few accept a hadith report from Asma concerning a sale having no *riba* in it. However the majority hold that this hadith should not be applied (*matrūk al-'amal*).

44. Ibn Ḥajar al-'Asqalānī, *Talkhīṣ al-Khabīr fī Takhrij Aḥādīth al-Rāfi'ī al-Kabīr* Vol. 3 (Cairo: Mu'assasa Qurṭuba, 1995), 379-80.

ample would be the case of a person's performing the ablution in the wrong sequence and then having an emission of blood.[45] His state of ritual purity would not have been invalidated had the actions occurred in two (separate) cases such as a person's having made his stained garment ritually pure according to the school of al-Shāfi'ī, then praying according to the school of Abū Ḥanīfa.[46]

It may be that there will be a debate about this due to the fact that the restriction on combining rulings from various schools (*talfīq*) (in a single case), if what is meant by it is that all of the actions performed by a person should not go outside of what is agreed on by either of the schools (on its own), then this is already the situation in rulings in any two separate cases. Alternatively, if what is meant by the restriction on combining schools (*talfīq*) is that this single case on its own should not fall outside of the consensus of the *madhhab* scholars, then it would be sufficient to make it a requisite condition that the case should concern an issue wherein *ijtihād* is allowed, as will follow.

5) Some scholars have predicated the permissibility of acting outside of a legal school on the opinion that a scholar advances about the ruling not being one that would annul a verdict that has been previously given by a judge. This condition is well-founded, and a person will be protected from this if he follows one of the four famous authoritative schools.

6) Some scholars say that they have an intuitive assurance about that case in which they follow someone other than their Imam. This is unimaginable except in the case of profoundly learned scholars.

7) Some say that if a scholar follows (*ittibā'*) the majority and the authoritative opinion then his going outside of the school of his Imam is proper, and if not, it is wrong.

This constitutes the summary of what is in their treatises with some revision and editing.

I prefer as a condition for permitting going outside of a legal school that the action should not invalidate a verdict that has already been given. This should apply whether this invalidation takes place due to combining two meanings, each of which would be valid (on its own), such as the acceptability of a marriage where the two witnesses are not present at the same time nor was there an announcement made, or due to some other invalidating factor.

---

45. In a combined case neither school would consider his state of ritual purity valid in this combined case, since Shāfi'īs require ablution to be performed in sequence and Ḥanafīs consider that blood flow nullifies the state if ritual purity.

46. That is, the Shāfi'īs require a certain order in the way ablution is performed in order for it to be valid and the Ḥanafīs consider that blood flow invalidates ablution, therefore neither will consider his state of ritual purity valid in a combined case.

In terms of allowing choice on the condition of (the scholar's feeling) of an intuitive assurance (6), I prefer that (it be based on) some element of the proof, or the large numbers of the pious ancestors who acted in this way, or on its being more comprehensive, or its being a way to obviate a difficulty without which a person would not have been able to obey (the divine law), as indicated in the Prophet's saying, "If I command you to do something, carry it out in so far as you are able."[47] (Going outside of a legal school) should be done on the basis of factors that should be taken into account in the divine law, not merely selfish desires or worldly ends.

I prefer as a condition in making it obligatory on a person to go outside of his *madhhab* that it concern some right of another person, so that the judge gives a verdict that requires him to act in variance from his school.

In the *Khizāna al-Riwāyat* it says that the case is mentioned in *Kashshāf al-Qinā'*,[48] "If a person follows a jurist in some matter, is it then possible to ask another jurist about it?"

The situation may take two forms.

> In one of them a person has not committed himself to following a specified legal school, such as the *madhhab* of Abū Ḥanīfa or al-Shāfi'ī or others.
>
> In the second a person has committed (to following a *madhhab*) and declared, "I am a committed follower (*mutabbi'*)."

About the first type of case Ibn Ḥājib said, "It is unanimously agreed (ittifāq) that a person should not ask for another opinion in a case where he already has performed an action on the basis of *taqlīd*. In the case of some other action, the preferred opinion (*mukhtār*) is that this (asking another jurist) is permitted as reflected in God's saying, "Then ask the people of knowledge (*al-dhikr*) if you do not know." (16:43)

Thus, holding it obligatory that a person must first ask the scholar whom he follows (for a ruling) about a case would constitute a qualification of the qur'ānic text and this would be tantamount to abrogating (the verse) according to what has been determined in legal methodology. A further proof (of the permissibility of asking a second jurist) is the Prophet's statement, "My Companions are like the stars, follow whichever one of them you want and you will be guided."[49]

In addition, the common people among the early generations used to

---

47. Hadith in al-Bukhārī I'tiṣām #6, Muslim and other collections.

48. *Kashshāf al-Qinā'* (*The Lifting of the Veil*) a Ḥanbalī work that is a commentary by Manṣur ibn Yūnus bin Ṣalāḥuddīn bin Ḥasan ibn Aḥmad al-Bahūtī (1051/1641) on the *Iqnā'* of al-Ḥujāwī al-Ḥanbalī (d. 1560) 6 vols. Beirut: Dar al-Fikr, 1402/1982.

49. The status of this hadith is discussed in detail by G. H. Haddad at www.abc.se/~m9783/compst_e.html

ask for legal opinions from the jurists without resorting to any particular individual and no one rejected this. This is tantamount to a consensus regarding its permissibility. This agrees with what is stated in the *Sharḥ* of Ibn Ḥājib.

As for the answer in the second type of case, that of a (*muqallid*) person who is committed to a specific *madhhab* such as that of Abū Ḥanīfa and al-Shāfi'ī, Ibn Ḥājib pointed out that there exists disagreement about this within his own legal school and also indicated where the scholars have differed about this, holding three views.

1) Some say that it is absolutely not permitted.

2) Some say that it is absolutely permitted.

3) The third opinion is that the ruling will be the same as in the first type of case i.e., that it is not permitted to ask for a second opinion in the event that he had already followed the first jurist and acted according to his ruling. However, it would be allowed (to ask a second jurist) in another case.

In the '*Umda al-Aḥkām* it is quoted from the *Fatāwā Ṣufiyya*[50] that Ibn Ḥājib was once asked about the following, "On the day of 'Īd al-Fiṭr we saw some people praying supererogatory (*nafl*) prayers in the congregational mosque at the time of the sunset. We forbade them to pray this *nafl* prayer and informed them that prayer has been forbidden at three times."[51] Ibn Ḥājib said, "Don't stop people from praying extra prayers lest you come under the scope of God's saying, 'Have you seen one who prevents a worshipper when he prays?'" (96:9-10) You are not absolutely sure of the exact time of sunset so perhaps it might be just before that time or just after it. Even if it is the time of sunset, it was reported from Abū Yūsuf that he did not hold it repugnant to pray this *nafl* prayer at sunset on Fridays, and al-Shāfi'ī did not deem it to be repugnant on any day. Thus if you objected to this person praying, it is no wonder that he answered you that he was performing *taqlīd* in that issue of a scholar who had deemed it permitted and that he could present the proof of this to you as did the scholar who had deemed it allowable. Thus, it is not allowable for you to deny the person who is performing *taqlīd* of a *mujtahid* or who can present a (*sharī'a*) proof. Also the '*Umda al-Aḥkām* cites similar cases and additional verdicts are quoted that perhaps the praying person was following. Thus the person who is carrying out an action wherein *ijtihād* has been performed or on the basis of imitating a *mujtahid* should not be criticized.

In the *Ẓahīriyya*, (it is stated that) when a *mujtahid* performs an action based on *ijtihād* or a person imitates a *mujtahid* in this action then there is

---

50. Muḥammad ibn Ayūb (15th C.) *al-Fatāwā al-Ṣufiyya fī Ṭarīq al-Bahā'iyya.* Cited in *Kashf al-Ẓunūn.*

51. At dawn, high noon, and sunset.

nothing shameful or disgraceful in this and it should not be rejected. In al-Bayḍāwī's *al-Minhāj* (it is stated that) if a husband considers that some utterance was in the nature of an allusion (*kināya*) to divorce while his wife thinks that it constitued a clear declaration of divorce, then he might be permitted to demand sexual intercourse from her and she might be allowed to reject it. Therefore the two of them would need to consult somebody else concerning the case.

Benefit

A Shāfiʿī individual thought that the disagreement of two expressions in *al-Anwār*[52] created ambiguity, so I gave him an answer in order to resolve the discrepancy. A discussion is found in the book of Judgement in the *Anwār* whose summary is that, once these four *madhhabs* were recorded, it became permitted for the *muqallid* to switch from the school of one *mujtahid* to the school of another. Likewise he would be permitted to follow one *mujtahid* in certain issues and another in certain others so that he could choose the more convenient ruling from each school. Examples include, if a Ḥanafī had blood let and wanted to adopt the Shāfiʿī way, so that he wouldn't have to perform an ablution, or if the Shāfiʿī had touched his own sexual organ or a woman and wanted to follow the Ḥanafī ruling, so that he would not have to repeat his ablution, and other similar cases where this (switching) would be allowed. This is the upshot of the discussion by the author of *al-Anwār* in the book of Judgement.

[Then in seeming variance with what] he had said in the chapter on "public morality" (*iḥtisāb*)—that if a Shāfiʿī saw another Shāfiʿī drinking wine or having intercourse with a woman whom he had married without her guardian's permission, then he would have a right to rebuke him because it is incumbent on every *muqallid* to follow his Imam, and he sins by acting at variance to him. However, if a Shāfiʿī were to see a Ḥanafī eating a lizard or eating an animal purposely slaughtered without having the formula "Bismillah" [phrase "In the name of God"] pronounced over it, then he should say to him, "Either you should admit that al-Shāfiʿī is more worthy of being followed (*ittibāʿ*) or you should stop eating these things." This is what the *Anwār's* author said in the chapter on "public morality" and there is an inconsistency between these two statements.[53]

I say that the solution to the conflict in my opinion, and God knows better, is that the meaning of his statement "he sins by acting at variance with him" is that a person sinned if he resolved to follow his Imam, whether in all cases or in that (specific) matter, then he acted at variance with him, for this is a sin without a doubt. However, if in that case he perfomed *taqlīd*

52. *Nur al-Anwār* is a commentary on al-Nasafī's, *al-Manār*.

53. Since in the first case it seems permitted for a *muqallid* to follow a different school in some cases while in the second this appears to be condemned.

of someone other than the first Imam, and he is a *muqallid* of that other scholar (in this case), then this is not opposing the first scholar. Or we may say that the second case (stated in the book on public morality) is based on the opinion of al-Ghazālī and some other scholars while the first one (from the Book of Judgement) is the opinion of the majority of the scholars (*al-jumhūr*). So understand this, since resolving this disparity (in *al-Anwār*) has posed some difficulty to certain of the compilers.

Issue #4

Know that there are two ways of performing *taqlīd* of *mujtahids*: obligatory and forbidden.

The obligatory form is in the nature of following (*ittibāʻ*) a hadith report as evidence. Its elaboration is that a person who is not conversant with the Qur'ān and the Sunna is not able on his own to trace reports; nor to draw inferences from texts, thus his duty is to inquire of a jurist concerning what the Prophet of God (ﷺ) ruled in a certain case. Then, once he is told, he should obey this ruling whether it is taken from an explicit pronouncement or inferred from it or analogized on the basis of a textual statement. All of these derive from the report transmitted from the Prophet (ﷺ), even if this is by way of a proof (*dalāla*)[54] and the Umma had agreed on the soundness of this, generation after generation; indeed all religious communities have agreed to things of this nature in their divine laws.

The mark of this *taqlīd* is that he should act according to the opinion of the *mujtahid* based on the condition that it is in conformity with the Sunna, and he should always inquire into the Sunna in so far as possible. Whenever a hadith comes to light contravening the *mujtahid*'s opinion, then he should act on the basis of the hadith. The Imams referred to this, for example, citing al-Shāfiʻī when he said, "If the hadith is confirmed to be sound then this is my opinion. If you find my words to be in disagreement with the hadith then act upon the hadith and beat my words against the wall."

Imām Mālik (ؓ) said, "There is no one whose words constitute a standard for acceptance or rejection except the Prophet (ﷺ)." Abū Ḥanīfa (ؓ) said, "The person who does not understand my proof must not give a fatwa based on my pronouncement," and Aḥmad (ؓ) said, "Do not follow me, nor Mālik, nor anyone else, and take the rulings from the Qur'ān and the Sunna as they took them."

The second situation (of *taqlīd* being forbidden) is that a person might imagine that his jurist had attained the utmost limit (of authority) and that it would be impossible for him to err. Thus, whenever a clear sound hadith came to his (the *muqallid*'s) knowledge opposing the jurist's opinion he would not dismiss the opinion, or he would suppose that since he had

54. That is, the ruling may not be explicit in the overt wording of the hadith, but needs to be derived from it by some approved means.

committed himself to being a *muqallid* of that jurist that God had made it incumbent on him to follow his verdict. Therefore such a *muqallid* is considered to be like the foolish person who is not competent to control his (inherited) property, even if he has reached the age of legal maturity so that if he finds out about a hadith and he assures himself as to its soundness, still he will not accept it due to his sense of responsibility, having become distracted by *taqlīd*.

This is a false belief and an unsound opinion that is neither founded on transmitted nor rational evidence. None of the preceding generations did this. Such a *muqallid* erred in supposing that someone he thought to be free from error was truly infallible or that he was infallible in terms of the propriety of [always] acting according to his opinion. He was also mistaken in supposing that God (ﷻ) had required him to obey this person's opinion, and that his responsibility was completely fulfilled by performing *taqlīd* of this scholar.

God's statement, "We are following in their footsteps." (43:23)[55] was revealed with respect to such situations and was not the going astray of previous nations due to this order (of misguidance)?

Issue #5

The scholars have disagreed about giving fatwas based on odd (*shādhdh*) or interdicted (*mahjūr*) reports.

In *Khizāna al-Riwāyāt*[56] it is quoted from the *Sirājiyya*[57] that the fatwa should (first) be issued according to the opinion of Abū Ḥanīfa (ﷺ), then on the opinion of Abū Yūsuf (ﷺ), then on the statement of Muḥammad ibn al-Ḥasan al-Shaybānī (ﷺ), then according to Zufar ibn Hudhayl and al-Ḥasan ibn Ziyād (ﷺ).[58]

Some scholars have held, "If Abū Ḥanīfa (ﷺ) was on one side and his two associates[59] on the other, it would be up to the *muftī* to choose.

The first option (choosing Abū Ḥanīfa's opinion) would be more sound if the *muftī* were not a *mujtahid*, because he was the most learned of his era so that al-Shāfi'ī said, "All of the people are the dependents of Abū Ḥanīfa (ﷺ) in jurisprudence. In *al-Muḍmarāt*[60] it was said, "If Abū Ḥanīfa (ﷺ) was on one side and Abū Yūsuf and Muḥammad on the other and the *muftī* had to choose, if he wanted he could use Abū Ḥanīfa's opinion and if not,

55. "We found our forefathers in a community and we are following their footsteps."

56. A Ḥanafī work by the Indian scholar Qāḍī Chakan d. 1514.

57. Opinions of Sajāwandī, Sirāj al-Dīn Muḥammad ibn Muḥammad, 12th cent.

58. In other words down the ranks of Ḥanafī jurists.

59. Abū Yūsuf and Muḥammad ibn Ḥasan.

60. *Jāmi' al-Muḍmarāt wa-l-Mushkilāt* a commentary on the *Mukhtaṣar* of al-Qudūrī by Yūsuf ibn 'Umar ibn Yūsuf al-Ṣūfī al-Kādūrī (832).

then that of the other two. However, if one of the two associates agreed with Abū Ḥanīfa, then he should certainly adopt the position held by the two of them. That is, unless the great scholars had seen a benefit in adopting that singly-held opinion and he followed them in their deeming it to be more beneficial. An example is the jurist Abū Layth preferring the opinion of Zufar in the case where an ill person remains seated during the prayer. This is that he should sit as one does while performing the *tashahhud* since this position would be easier for the sick person, even though our associates (in the Ḥanafī school) have said that at the time for standing up the sick person should sit cross-legged or with his feet drawn up so that there would be a differentiation between his standing and sitting, which is one of the rules of the prayer in the standing position. However, this would constitute a hardship for the sick person since he is not accustomed to sitting in this position.

Another example is when most *'ulamā'* prefer securing the informer when he reports to the sultan without a royal decree. This is the opinion of Zufar that would close the door on slander although the rest of the 'ulamā' hold that security is not obligatory because the informer has not lost any property because of it.

The great scholars permit adopting the opinion of one of our associates as a course of action for the sake of a benefit. In the *Qunya* in the chapter on "what concerns the mufti in rare cases" he said with respect to giving judgments that they should be according to the opinion of Abū Yūsuf since he was the more experienced. In the *Muḍmarāt* it is stated that it is not correct for a *muftī* to avail himself of certain rejected opinions when issuing a *fatwā* out of the desire to provide a benefit, because the harmfulness of this course of action in this world and the next is more complete and general. Rather he should adopt the opinions of the great scholars, preserving their precedence and honor.

In the *Qunya* in the section about the proper conduct of the judge, there is a chapter containing diverse issues. In one of these cases connected with court judgments it is stated that Abu Yūsuf's opinion should be used in issuing fatwas, because he has more knowledge based on experience.

In the *'Umda al-Aḥkam* it is reported from al-Bazdawī's book in the *Kashf*,[61] that it is recommended for the *muftī* to allow dispensations that make things more convenient for the common people. Examples are being able to perform ablution with one's bath water and being able to pray in any ritually clean places without having a prayer carpet and not worrying about the mud from the streets in areas that the *'ulamā'* have already ruled ritually pure. These dispensations are not for the sake of those in religious retreat, rather it is better that they be cautious, and in their case acting according to

61. *Kashf al-Asrār*, a commentary by the Ḥanafī, 'Alā' al-Bukhārī (d. 730/1329-30) on the *Uṣūl al-Dīn* of al-Bazdawī.

the *'aẓīma*[62] is preferable.

Also reported from *al-Qunya* is that the mufti should issue opinions for people that would be more easy for them as al-Bazdawī has mentioned in *Sharḥ al-Jāmī' al-Saghīr*. "It is incumbent on the *muftī* to adopt what is easier in the case of another person, especially in the case of the weak due to the Prophet's saying to Abū Musā al-Ash'arī and Mu'ādh when he sent them to Yemen, "Be easy on the people and do not make things more difficult."[63]

It is reported in *'Umda al-Aḥkām* in the chapter on repugnant things that small dogs and pigs are ritually polluting, and Mālik and others disagreed with this, and if a *muftī* had given a *fatwā* according to Imām Mālik then this would be correct. In the *Qunya* it is reported that a jurist gave a *fatwā* according to the opinion of Sa'īd ibn al-Musayyab and remarried a woman who had been divorced by the triple formula to her previous husband, thus she remained divorced and the jurist was punished. Another jurist used a legal fiction (*hīla*) in the case of a woman divorced by the triple formula and took a bribe for that and remarried the woman to the original husband without her having been married to another husband. Is this marriage legal and what should be the punishment for the person who allowed this? The scholars say he should have his face blackened and he should be exiled.

In the *Fatāwā al-I'timādiyya*[64] it is quoted from the *Fatāwā al-Samarqandī*[65] that Sa'īd ibn Musayyab retreated from his opinion that a triply divorced woman could remarry the first husband without having been married to someone else in between. Now, if any judge issues a verdict, ibn Musayyab's (original) opinion would not be applicable, and if a jurist ruled using it, his ruling would not be correct and he would be liable to punishment.

In the *Tuḥfa,* the commentary on *al-Minhāj (by Ibn Hajar al-Haytamī)*:

> Al-Qarāfī reported that there was scholarly consensus regarding a muqallid's being able to choose between two opinions of his Imam, that is, he could sometimes act according to one and sometimes another, but not both at once. Such an option would apply when the reason for preferring either one of the opinions was not obvious. It seems that what he meant by this *ijmā'* was the consensus of the leading scholars of his *madhhab* (Shāfi'īs). How could this be the case because the requirement of our school is what al-Subkī, said forbidding this in cases of judgement and issuing fatwas, but not in the case of one's own per-

62. The regular *sharī'a* ruling as opposed to a dispensation (*rukhṣa*).
63. For example, al-Bukhārī 9, Book 89 #1284.
64. Perhaps this is a misprint for the *Fuṣūl 'Imādiyya* since that work bears on marriage law.
65. *Fatāwā of* Abū Layth al-Samarqandī (d. 983).

sonal actions. Through this he reconciled the opinions of al-Māwardī, who said that choosing between two opinions was permitted in his (the Shāfi'ī) school, and al-Ghazālī supported al-Māwardī's opinion on this (just as it is permitted for a person who determines through ijtihād two equally plausible locations for the qibla to pray facing whichever of them he wishes, on the basis of consensus), with the opinion of the Imam, who forbade the muqallid from selecting between two opinions if the two opinions were mutually contradictory, such as a thing's being both obligatory and forbidden, in contrast to cases similar to the various expiatory penalties (where an individual may have a choice). al-Subkī proceeded like this and others followed him in acting in contravention to the four legal schools, that is when a person's affiliation was known to be with a mujtahid whose authority could be followed and who possessed all the conditions for ijtihād. Ibn al-Ṣalāḥ's opinion bears on this i.e., "It is not permitted to perform taqlid of anyone other than the four founders of the legal schools in rendering judgments and in issuing fatwas." The situation wherein this (choice) and other permutations of performing taqlīd may be valid is that a person should not be seeking exemptions so as avoid religious obligation altogether, and there is no sin (*ithm*) in this. Some scholars say such a person has transgressed (*fasaqa*), and this is a contested opinion. The weak point of the argument is that such a person may confine himself to seeking exemptions from within the recognized and authoritative schools of law, for if he does not, then surely this person has transgressed.[66]

### The layperson (*'āmmī*)

Know that the layperson does not have a *madhhab*, rather his *madhhab* is the legal ruling from a *muftī*. As it was stated in the *Baḥr al-Rā'iq* that if a person had blood drawn by leeches or engaged in backbiting and he thought that by these actions he had broken his fast, so he ate—if he has not asked an opinion from a *muftī* and no report on this has reached him then he must pay a penalty because he is merely ignorant, and he has no excuse for that due to residing in an Islamic realm.

In the event that he had asked a legal scholar who had told him to break his fast, then no penalty is incumbent upon him because it is required that the layperson perform imitation (*taqlīd*) of the learned one. If he relied on the *fatwā*, then he is excused in what he did even if the *muftī* were incorrect in what he ruled. If he hadn't asked for an opinion but rather the reports had reached him that the Prophet said, "The cupper and the cupped have each

66. Ibn Ḥajar al-Haytamī (1567), *Tuḥfa al-muhtāj bi sharḥ al-Minhāj* I [*The gift of him in need: an explanation of "The Way"*], (Beirut: Dār al-Kutub al-'Ilmiyya 2001), 23. This work is a commentary on Nawawī's *Minhāj al-Ṭālibīn* [*The Seekers' Way*]. The translation here is based on the *Tuḥfa's* text.

broken their fast," and, "Backbiting breaks the fast of the fasting person," if he doesn't know that these are abrogated nor their interpretation, then he faces no penalty in either of the two cases because the apparent meaning of the hadith should be implemented. Abū Yūsuf opposes this view because it is not required of the layperson to implement the hadith due to his lack of knowledge about the abrogating or abrogated pronouncements.

If a person touches a woman or kisses her out of lust or uses kohl and it is supposed that these actions invalidated his fast so that he broke the fast, then he must undertake some act of expiation unless he had asked a legal expert who had told him to break his fast or he had heard some hadith report to this effect. If he made the intention of fasting before noon (*zawāl*), then he broke his fast, he is not required to make an act of expiation according to Abū Ḥanīfa, in contradistinction to the two associates. This is found in *al-Muḥīṭ*.

From this it is known that the procedure of the layperson is asking his *muftī* for an opinion. There is more on this (in *al-Baḥr al-Rā'iq*) under the topic of judgments concerning missed prayers where the compiler speaks of prayer missed due to lack of time and forgetfulness.[67] If someone is a layperson and he doesn't have a specific *madhhab,* then his procedure is asking his *muftī* for a fatwa and he should follow the fatwa of his *muftī* as they (the scholars) clearly state. Thus if he asks an opinion from a Ḥanafī he will repeat the afternoon and sunset prayers and if he asks a Shāfi'ī he will not repeat them and his own opinion will not be taken into account. If he does not ask any scholar for a opinion and he has prayed correctly according to the school of any *mujtahid*, then this is permitted and he does not have to repeat the prayers. (End of citation from *al-Baḥr al-Rā'iq*)[68]

In the *Sharḥ of al-Minhāj* of al-Bayḍāwī by Ibn Imām al-Kāmiliyya[69] it is reported that if a situation arises for a lay person and he asks a *mujtahid* about it and acts upon it according to the fatwa of that *mujtahid* then he may not have recourse to the opinion of a different *mujtahid* about the very same matter on the basis of juristic consensus as Ibn Ḥajib and others reported. In the *Jam' al-Jawāmi'* there is a disagreement about this, i.e., if this applies before he has acted on it, al-Nawāwī says the preferred opinion is what al-Khaṭīb and others have transmitted, that if there is no other *muftī*

---

67. The case is that of a person who missed the afternoon (*'aṣr*) prayer and then performed the sunset prayer. He then remembered and prayed the afternoon prayer. The order of prayers is important in the Ḥanafī school so a Ḥanafī jurist will require that both be repeated. The Shafi'ī will consider both prayers valid.

68. Zayn al-'Ābidīn ibn Nujaym, *al-Baḥr al-Rā'iq* II (Beirut: Dār al-Ma'rifa, 1993/4, 90.

69. This commentary on the *Minhāj* was composed by Muḥammad ibn Muḥammad ibn 'Abd al-Raḥmān ibn 'Alī Yūsuf ibn Manṣūr al-Qāhirī Kamāl al-Dīn (874/1459). He was a Shāfi'ī also known as Imām al-Kāmiliyya.

available, he must act according to his legal opinion (*fatwā*). If his conscience is not satisfied and if there is another *muftī* available, then he does not need to proceed according to that scholar's *fatwā*. Rather he may ask someone else about that case and perhaps he will disagree with the first one and this will result in a case of disagreement between the *muftīs*.

However, should some other situation arise for this individual, it would be more sound if he were to seek a legal opinion from someone other than the scholar he consulted in the first instance. Karābisī[70] said definitively that it is incumbent on the ordinary person to commit himself to a specific legal school. He preferred the opinion in the *Jam' al-Jawāmi'*[71] that the ordinary person should be required to commit to following a specific legal school and that he should not do this merely on the basis of personal desire but that rather he should choose a legal school to follow believing that it is better in every instance or at least equivalent to the others and not inferior to them.

Al-Nawawī said, "The thing that requires a proof is that the layperson is not required to affiliate to a school but rather is required to ask for a legal opinion from whoever he wishes, as long as this is without the intent of garnering allowances. Perhaps what prohibits the layperson (from asking whichever scholar he wishes) is that it cannot be assured that he will not be trying to get allowances. Once he commits to following a specific legal school then it is allowed for him to go outside of it as required by a more sound opinion."

In the book *Zubad* of ibn Raslān[72] there is a poem:

Al-Shāfi'ī, Mālik and Nu'mān
Aḥmad bin Ḥanbal and Sufyān,
and others among the Imams
are all rightly guided and juriṣtic disagreement is a mercy.

In the commentary on this book (*Zubad*) called, *Ghāyat al-Bayān*[73] it is stated that if the answers of two *mujtahids* of equal status disagree, then the better course of action for the *muqallid* is to choose the opinion of whichever of them he wishes. The book, *al-Tuḥfa,* was previously cited concerning the same issue.

70. As'ad b. Muḥammad, a Ḥanafī jurist (570/1174).

71. By al-Subkī, a Shāfi'ī work on the principles of jurisprudence.

72. Ibn Raslān al-Ramlī, Aḥmad ibn Ḥusayn, ca. 1371-1441.

73. Muḥammad ibn Aḥmad Ramlī, (1513-1596), *Ghayat al-Bayān* a commentary on the *Zubad* of Ibn Raslān. (Beirut: Dār al-Kutub al-'ilmiyya, 1995), 21-2. The *Zubad* is composed entirely in verse that the commentary elucidates.

# Chapter 5
# Maintaining Balance in *Taqlīd*

This chapter deals with what we previously mentioned with regard to *taqlīd*, i.e., that there is a path between the extremes on which the majority of scholars who followed the four schools walked and that the founders of the schools have bequeathed to their students.

Shaykh 'Abd al-Wahhāb al-Sha'rānī said in his *al-Yawāqīt wa'l-Jawāhir* (Sapphires and Jewels):

> It is reported that Abū Ḥanīfa (رضي الله عنه) used to say, "One who does not know my argument (*dalīl*) must not give a fatwa based on my opinion." Whenever he gave a fatwa he (رضي الله عنه) used to say, "Al-Nu'mān ibn Thābit, i.e., his own name, holds this view and this is the best we were able to do, so if someone comes up with something better, this would be more correct. Imām Mālik (رضي الله عنه) used to say, "Anyone's opinion may either be accepted or rejected except that of the Prophet of God (ﷺ)."
>
> Al-Ḥākim and al-Bayhaqī reported that al-Shāfi'ī used to say, "If there is a sound hadith, that becomes my opinion," and in another report, "If you see that my opinion opposes this hadith, then act according to the hadith, and beat my opinion against the wall." One day he said to Mazanī, "O Ibrāhīm, don't emulate me in everything I say, but look into it on your own, for this is religion." He (رضي الله عنه) used to say, "There is no final word (*ḥujja*) in anyone's opinion except that of the Prophet of God (ﷺ), even if there are many who hold such a view, and neither in an analogy (a proof), nor in anything else and you must obey God and his Prophet with full acceptance." Imām Aḥmad (ibn Hanbal) (رضي الله عنه) used to say, "No one is allowed to argue with God and his Prophet." He also said to a man, "Neither perform *taqlīd* of me, nor Mālik, nor al-Awzā'ī, nor Nakha'ī, nor anyone else, and take the rulings from where they took them, the Qur'ān and the Sunna."[1]

Then he (Sha'rānī) related from a large group of the scholars of the legal schools that from the time of the founders of the schools until his era they used to practice and give opinions from across the schools without being exclusively committed to any one school. The way he explained this entailed that this had been a consistent practice of the scholars from the early times until the present such that it has achieved the status of unanimous acceptance and become a practice of Muslims that cannot properly be opposed. Thus there is no need for us, given what 'Abd al-Wahhāb al-Shar'ānī mentioned and expounded upon, to report their statements. Still, there will

---

1. 'Abd al-Wahhāb ibn Aḥmad al-Sha'rānī, 1493-1565/6, *al-Yawāqīt wa'l-Jawāhir* II (Cairo: Dār al-Fikr, n. d.), 96.

be no harm in mentioning at this time something of what we recall.

Al-Baghawī said in the opening of *Sharḥ al-Sunna*, "In most of my adducing, in fact in almost all of my adducements, I follow others, except for in a very few instances that became clear for me due to some type of evidence in cases of interpretating multivalent expressions, through clarifying the ambiguous, or through determining the preferable opinion."

He also stated in the *Sharḥ al-Sunna* in the chapter concerning "The Invocations which are pronounced at the commencement of the Prayer" after he mentioned the phrases of *Taujīh* (*innī wajihtu*) and "Glory be to you, O God" (*subḥānaka Allahuma*), that alternative invocations for commencing the prayer have been reported in the hadith, and that this is a case of permitted variations and whichever one of these is used at the commencement of the prayer, it is allowed.

He said in the chapter entitled "A woman should not undertake a journey without a male relative (*maḥram*)" that this hadith indicates that a woman is not required to make the Hajj unless she has a *maḥram* male to travel with her. This is the opinion of al-Nakha'ī and Ḥasan of Baṣra, and it was also held by Aḥmad and Isḥāq and the practitioners of personal opinion (*ra'y*). Another group of scholars holds that she is required to perform the Hajj amid a company of women and this is the opinion of Mālik and al-Shāfi'ī while the first opinion is preferred due to its being closer to the overt meaning of the hadith.

Al-Baghawī said about the hadith reported from Birwa' bint Wāshiq[2] that al-Shāfi'ī (ﷺ) had said, "If the hadith of Birwa' bint Wāshiq is true, then there is no conclusive argument in the statement of anyone other than the Prophet (ﷺ)." This hadith has been reported on the authority of Ma'qil ibn Yasār and another time from Ma'qil ibn Sinān and another time from other valorous persons.[3] If this hadith were not sound then a woman in that situation would not receive a marriage payment, while she would receive an inheritance share. This ends the citations from al-Baghawī.

2. This concerns the situation of a woman whose husband married her without specifying the *mahr* and who had not yet consummated the marriage before he passed away. This case was put before 'Abd Allāh ibn Ma'sūd and he tried for a month to find an answer by asking about hadith reports. Finally he decided to rule based on his own opinion, ruling that her dowry and full inheritance share should be paid and that she should observe the three month waiting period. At that time Ma'qal ibn Sinān said that ibn Ma'sūd's opinion corresponded to what the Prophet had ruled in the case of Birwa' bint Wāshiq. see *al-Inṣāf* p. 9.

3. As discussed in al-Shāfi'ī's, *al-Umm*, the Prophet gave her a dowry and inheritance according to some hadith reports but some Companions including 'Alī, Zayd ibn Thābit, and Ibn 'Umar disagreed about this instance. (*al-Umm* chapter on "*Tafwīḍ*," p. 2362.) That is, there is some doubt about its soundness due to confusion in the chain of transmission.

Al-Ḥākim, after first relating the statement of al-Shāfi'ī where he stated, "If the hadith of Birwa' bint Wāshiq is sound, then I will uphold it," then gave an account of how one of his teachers used to say, "If I were in the presence of al-Shāfi'ī, I would have stood up in the middle of his students and said, 'The hadith is sound, so rule according to it.'" (End of report from al-Ḥākim).

In the same way al-Shāfi'ī desisted from implementing the hadith of Burayda al-Aṣlimī concerning the timings of prayer[4] while the hadith was determined to be sound by Muslim. For this reason many hadith scholars did not leave this hadith aside.

A similar case is that of clothing dyed yellow with safflower[5] in which al-Bayhaqī emended al-Shāfi'ī based on the hadith of 'Abd Allāh ibn 'Umar. Al-Ghazālī emended al-Shāfi'ī in the case of the ritual impurity of water being less than the amount contained in two large pitchers in a discussion found in the book, *Iḥyā'*.[6] Al-Nawawī objected that selling without offer and acceptance of the contract (*mu'āṭā*) was allowed, in disagreement with the pronouncement of al-Shāfi'ī .

Al-Zamakhsharī emended Abu Ḥanīfa in certain cases. Among them is what he said about the verse concerning performing ablution with earth (*tayammum*) in the qur'ānic Chapter V, "The Table Spread." (5:6) Zajāj[7] said that by "*ṣa'īd*" is meant the surface of the ground whether it is earth or something else. If this surface is rock and there is no earth on it, still, if the person who is performing the ablution with earth strikes his hand on it and wipes it over himself, that will render him ritually pure, which is the opinion of Abū Ḥanīfa.

If you held this view, then how would you interpret God's (ﷻ) other statement in "The Table Spread": "Then rub *some* of it on your faces and hands," (5:6) that is the expression, '*some* of it,' which cannot make sense in this instance since there is no earth on the rock?

I would respond, "They (the scholars) say that the Arabic word '*min*' in this sentence is not meant in the sense of 'some of' but rather marks the beginning of the next clause. If you agree with their statement that it sig-

4. According to this hadith reported by al-Nasā'ī. Burayda asked the prophet about the prayer timings and was told to stay with him for two days. The first day he prayed the prayers near the beginning of their times and the second day near the end. The Prophet told him that the correct timings should be between those two timings.

5. Nisā'ī reported a hadith related from 'Abd Allāh ibn 'Umar. He came to the Prophet one day in clothing dyed in this yellow color and the Prophet said, "You are wearing the clothing of the unbelievers." Al-Shāfi'ī had permitted wearing clothing of this color.

6. Al-Ghazālī, *Iḥyā'*, Vol. 1, part 3, "The Mysteries of Purification."

7. A grammarian.

nals the beginning of the second clause, this is taking undue license in interpreting the meaning in a way that would not be a normal understanding. If you hold that the statement in Arabic, 'I rubbed my head with oil, with earth, and with water,' could be taken in anything other than the sense, 'I wiped *some of* these things on my head,' so that, in other words, the Arabic word '*min*' should rather be understood in the sense of 'some,' then I would agree with what you say. Acknowledging the truth is better than quarreling." (End of quote from al-Zamakhsharī.)[8]

These types of citations that the scholars take from their Imams, especially from the hadith experts, are innumerable. For instance, my shaykh, Shaykh Abū Ṭāhir al-Shāfi'ī,[9] related to me that his Shaykh, Shaykh Ḥasan al-'Ujaymī al-Ḥanafī[10] told him that we should not be too hard on our women in matters concerning minor ritual impurities due to it being a source of severe hardship. What he commanded us to follow in that case was the school of Abū Ḥanīfa in excusing what is less in size than a *dirham*.[11] Our shaykh, Abū Ṭāhir, was pleased with that statement and used to implement it himself.

In *al-Anwār* it is stated that the qualification for *ijtihād* is achieved when a scholar knows certain things:

1) The first is the Qur'ān. It is not a condition that he know all of the Qur'ān but at least he should know whatever is concerned with legal rulings, and it is not a required condition that he has memorized all of it by heart.

2) The second is the Sunna of the Prophet of God (ﷺ) in terms of the elements of it related to the legal rulings, not its entirety. The requisite condition that he recognize within these two (Qur'ān and Sunna) the particular and the general, the absolute and the restricted, the ambiguous (*mujmal*) and the clear (*mubayyan*) elements, and the abrogating and the abrogated statements. About the Sunna he must know the abundantly transmitted (*mutawātir*) and the single hadiths (*aḥād*)[12] and those whose chains of transmission omit the name of

---

8. This passage is from Al-Zamakhsharī's work *al-Kashshāf* Vol. 1 ed. Muṣṭafā Ḥusayn Aḥmad. (Beirut: Dār al-Kitāb al-'Arabī, 1987) pp. 514-5 with regard to verse 4:43, rather than the similar verse in Chapter 5 cited here.

9. Shaykh Abū Ṭāhir Muḥammad ibn Ibrāhīm al-Madanī al-Kurdī (d. 1145/1733).

10. Shaykh Ḥasan ibn 'Alī al-'Ujaymī (1049/1639-1113/1702).

11. This refers to the rules for ritual impurity. According to Hanafīs a small amount, less than a dirham, will not render clothing etc. ritually impure.

12. Those transmitted by a few narrators or a single narrator.

a Companion (*mursal*),[13] the supported (*musnad*) hadith,[14] the connected (*muttaṣil*) hadith,[15] and those hadith whose chains are broken (*munqaṭi'*), as well as the status of the transmitters, as being either impugned or veracious.

3) The third is knowing the opinions of the scholars among the Companions and those who followed them, and whether these opinions are consensual or contested.

4) The fourth is analogy, whether overt or concealed, and distinguishing correct analogies from false ones.

5) The fifth is the Arabic language, its words and vocalization.

Total mastery of these fields of knowledge is not a requisite condition, and having an overall grasp of them to a proper extent will suffice. There is also no need to trace back all the hadith in their diversity. Rather it is sufficient that a scholar have a sound (*ṣaḥīḥ*) compendium that gathers together the hadith underlying the (*sharī'a*) rulings such as the *Sunan* of al-Tirmidhī and al-Nasā'ī and other books like them such as Abū Dāwūd.

It is not a requisite condition to have precise knowledge about all the occurrences of consensus or disagreement. Rather it suffices a scholar to know that in the given issue wherein he is judging, his opinion does not conflict with (juristic) consensus. This is achieved if he knows that he agrees with some of the previous scholars or he is quite sure that the early scholars did not address the case and that this situation only emerged during his era. The case of recognizing the abrogating and the abrogated is similar.

In the case of hadith reports that past scholars agreed by consensus to accept or whose reporters' competency was acknowledged at the rank of abundance (*tawātur*), there will be no need to inquire into the honesty of the transmitters. In the case of other hadiths, the integrity of the transmitters should be investigated.

The confluence of all five of these disciplines is only required in the case of the absolute *mujtahid* who gives opinions in all departments of the divine law, and it is permitted for a scholar to be a *mujtahid* in one topic and not another.

A further condition for *ijtihād* is knowledge of the principles of belief.

---

13. If the link between the Successor and the Companion is missing, the hadith is termed *mursal* ("hurried"), i.e., when a Successor says, "The Prophet said," thereby omitting the name of a Companion. However, if a link anywhere before the Successor (i.e., closer to the hadith scholar recording the hadith) is missing, the hadith is *munqaṭi'* ("broken").

14. *Musnad* (supported) hadith have sound chains whose reporters are verified to have heard the reports from each other in redundant transmissions reaching back to the Prophet.

15. *Muttaṣil* hadith have connected chains but may either reach back to the Prophet or start at the level of a Companion.

Al-Ghazālī said, "It is not a condition to know them according to the methods of the theologians with the proofs that they adduce. A heretic whose testimony (*shahāda*) would not be accepted cannot be followed in matters of legal judgement. Likewise it is unacceptable to perform *taqlīd* of those who do not believe in the principle of consensus as is the case of the Khawārij,[16] or of those who reject the single (*aḥād*) hadith reports, such as the Qadariyya,[17] or of those who reject analogical reasoning (as a principle of law), such as the Shi'a."

It is also reported in *al-Anwār* that it is not a requisite condition that the *mujtahid* belong to a recorded legal school. Once the legal schools had been recorded, then it became permitted to the *muqallid* to transfer from one school to another. According to the legal theorists (*uṣuliyīn*), if a follower (*muqallid*) has already acted in a matter according to the rulings of one school, then it is not allowed for him to change to the ruling of another school in the same matter, while in other cases it is allowed. If he has not already acted according to the first school in that matter then in that and other cases he may act according to the rulings of either that legal school or another one. If he has performed *taqlīd* of one Imam in certain issues and another scholar in certain other issues, this will be permitted.

If the follower (*muqallid*) chooses whatever is the easiest from every school, Abū Isḥāq[18] says that he commits a sin, and Ibn Abī Hurayra says he has not, which is the preferred opinion according to certain commentaries.

It is also stated in *al-Anwār* that persons affiliated with the schools of al-Shāfi'ī, Abū Ḥanīfa, Mālik, and Aḥmad (ﷺ), are at various levels:

a) The first of them are the laypeople, and their performing *taqlīd* of al-Shāfi'ī is based on their performing *taqlīd* of the *mujtahids* affiliated with his school.

b) Second are scholars who have attained the rank of *ijtihād*. A *mujtahid* does not perform *taqlīd* of another *mujtahid* but rather may be affiliated with him (for example with al-Shāfi'ī) due to his proceeding according to his methodology in *ijtihād*, employing his evidence, and basing some of the proofs upon others.

c) Thirdly, there are scholars at the intermediary levels who do not attain the rank of *ijtihād*. However, they are aware of the principles of the founder of the school and are able to draw analogies between situations where they do not find anything directly reported and cases about which they have proof texts. These scholars are *muqallids* of the

16. Kharijites. An early sectarian movement that seceded from the main community of Muslims.

17. Qadariyya. An early Islamic theological movement known as "libertarians" who allowed more scope for human free will and held variant views on a number of other doctrines.

18. Abū Isḥāq al-Shīrāzī.

founder of the school and so are the laypersons who follow their opinions. It is well-known that these scholars are not followed in their own right since they are themselves *muqallids*.

Abū Fatḥ al-Ḥarawī[19] who was a student of the Imam (Abū Ḥanīfa) said, "The opinion of most of our (Ḥanafī) associates regarding juristic principles is that the layperson has no legal school, so that if he finds a *mujtahid* he will follow his ruling. If he does not locate such a *mujtahid* scholar but instead finds one profoundly learned in a legal school, then the layperson can still perform *taqlīd* of him for this scholar will only issue him opinions based on his own school. This statement makes it clear that the layperson would be performing *taqlīd* of the highly learned scholar in his own right.

The preferred option among the jurists is that the layperson who is affiliated to a legal school belongs to that school and he should not act at variance with it.

If such a layperson is not affiliated with a school, would it be possible for him to choose and follow whatever school he wants?

There is juristic disagreement about this case based on the issue of whether the layperson is required to follow a particular school or not. There are two views on this.

1) al-Nawawī said, "What the argument entails is that the layperson does not need to be committed (to only one school) but that he may seek legal opinions from whichever scholar he wants and whomever is in agreement, so long as he is not scrounging for allowances."

In the book *Ādāb al-Qāḍī* from *Fatḥ al-Taqdīr*[20] it is stated, "Know that whatever the author said about the judge applies to the *muftī* as well, i.e., that only *mujtahids* should give legal opinions." The opinion of the legal theorists has settled on the need for the *muftī* to be a *mujtahid*. A non-*mujtahid,* who has memorized the statements of a *mujtahid*, cannot operate as a *muftī*. It is incumbent upon him, if he is asked to rule on an issue, to cite the opinion of the *mujtahid* in the mode of reporting it, for example, "Abū Ḥanīfa, by way of reporting." Thus it may be known that fatwas given by our contemporary scholars are not fatwas (in the original sense) but rather are reports of the opinions of *mujtahid muftī*s (of the past) to those questioners seeking legal opinions to act upon.

The practice of the *muftī* in transmitting these statements of *mujtahids*, should be in accord with either one of two ways.

Either (a) there should be an authentic chain of transmission going back to the *mujtahid* in this matter; or (b) the fatwa should be taken from a well-known and approved book that has been widely circulated such as the book

19. Abū al-Fatḥ Naṣr ibn Ibrāhīm al-Harawī (510/1116) who compiled a *Musnad* hadith collection.

20. This seems to be an error for *Fatḥ al-Qadīr*.

of Muḥammad ibn Ḥasan or this type of compilations that are well-known among the *mujtahids*. This is because they are at the level of the abundantly transmitted or the authoritative (*mashhūr*) hadith report. al-Rāzī also mentioned this.

On this basis, if some manuscripts of the *Nawādir*[21] were to be found in our era, it would not be permitted to attribute their contents to Muḥammad (ibn Ḥasan) or Abū Yūsuf because these books were not widely approved in our age and in our lands and they did not circulate widely. Of course, if we were to find some reports taken from *al-Nawādir*, for example, in well-known and accepted books such as the *Hidāya* and the *Mabṣūṭ* then this (acceptance of the *fatwā*) would depend on that book.

If a *muftī* has memorized various opinions of *mujtahids* while he did not know their proofs and he has no ability to carry out *ijtihād* in order to determine the preferred opinion, then he cannot give a ruling that one opinion is conclusive nor issue a legal opinion. He can, however, convey these various opinions to the individual who sought a legal opinion. It is then up to that individual to choose the one that is more correct, based on what his conscience determines. This is mentioned in certain of the Jāmi' collections.

My view is that it is not required for him (the *muftī*) to relate all of these opinions. Rather it would suffice for him to relate one of them and it would be up to the *muqallid* to follow whichever *mujtahid* he wanted. If the *muftī* mentions one of the *mujtahids*' rulings and the questioner follows it, then the intended result is obtained. Of course this one opinion is not decisively established so the *muftī* should not say, "The response to your question is as follows." He should rather say, "Abū Ḥanīfa said that the ruling in this case is such and such."

Certainly, if all the opinions have been cited, it would be better that the one who asked for an opinion acted upon the one that he feels is most correct. (However), in the case of the layperson there would be no taking into account of what he might feel regarding the correctness or error of a ruling. Due to this fact he can ask for opinions from two jurists, I mean, *mujtahids*, then if they disagree about the case it would be better that he adopt the opinion of the person to whom his heart feels more inclined.

I hold that if he acted according to the ruling of the scholar to whom he felt less inclined, it would still be permitted because the layperson's liking and disliking something are equivalent. What is required of him is performing *taqlīd* of a *mujtahid* and he has fulfilled this whether that *mujtahid* was correct or in error.

2) Other jurists hold that the layperson who switches from one legal school to another on the basis of *ijtihād* and rational proof has sinned, and therefore he should be punished. Thus the individual who switches legal

21. The books of Hanafī reports that are not considered authoritative.

schools before a process of *ijtihād* and proof has occurred, will be considered a sinner, as in the first instance.

Necessarily what is meant by *ijtihād* in this sense is trying to find out the best answer and the heart's judgement, because the layperson cannot (technically) perform *ijtihād*. Therefore, in fact, switching his legal school can only happen when there is a ruling about a specific case in which he had performed *taqlīd* and already acted on a ruling.

Otherwise, for example, a *muqallid*'s statement, "I performed *taqlīd* of Abū Ḥanīfa in a case where he had issued a fatwa and I committed myself to act accordingly," must be taken in a general sense, while he does not recognize the forms (of these cases). This is not in reality a case of *taqlīd* but rather, this is in actuality making a verbal commitment to performing *taqlīd* or promising to perform it. This is tantamount to a layperson's committing himself to act according to the rulings of Abū Ḥanīfa in whatever specific cases actually arise for him.

If the scholars meant this sort of commitment (to following a legal school), then there is no proof that a layperson is obligated to follow (*ittibā'*) a specific *mujtahid* on the basis of his having committed himself to a legal school, whether this was by verbal declaration or by inner intention, according to the *sharī'a*. Rather, the proof and the requirement to act according to the ruling of a *mujtahid* in situations where this might be necessary are found in this qur'ānic verse, "Ask the people of knowledge if you do not know." (21:7)

Such questioning can only take place when a person seeks a ruling on a particular case that comes up. In this instance, if the opinion of the *mujtahid* becomes established for a layperson, then implementing it becomes compulsory for him.

Most probably the scholars made these sorts of commitments to following legal schools obligatory for people in order to prevent them from seeking out allowances and so that the layperson would not adopt in every case the ruling of the *mujtahid* that was easiest for him.

I am not aware of any revealed texts or rational proofs that would prevent a person from seeking whatever ruling would be easiest for him from a qualified *mujtahid*. Neither have I come to know of anything in the divine law censuring the practice. The Prophet (ﷺ) used to like whatever would be easy on his community, and Allah (ﷻ) knows best which is correct.

This is the conclusion of what we wanted to expound in this treatise, and praise be to Allah at the first and the last.

# Qur'ānic Citations



# Hadith Citations

# Bibliography


Editions of *al-Inṣāf fī Bayān Sabab al-Ikhtilāf*

*al-lnṣāf fī-Bayān Sabab al-lkhtilāf.* (Arabic). Edited by Rashīd Aḥmad Jelandurī. Lahore: Hi'at al-Auqāf bi-Ḥukūmat al-Banjāb, 1971.

*al-Inṣāf fī Bayān fī Sabab al-Ikhtilāf.* Cairo: Muḥibb al-Dīn al-Khaīṭīb, 1965.

*al-Inṣāf.* edited by 'Abd al-Faṭṭāh Abū Ghuddah. Beirut: Dār al-Nafā'is, 1978.

*As'āf min Tarjumat il-Inṣāf.* Urdu translation of al-Inṣāf by Muḥammad 'Abd Allāh Balyavī. Lucknow, 1304 (1886)

*Kashshāf fī Tarjama al-Inṣāf.* Urdu translation of al-Inṣāf by Muḥammad Aḥsan Siddīqī. Delhi: Mujtabā'ī, 1891.

*al-lnṣāf fi-Bayān Sabab al-lkhtilāf.* Sindhi translation by Ghulām Muṣṭafā Qāsimī. Hyderabad: Shāh Walī Allāh Academy, 1973.

*Hadhihi Majmū'ah mushtamilah 'alá thalathat rasā'il* Cairo: Maṭba'a Shirkat al-Matbū'āt al-'Ilmiyya, 1909.

*Difference of Opinion in Fiqh.* English translation by Dr. Muhammad Abdul Wahhab. London: Ta Ha, 2003.

Editions of *'Iqd al-Jīd*

*'Iqd al-Jīd fī-Aḥkām al-ljtihād wa-l-Taqlid.* (Arabic). Cairo: Maktaba al-Salafiyya, 1965.

*Silk al-Mawārīd.* (Stringing the Unbored Pearls). Arabic text with Urdu translation by Maulānā Muḥammad Aḥsan Ṣiddiqī Nānautvī. Delhi: Maṭba'a Mujtabā'ī, 1344/1925-6.

*'Iqd al-Jīd.* Arabic text with Urdu translation by Maulānā Muḥammad Ḥusayn. Delhi: Maṭba'a Fārūqī, 1290/1873-4.

Rahbar, Da'ud. "Shah Waliullah and Ijtihād," *The Muslim World* 45 (December 1955): 346-358. Partial translation.

Other Works of Shāh Walī Allāh

For annotated bibliographies attempting to make a chronology of his works see J.M.S. Baljon. *Religion and Thought, pp.* 9-14, S.A.A. Rizvi. *Shāh Walī Allāh and His Times*, pp. 220-228, and in G. M. Qasimi's introduction (in Arabic) to *al-Tafhīmat al-Ilāhiyya.* vol. 1, pp. 15-37.

*Anfas al-'Ārifīn.* Urdu translation by Muḥammad Fārūq al-Qādirī. Lahore: Ma'ārif, 1974.

*Fuyūḍ al-Ḥaramain.* Arabic with Urdu translation. Karachi: Muḥammad Sa'īd, n.d.

*Ḥujjat Allāh al-Bāligha.* (Arabic). Vols. 1 & 2. ed. al-Sayyid Ṣābiq. Cairo: Multazim al-Ṭab' wa-l-Nashr Dār al-Kutub al-Ḥadīth. 1952–1953. There is also an edition of Cairo: Dār al-Turāth, 1355/1936 and subsequent reprints that are more readily available.

*Ḥujjat Allāh al-Bāligha.* (Arabic). Vols. 1 & 2. ed 'Uthmān Jum'a al-Dumayriyya. Riyādh: Maktaba al-Kawthar, 1999. A critical edition with annotations and citations.

*Ḥujjat Allāh al-Bāligha.* English translation Vol. 1 by Marcia K. Hermansen. Leiden: E. J. Brill, 1996.

*Ḥujjat Allāh al-Bāligha.* Urdu translation *Ni'mat Allāh al-Sābigha* by Abū Muḥammad 'Abd al-Ḥaqq Ḥaqqānī. Karachi: Aṣaḥḥ al-Maṭābi'. n.d.

*Ḥujjat Allāh Al-Bāligha.* Urdu translation and critical commentary by Sa'īd Aḥmad bin Yūsuf Pālanpūrī. 5 vols. Deoband: Maktaba Ḥijāz, 2005.

*Irshād 'ilā Muhimmat 'ilm al-isnād.* Lahore: Sajjād Publishers, 1960.

*Ittiḥāf al-Nabīh* (the latter two sections of *al-Intibāh fī Salāsil Awliyā' Allāh).* Lahore: al-Maktaba al-Salafiyya, 1969.

*al-Khair al-Kathīr.* (Arabic). Cairo: Maktaba al-Qāhira. 1974. English translation by G.H. Jalbani. Hyderabad. Sindh: Shah Waliullah Academy. 1974.

*Al-Juz' al-Laṭīf fi-Tarjamat al-'Abd al-Ḍa'īf.* (Persian original). In *Journal of the Asiatic Society of Bengal* 14 (1912), 161—175 with English translation by M. Hidayat Ḥusain.

*Musawwā Muṣaffā.* (Arabic/Persian). 2 vols. Karachi: Muḥammad 'Alī Karkhāna-e-Islāmī Kutub, 1980.

*al-Tafhīmāt al-Ilāhiyya.* (Arabic and Persian) 2 vols. Hyderabad, Sindh: Shah Waliullah Academy, 1970.

Secondary Works on Shāh Walī Allāh and His Circle

Aḥmad, 'Azīz. "The Waliullahi Movement." In *Islamic Culture in the Indian Environment.* Oxford: Oxford University Press., 1964.

Ansari, A. S. Bazmee. ''Al-Dihlavī, Shāh Walī Allāh." In *Encyclopedia of Islam* . New Edition. Leiden: E. J. Brill. 19 54 .

Baljon. J. M. S. *Religion and Thought of Shāh Walī Allāh Dihlavī.* Leiden: E. J. Brill. 1986.

Baqā, Maẓhar.*Uṣūl-i-Fiqh aur Shāh Walī Allāh.* Islamabad: Idāra Taḥqīqat Islāmī, 1979.

Hermansen, M. K. "Tension between the Universal and the Particular in an Eighteenth Century Theory of Religious Revelation: Shāh Walī Allāh of Delhi's *Ḥujjat Allāh al Bāligha. Studia Islamica* 63 (1986): 143-157.

———. "The Current State of Shāh Walī Allāh Studies." *Hamdard Islamicus* XI (3, 1988):17-30.

Husain, M. Hidayat. "The Persian Autobiography of Shāh Walīullāh bin 'Abd al-Raḥīm al-Dihlavī." *Journal of the Asiatic Society of Bengal* (1912): 161-175.

Jalbani, Ghulam Hussain. *Life of Shah Waliyullah.* Lahore: Ashraf, 1978.

al-Nadwī, Salmān al-Ḥusaynī. *Ārā' al-Imām Walī Allāh al-Dihlawī fī Ta'rīkh al-Tashrī' al-Islāmī*. Lucknow: Dār al-Sunna li-l-Nashr wa-l-Tawzī', 1407/1986. (A study of *al-Inṣāf fī Bayān Sabab al-Ikhtilāf).*

Rahbar, Da'ud. "Shah Waliullah and Ijtihād." *The Muslim World* 45 (December 1955): 346-358.

Rahman, Fazlur. "The Thinker of Crisis--Shāh Waliy-Ullah." *The Pakistan Quarterly* (Summer 1956): 44-48.

Rizvi, Sayyid Athar. 'Abbas *Shāh Walī Allāh and His Times.* Canberra: Ma'arifat. 1980.

Relevant Reference Works and Articles on Islamic Thought

Gaborieau, Marc. "A XIXth Century Indian Wahhabi Tract against the Cult of Muslim Saints: al-Balāgh al-Mubīn," in: Christian W. Troll (ed.), *Muslim Shrines in India.* Delhi: Oxford University Press, 1989, 198-239.

Knysh, Alexander. "Ibrāhīm al-Kūrānī (d. 1101/1690), an Apologist for waḥdat al-wujūd" in *Journal of the Royal Asiatic Society* Series 3, 5, 1 (1995): 39-47.

Nafi, Basheer M. "Taṣawwuf and Reform in Pre-Modern Islamic Culture: In Search of Ibrāhīm al-Kūrānī," *Die Welt des Islams* 42 (3, 2002): 264-273.

______. "A Teacher of Ibn 'Abd al-Wahhāb: Muḥammad Ḥayāt al-Sindī and the Revival of Aṣḥāb al-Ḥadīth's Methodology,",*Islamic Law and Society13* (2, 2006): 208-241.

Peters, Rudolph. "Idjtihad and Taqlīd in 18th and 19th Century Islam," *Die Welt des Islams* 20 (3-4,1980): 131-145.

Riexinger, Martin. *Sanaullah Amritsari (1868–1948) und die Ahl i Hadis im Punjab unter britischer Herrschaft Mitteilunungen zur Sozial und Kulturgeschichte der Islamischen Welt.* Würzburg, Germany: Ergon, 2004.

Voll, John O. "Hadith Scholars and Tarīqahs: An 'Ulema' Group," *Journal of Asian and African Studies* 15 (July-October 1980): 264-273

*Hadith* Collections

al-Bukhārī. *Ṣaḥīḥ al-Bukhārī* trans. Muhammad Muhsin Khan. Chicago: Kazi Publications, 1979.

al-Dārimī. *Sunan.* Beirut: Dār Iḥyā' al-Sunna al-Nabawiyya, 1974.

Ibn Hanbal. *Musnad.* Reprint of Cairo 1985 edition. Beirut: Maktaba al-Kutub al-Islāmī, 1969.

Mālik. *al-Muwaṭṭa'*, trans. Muhammad Rahimuddin. Lahore: Ashraf, 1980.

Muslim. *Ṣaḥīḥ Muslim,* trans. Abdul Hamid Siddiqi, Lahore: M. Ashraf, 1971-75.

al-Nasā'ī. *Sunan,* Cairo: Muṣṭafā al-Bābī al-Ḥalabī, 1964.

Robson, James. English trans. *Mishkāt al-Maṣābiḥ* of al-Tabrīzī. Lahore: Ashraf, 1963.

al-Tirmidhī. *Sunan: al-Jāmi' al-Ṣaḥīḥ* ed. 'Abd al-Raḥmān Muḥammad 'Uthmān. Dār al-Fikr Beirut, 1983. Five volumes.

Works on Islamic Law

al-Āmidī. *al-Iḥkām fī Uṣūl al-Dīn.* Cairo: Dār al-Ḥadīth, 1984.

Brunschwig, Robert. "*Raissonnement Juridique par analogie d'après al-Ghazālī,*" *Studia Islamica* 34 (1971), 57-88.

Calder, Norman. "al-Nawawī's Typology of Muftis and its Significance for a General Theory of Islamic Law," *Islamic Law and Society* 3 (2, 1996): 137-164.

al-Ghazālī. *Iḥyā 'Ulūm al-Dīn.* Beirut: Dār al-Ma'rifa, 1982.

———. *al-Mankhūl fī Ta'līqāt al-Uṣūl.* ed. Muḥannad Ḥasan Hitu. Damascus, 1970.

———. *al-Mustaṣfā.* 2 vol. Cairo: Maṭba'a al-Amīriyya, 1334 A.H.

Hallaq, Wael. "Development of Logical Structure in Sunni Legal Theory," *Der Islam* 64 (1987): 42-67.

———. "On the Origins of the Controversy About the Existence of Mujtahids and the Gate of Ijtihād," *Studia Islamica* 63 (1986): 129-142.

———. "Was the Gate of Ijtihād Closed?" *International Journal of Middle East Studies* 16, (1984): 3-41.

———. "Notes on the Term Qarīna in Islamic Legal Discourse", *Journal of the American Oriental Society* 109 (1989): 475-480.

———. "Non-Analogical Arguments in Sunni Juridical Qiyās" in *Arabica* 36 (1989): 286-306.

———. *A History of Islamic Legal Theories: An Introduction to Sunni Uṣūl al-fiqh.* Cambridge: Cambridge University Press, 1997.

Ibn Ḥājib. *Mukhtaṣar al-Muntahā al-Uṣūlī.* Beirut: Dār al-Kutub al-'Ilmiyya, 1983.

Ibn Rushd, *Bidāyat al-Mujtahid wa-nihāyat al-muqtaṣid* l, trans. as *The Distinguished Jurist's Primer* 1 & ll by Imran Ahsan Nyazee. London: Garnet Publishing, 1994-6.

al-Jazīrī. *al-Fiqh 'alā Madhāhib al-Arba'a.* Beirut: Dār al-Fikr, 1392/1972.

Juynboll, G.H.A. *Muslim Tradition.* Cambridge: Cambridge U. Press, 1983.

Kamali, Mohammad Hashim. *Principles of Islamic Jurisprudence.* Cambridge: Islamic Texts Society, 1991.

Makdisi, George. "The Juridical Theory of al-Shāfi'ī," *Studia Islamica* 59, (1984): 5-47

Nyazee, Imran Ahsan. *Theories of Islamic Law.* Islamabad: Islamic

Research Institute, 1994.
Rahman, Fazlur. *Islam*. Chicago: University of Chicago Press, 1971.
al-Sarakhsī. *Kitāb al-Mabsūṭ*. Cairo: Maṭba'a al-Sa'āda, 1907/8.
al-Shāfi'ī. *al-Risāla*. trans. Majid Khaddouri. Baltimore: Johns Hopkins, 1962.
———. *Kitāb al-Umm*. Beirut: Dār al-Ma'rifa, n.d.
al-Sindhī, Muḥammad Ḥayāt. *al-Iqāf 'alā Sabab al-Ikhtilāf* in *al-Ittibā'*. Lahore: Maktaba al-Salafiyya, 1981, 107-115.
———. *Tuḥfa al-Anām fī-l 'Amal bi-Ḥadīth al-Nabī*, ed. Abū Bakr Ṭā Ḥā Bū Sarī. Beirut: Dār Ibn Ḥazm, 1993.
al-Suyūṭī, Jalāl al-Dīn. *Al-Radd 'alā man akhlada 'alā Arḍ wa jahila anna al-Ijtihād fī kulli 'Aṣr Farḍ*, ed. Shaykh Khalīl al-Mais. Beirut: Dār al-Kutub al-'Ilmiyya, 1983.

# General Index


A

ablution 10, 44, 62, 70, 89, 90, 91, 92, 107, 116, 119, 122, 129-130

*adab* 103

*adilla* (pl of *dalīl,* proofs) 47, 81, 99

*aḥād* (singly transmitted hadiths) 65, 130, 131

Ahl al-Ḥadīth (South Asian movement) xv, xvi, xxviii

Ahl al-Ḥadīth (classical scholars emphasizing use of hadith texts) 26, 35, **38-43**

*amāra, amārāt* (textual sign) 8, 82, 83

*'āmm* (general in meaning or application) 61, 63, 64, 87

*'āmmī* (the common or layperson) 110, 112, 117, 124-126, 133, 135

analogical reasoning (see *qiyāṣ*)

*'azīma* (regular sharī'a requirement) **84**, 123

B

Bareilvis xxviii

*bid'a* (heretical innovation) xv, 48

blood

- having blood drawn 70, 111, 124-5
- menstrual 10, 90, 130

C

categories of actions 79

consensus (see *ijmā'*) 78, 79, 80, 85, 96, 98, 100, 103, 104, 114, 116, 118, 125, 131, 132

D

*dalāla* 99, 120

*dalīl* (indicant, proof, see pl. *adilla*) 37, 106, 127

Deoband xv, xvii

divorce 9, 62, 123

F

fasting 65, 84, 89, 111, 125

*fatwā, fatāwā* (legal opinion-fatwa) 14, 15, 38, 60, 90, 100, 102, 107, 108, 109, 110, 111, 120, 121, 123, 124, 125, 126, 133, 135

four legal schools 94, 96, 102

*furū'* (applied cases, positive law) 3, 5 ff., 19, 20, 21, 42, 47, 53

G

*ghālib al-ra'y* (preponderant opinion) 85

*ghālib al-ẓann* (preponderant conjecture) 9, 113

H

Hadith terminology

- *fādhdh* 33
- *līn* (without defect) 34
- *marfū'* ("elevated" chain back to the Prophet) 31
- *mawqūf* (interupted transmission) 16
- *munqaṭi'* (interrupted) 21, 131
- *mursal* (hadith chain lacks link to Prophet) 21, 22, 32, 53, 79, 131
- *musnad* 16, 21, 79, 131
- *mutabi'āt* (corroborating hadith) 27
- *muttaṣil* (connected) 32, 131
- *mutawātir, tawātur* (abundantly transmitted) 29, **30**, 109, 130
- *shādhdh* 33, 106, 121
- *shāhid, shawāhid* (supported hadith) 27, **103**

Hajj 10, 11, 12, 68, 89, 128

Ḥanafī school xi, xiii, xiv, xv, xvi, xix, xxix, xxxi, xxxii, **20-21**, 23, 37, 53, 57, 58, 60, 100, 105, 106, 107, 109, 110, 116, 117, 118, 119, 121, 125, 126, 130, 133, 134

Hanbalī school xxx, xxxii, 58, 68, 114

Hijāzis 115

*hīla* (legal artifice) 123

*ḥukm, aḥkām* (ruling) 101

I

*'Īd (holiday)* 68, 88, 89, 118

*ijāza* xxiii, xxiv

*ijmā'* (consensus) 78, 79, 80, 85, 96, 98, 100, 103, 104, 114, 116, 118, 125, 131, 132

# Names Index

# Works Cited by Shāh Walī Allāh Index